Recovering Scotland's Slavery Past

Recovering Scotland's Slavery Past

The Caribbean Connection

Edited by T. M. Devine

EDINBURGH
University Press

For Evan and Lena

© editorial matter and organisation T. M. Devine, 2015
© the chapters their several authors, 2015

Edinburgh University Press Ltd
The Tun – Holyrood Road
12 (2f) Jackson's Entry
Edinburgh EH8 8PJ
www.euppublishing.com

Typeset in 10.5/13pt Sabon by
Servis Filmsetting Ltd, Stockport, Cheshire
printed and bound in Great Britain by
CPI Group (UK) Ltd, Croydon CR0 4YY

A CIP record for this book is available from the British Library

ISBN 978 0 7486 9808 0 (hardback)
ISBN 978 1 4744 0880 6 (paperback)
ISBN 978 0 7486 9809 7 (webready PDF)
ISBN 978 1 4744 0881 3 (epub)

Contents

Illustrations and Tables

The Contributors

David Alston is an independent researcher living in the Highlands

Sir Thomas Martin Devine is Sir William Fraser Professor of Scottish History and Palaeography Emeritus in the University of Edinburgh

Nicholas Draper is Co-Director of the *Structure and Significance of British Caribbean Slave-ownership 1763–1833* project at University College London

Eric J. Graham is an Honorary Post-Doctoral Fellow in the Scottish Centre for Diaspora Studies at the University of Edinburgh

Catherine Hall is Professor of Modern British Social and Cultural History at University College London

Philip D. Morgan is Harry C. Black Professor of History at Johns Hopkins University Baltimore USA

Michael Morris is Lecturer in English Literature and Cultural History at Liverpool John Moores University

Stephen Mullen is Research Associate in History, University of Glasgow

Stuart M. Nisbet is a freelance researcher and Honorary Research Fellow in the School of Humanities, University of Glasgow

Suzanne Schwarz is Professor of History at the University of Worcester

Iain Whyte is an Honorary Post-Doctoral Fellow in the Scottish Centre for Diaspora Studies at the University of Edinburgh

Acknowledgements

I AM GRATEFUL TO each of the contributors for their loyal support in helping to see the Scotland and Slavery project through to this stage since it was first discussed in 2013.

The Economic and Social Research Council funded an event in the Mitchell Library, Glasgow on 3–4 October 2014 as part of the ESRC three-year seminar series on 'Scotland's Diasporas in Comparative International Perspective' (Universities of Edinburgh, Hull and Otago).

The authors presented short preliminary papers, based on their proposed chapters, to an audience of fellow scholars and members of the general public. In addition, contributors and invited experts held a private seminar the day afterwards to consider key issues associated with the volume.

We are most grateful to Professors Angela McCarthy (Otago), John Oldfield (Hull) and David Richardson (Hull), who acted as commentators and reviewers during the discussion session of that seminar. Their advice helped not only with the preparation of the book as a whole but also with the shaping of individual chapters.

Dr Nick Evans of the Wilberforce Institute for the Study of Slavery and Emancipation at Hull organised the entire event with aplomb and efficiency; we also thank the University of Hull and its Alumni Office for additional financial support for it.

The Mitchell Library provided an excellent environment for the conference and we warmly acknowledge the support of Dr Irene O'Brien of Glasgow City Archives, which celebrated its fiftieth anniversary in 2014, and the Mitchell's AV technical staff for their professional input to the success of the seminar.

As editor I am particularly indebted to Professor Phil Morgan of Johns Hopkins University, USA, for agreeing to write the Foreword to the book and to Professor Jim Walvin, formerly of the University of York, for his perceptive comments on my own draft contributions. I am also deeply grateful to an external reader who considered the whole book in draft form and made several acute and useful observations on the text as it developed towards final form.

The staff of Edinburgh University Press, especially John Watson, Ellie Bush, Eddie Clark and Ian Davidson, were as usual most helpful and efficient.

The editor could not have completed his work without the expert and characteristically reliable support of Margaret Begbie.

Tom Devine
The University of Edinburgh
31 January 2015

Foreword

Philip D. Morgan

SCOTLAND'S CONNECTIONS TO SLAVERY can seem tenuous, almost non-existent. After all, few vessels left Scottish ports for Africa to participate in the horrific slave trade. By the end of the eighteenth century, when England had a black population of about 15,000, perhaps fewer than one hundred black slaves resided in Scotland. Furthermore, Scots were in the vanguard of the abolitionist movement; and Scotland can pride itself as a pioneering abolitionist nation. A country that was about 10 per cent of the United Kingdom population contributed at times about a third of the petitions to Parliament advocating abolition of the slave trade. Iconic figures such as James Ramsay and William Dickson were in the forefront of the opposition to the slave trade. Moreover, in Duncan Rice's view, scholars of the Scottish Enlightenment 'perfected most of the eighteenth century's rational arguments against slavery'. Scottish philosophers discussed slavery at greater length than their continental counterparts. Adam Smith's famous *The Wealth of Nations* contains a condemnation of the slave trade and slavery not only as morally repugnant but as economically inefficient. Is it any surprise that many general histories of modern Scotland fail to mention slavery at all?

But the essays in this impressive collection make clear that, if Scots think their country has few or no connections to slavery, they are sorely mistaken. In effect, they are engaging in a form of collective amnesia, for in fact Scotland's connections to slavery were extensive. Scots participated fully in slave trading from ports such as Liverpool, Bristol and London. At the height of the slave trade, a fifth of the ship captains and two-fifths of the surgeons manning slavers out of Liverpool, the world's major slave-trading port at the time, were Scots. The image of Scots, dressed in tartan, playing golf by the slaving fort of Bance Island, Sierra Leone, points to the quotidian nature of Scottish involvement in that nefarious business. One Scottish slave trader thought so familiarly of slavery that he named his vessel after his daughter. This book shows that Scots owned and managed enslaved people in many New World slave societies – from Maryland to Trinidad, from St Croix to St Kitts. Scottish slave owners named many of their slaves and their plantations in ways to remind themselves of home. According to Edward Long, the historian of late eighteenth-century Jamaica, one-third of the whites on that island were Scots. Other societies such as Grenada and the other Windward Islands, as well as Demerara and Berbice, also experienced heavy Scottish influxes. In the early nineteenth century, Scots accounted for about a third of the planters on St Vincent. Scots fulfilled many roles within New World slave societies: from indentured servants to book-keepers, from merchants to bankers, from attorneys to planters, from nurses to doctors. The scale of Scottish involvement in the slave econo-mies and societies of the New World was therefore wide and deep. If Scotland can boast of its abolitionists, it should also take ownership of the many Scots who defended and profited from the institution. Even the slaves themselves took note of Scots: in one colony they tagged shellfish that clung to one another as clannish Scotchmen.

The economic links between Scotland and New World slave societies were impressive. Slave societies provided markets for Scottish textiles, herring and a range of manufactured goods. In turn, those societies sup-plied Scotland with tobacco, sugar, rum, coffee and cotton. Capital from the Chesapeake and the Caribbean made its way into Scottish industries and landownership. Indeed, as Sir Tom Devine suggests in Chapter 11, the small scale of the Scottish domestic market and the nation's relative poverty probably accentuated the impact of the slave-based economies of the Atlantic. As he notes, there is evidence pointing to 'an even greater per capita Scottish stake' in British imperial slavery than for any of the other nations of the United Kingdom.

At the same time, this outsized Scottish involvement in the slave-based economies of the Atlantic must not be exaggerated. The Scots were not much of a presence in Barbados or some of the Leeward Islands. Between 1750 and 1834 only about 34,000 Scots travelled from Scotland to the West Indies, a small proportion of the Scottish popula-tion of just over 1.5 million in 1801. Furthermore, the Caribbean was a graveyard not just for slaves but for immigrant whites, many of whom died within a few years of arrival. A commercial handbook published in 1766 for 'men of business' in Glasgow recommended sending 'two, three or more' factors to the West Indies so 'that on the death of one', others could replace him. The famous volatility of the Antilles took its toll on Scots. The impact of slavery on the homeland was also limited in some respects. As Nicholas Draper emphasises in Chapter 8, only 'between 5 and 10 per cent of British elites were close enough to the slave-economy to appear in the compensation records, as owners, mortgagees, legatees, trustees or executors'. The other 90 to 95 per cent had no discernible connections to slavery. Scotland, it is true, is over-represented among absentee slave-owning claimants, accounting for 15 per cent of them. Still, the point Draper makes about the general significance of slavery also applies to the Scots, namely that 'slave wealth could be incidental in the sense that other sources of wealth appear to dwarf it in the composition of an individual's overall net worth'.

More work therefore remains to be done precisely linking slavery to Scots at home and in the diaspora. The impact on Scotland – not just measured in investments but in everything from diet to country houses to material culture – will also need careful and precise calibration. But any claim that Scotland grew rich from slavery may not be easily sustained. The flow of profits from slaving and slave-related business, while notable, probably accounted for only a small proportion of domestic capital formation. The value added by the Caribbean sugar sector was approximately 2 per cent of British national income. As Devine notes below, 'the origins of industrialism were far from being monocausal'. Rather, he adds, 'the commitment of the landed elites to economic improvement, indigenous levels of literacy, the practical impact of improving Enlightenment thought, English markets within the Union, new technologies and the indigenous natural endowment of coal and ironstone resources, *inter alia*, were all part of the mix'. Slavery was important to Scotland's development, as these essays abundantly and rightly demonstrate, but quite how profound the institution's impact was awaits further investigation. Still, these splendid path-breaking essays point the way forward, by providing a sturdy foundation on which others can build.

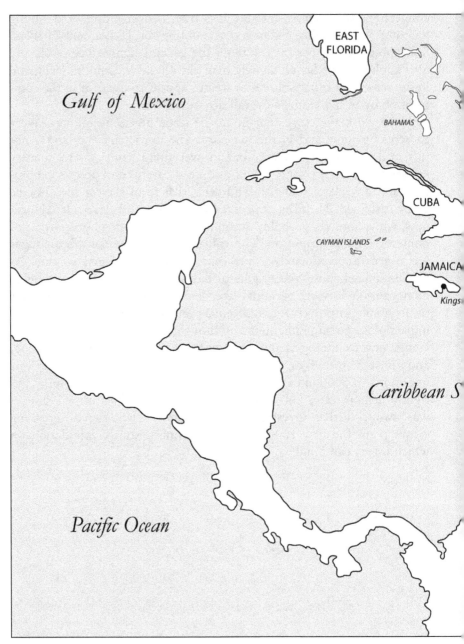

Map The West Indies based on a map by Aaron Arrowsmith and Samuel Lewis (1812).

Atlantic Ocean

ST DOMINGUE

BRITISH VIRGIN
ISLANDS

ST KITTS

NEVIS   ANTIGUA

MONTSERRAT

LEEWARD
ISLANDS   DOMINICA

MARTINIQUE

ST LUCIA

ST VINCENT   BARBADOS

GRENADA

TOBAGO

TRINIDAD

Georgetown

BRITISH
GUIANA

Introduction

Scotland and Transatlantic Slavery

T. M. Devine

I

BETWEEN THE EARLY DECADES of the seventeenth century and the abolition of the British slave trade in 1807, ships of the Empire carried over 3.4 million Africans to a life of servitude, and often an early death, in the plantations across the northern Atlantic. That figure accounted for as many slaves delivered to that part of the New World over the period as the vessels of all other European nations combined. At the peak of the business in the 1760s, annual shipments reached an average of 42,000 slaves a year. As far as the history of black slavery in the northern Atlantic was concerned, Britain by all measures was the dominant force.

The system of bondage practised was chattel slavery, where the enslaved became the property of their masters until death, like their beasts of the field or their household plenishings, with no legal right to be treated as humans and with all the potential for exploitation and degradation which could accompany that helpless condition. The progeny of enslaved women also became the property of their masters at birth, either to be sold on from the plantation where they had been born or to spend their lives in hard labour within its bounds in perpetual servitude. Those modern sceptics who consider the contemporary poor at home, often eking out a miserable existence, or the indentured white servants in the transatlantic colonies, to be just as oppressed as black slaves, fail to take account of that stark and fundamental distinction. Colonial servants were bondsmen, indentured to labour, often under harsh conditions, but their contracts were not for life but for specific periods, usually an average of four to seven years, and were enforceable at law.

Throughout the Americas, the enormous increase in the output of the exotic commodities of sugar, tobacco, cotton, indigo and rum destined for consumption in Europe would have been impossible without the magnitude of black enslavement. The extreme risks to the health of whites in the tropics and the arduous climatic conditions of the transatlantic plantations made it impossible to attract European field workers by the late seventeenth century on anything like the numbers required by the intensity of the new capitalist agriculture. Indeed, the British state for a long period had viewed the Caribbean as a place of terror and punishment, fit for transported criminals, traitors and other miscreants, but not a suitable location for free settlement. The notorious kidnapping trade in young lads, forcibly transported from their homeland to indentured service in the colonies by unscrupulous sea captains and crooked traders (immortalised in Robert Louis Stevenson's classic novel *Kidnapped*, set in the mid-eighteenth century), testifies to the emerging problem of white labour scarcity across the Atlantic.

At the same time, the growing addiction of the peoples of Britain and the Continent to sugar and tobacco became the decisive influence shaping the colossal expansion of the slavery system in the Americas. Ordinary consumers became just as dependent on the trade as merchants, slavers, shipowners, mariners and plantation owners. The mass enslavement of Africans was the inevitable consequence of the new and vast demand in the West for sweetness in all things, Britain alone taking around a third of all the sugar imported to Europe in the eighteenth century.

Recovering Scotland's Slavery Past is a study of the origins, nature and effects of involvement with slavery and the slave trade in one European country. It focuses mainly on the Scottish connection with the sugar islands of the Caribbean from the seventeenth to the early nineteenth centuries; the important American dimension of the tobacco colonies, with which Scotland had such a vital commercial relationship especially before 1776, is treated only briefly in this Introduction and again in Chapter 11. That topic will merit extended future study. Nor does the book consider abolitionism in detail but concentrates for the most part on the Scottish linkages with chattel slavery itself and the under-researched subject of anti-abolitionism. Studies of the important Scottish role in the successful movement for slave emancipation have already been published by C. Duncan Rice (1981) and Iain Whyte (2006). This volume does not claim to be the final word on a subject which has been long lost to history. Rather, as a pioneering study in the field, its primary purpose is to provide a platform of evidence from which future scholarship can develop the themes examined here and so progress into fresh avenues of research. The book focuses mainly on material, economic and migration aspects, and much scope therefore remains for future work which can place the Scottish experience in a clearer international comparative context and consider also the political, intellectual, cultural and gender issues associated with the subject. This volume is an integrated study which looks both outwards and inwards by exploring the Scottish role in slavery on the one hand and the effect of that connection on Scotland itself on the other. Within that framework, five main topics are considered.

T. M. Devine and Michael Morris begin the book by probing collective slavery amnesia in both history and literature, and ask why it has taken so long to come to grips with an understanding of this dark episode in Scotland's past. Only in the last fifteen years or so has serious work started to be published on the country's historical links with slavery by scholars in Scottish universities. Most creative writing on the subject in Scotland also more or less dates from the same period.

The chapters which then follow seek to provide hard evidence of Scottish involvement in all aspects of West Indian slavery on the basis of original archival-based research. Stuart Nisbet, Eric Graham, David Alston and Stephen Mullen trace the development of increasing interest in the islands of the Caribbean and mainland South America from the seventeenth century to the 1830s. They demonstrate the impressive scale of Scots migration to the West Indies which at times and in specific locations was more extensive than that from the other nations of the United Kingdom when measured by the respective size of their base populations. These adventurers, unlike their mainly poorer predecessors who ventured to the Caribbean in the seventeenth century, were increasingly drawn from the minor landed, middling and artisan ranks of Scottish society. They sailed across the Atlantic in search of business opportunities and quick fortunes. Suzanne Schwarz in her contribution adds to this picture by describing the extensive part played by Scots mariners, and more especially physicians, in the slavery business of Liverpool, at that time the most successful slaving port not only in the British Isles but in the Atlantic world as a whole. Another striking feature was the very significant Scottish investment from the later 1790s in the 'frontier' lands of the former Dutch colonies of Demerara, Essequibo and Berbice (British Guiana from 1836, now Guyana) situated on the South American mainland. Even in the years immediately before the end of slavery in the Empire in 1833, these territories were still yielding substantial profits for plantation proprietors and slave owners.

These case studies illustrate the geographical range of the Scottish regions with strong migrant connections to the Caribbean. They spread across the western Highlands, the north, the north-east and the south-west Lowlands. Hardly any part of Scotland was excluded. The chapters also describe the great wealth that some attained from the slave-based economies, with a minority returning to the homeland with princely fortunes beyond the dreams of avarice to become country gentlemen with elevated positions in society. Their dazzling material success inevitably inspired many more to follow in their footsteps to the sugar islands. Less well recorded, however, are the lives of those who succumbed to the diseases of the tropics or failed to make a substantial mark on the West Indies. They, unlike their wealthier peers, have left little documentary trace for the historian to research and assess.

Key questions arise from these contributions as the bigger picture is considered. Why did there appear to have been proportionately more Scots in relation to their share of British population throughout the plantations by the later eighteenth century? Was the Scottish presence there in any way distinctive in comparative terms? What impact did migration to the Caribbean and the profits made by the sojourners there have on the economy and society of the homeland? These broader issues are examined later in this Introduction and also in some of the chapters which follow.

Nicholas Draper then considers the vast sums paid out in compensation to slave owners for the losses of their 'property' when slavery came to an end in the British Empire in 1833. Crucially, he shows that at abolition the extent of Scottish slave ownership relative to population size was more than England's and much more than that of Ireland and Wales. Moreover, he finds that of the fifteen major British mercantile syndicates receiving most compensation after abolition, ten were either Scottish-based firms or businesses trading from England with earlier founding patterns of known Scottish origin.

Iain Whyte and Catherine Hall follow by examining the passionate public debates which were triggered around the momentous issue of slavery abolition. They focus also on the less familiar, though widespread, opposition in Scotland to emancipation. Not until the 1760s did chattel slavery begin to attract much moral criticism in the public sphere either in Scotland or Britain more generally. Before then the mass enslavement of Africans in the plantations was considered an unexceptional fact of life. Although some of the ideas of the Scottish Enlightenment eventually provided much of the intellectual tool kit for the abolitionist campaigns, their impact overall did not become really significant until later in the eighteenth century, in part because the writings of several of the literati on slavery were sometimes complex, ambiguous in approach and not always entirely critical (see Chapter 9).

The cause célèbre at the Court of Session in Edinburgh in 1778 resulting in the liberation of the runaway slave Joseph Knight, brought by his master John Wedderburn of Ballindean from the Caribbean, was indeed a landmark judgement and served to increase awareness of the rarely publicised incidence of slavery in Scotland. The decision effectively outlawed chattel slavery in the home country more than half a century before it was declared illegal in the British Empire. But the judgement had no effect on the functioning of the mass system of bondage in the Americas. The Sheriff of Perth found in 1777, when Knight appealed to him, that 'the regulations of Jamaica, concerning slaves, do not extend to this kingdom'. That ruling was confirmed by a majority of judges in the Court of Session a year later. It might equally have been said, however, that conversely, nor did the 'regulations' of Scotland apply to Jamaica.

Finally, T. M. Devine analyses the impact of profits derived from the slave-based plantations and their markets on Scottish economic trans-formation before c. 1830. He argues that these capital transfers together with the expansion of transatlantic demand for manufactured goods at the same time were influential factors among others in the origins of the Industrial Revolution in Scotland. The discussion also suggests that the economic effects of slavery in all its aspects may have been more impor-tant to industrialisation north of the Border than in England.

The next two sections of the Introduction broaden the lens by exam-ining the slave economy of the West Indies in general terms and then provide an overview of the Scottish factor throughout the islands during the many decades from the early seventeenth century when the slavery system remained unchallenged.

II

In the eighteenth century Britain's West Indian colonies were univer-sally regarded as crucial to the imperial economy. Even Adam Smith, the most eminent contemporary critic of the colonial system, waxed eloquent about their immense value: the profits of a sugar plantation in the Caribbean, he noted, 'were generally much greater than those of any other cultivation that is known either in Europe or America'.[1] Edmund and William Burke also asserted in 1757 that nowhere in the world could great fortunes be made so quickly as in the West Indies. Their importance to the British state and economy was widely acknowl-edged. In 1700 the British islands accounted for about 40 per cent of all transatlantic sugar consignments. By 1815 the figure had reached 60 per cent. At the end of the eighteenth century the Caribbean colonies employed, directly or indirectly, half the nation's long-distance shipping, their fixed and moveable wealth was reckoned at more than £30 million sterling, duties on West Indian produce accounted for an eighth of Exchequer revenues and the credit structures linked to the plantation economy were crucial elements in UK financial markets.[2]

The expansion of the British West Indian colonies was forged in the violent crucible of the titanic conflicts with France over transatlantic hegemony. The sugar islands were first settled by British adventurers from the 1620s, and by c. 1750 Barbados, the Leeward Islands (Antigua, St Kitts, Nevis, Montserrat) and Jamaica had all been conquered or annexed. Further large-scale territorial gains took place after both the Seven Years War (ending in 1763) and the Napoleonic Wars (ending in 1815). As a result of the first, Britain added Grenada, Dominica, St Vincent and Tobago (the Ceded Islands). By the second, the Empire absorbed Trinidad, Demerara, Berbice, Essequibo and St Lucia. The development of these new colonies depended on a number of factors. The British Laws of Trade and Navigation gave the islands a virtual monopoly of the protected home market for the products of tropical agriculture, where commodities such as sugar by the 1750s were selling at prices some 50 per cent higher than in continental Europe. The West Indies at that time also became the great source of rum for the crews of a massively expanding Royal Navy during the long wars after 1756. Then, after c. 1760, the plantations also fed the factories of the early Industrial Revolution with numerous cargoes of raw cotton. But sugar was king. It is reckoned that sugar consumption in England and Wales alone increased about twenty-fold in the period from 1663 to 1775. Between 1771 and 1775, colonial imports topped 1.8 million cwt. Consumption per head in Britain rose spectacularly from about four pounds in 1700 to ten pounds by 1748, and then to twenty pounds in 1800. Britons seem to have had a uniquely sweet tooth. As late as the 1780s, for instance, the French were only consuming about two pounds per head. The voracious national appetite for sugar and its derivatives was intimately linked to the new obsession for tea-drinking, which set in from the middle decades of the seventeenth century. Consumption per head of tea quintupled in the UK from 0.32lb per head in 1730–9 to 1.78lb in 1804–6. This was partly related to the much faster rise of real incomes in Britain in the eighteenth century compared to the countries of continental Europe. But an even more fundamental influence was the British rate of urbanisation. Under conditions in town and city tea was more convenient than milk and, until Indian leaf displaced the Chinese after 1865, tea was usually taken without milk. In Britain as a whole, there was a very close correlation between the spread of tea-drinking and the rapid urbanisation of the country. In Scotland, in particular, tea was most commonly consumed in cities and towns before 1800. Sugar as a sweetener came in sugar loafs and semi-hard cones that required a sugar axe or hammer to break them up, and 'nips', a pliers-like tool, to reduce the sugar to usable pieces.

The Caribbean response to the burgeoning sugar markets in Europe was built on two key foundations – the evolution of the plantation system and the massive use of enslaved labour. Conceivably, given the vital dependency on African slaves, the plantations ought to have located in West Africa close to plentiful supplies of labour. But tropical Africa had a notorious reputation as the white man's grave and also, it was argued, slaves might more easily escape back to their homelands. Transporting Africans half way across the world, on the other hand, had several advantages. The Caribbean islands were certainly host to such virulent pestilences as cholera, smallpox and dysentery. But they were not only relatively free from malaria but also were regarded as less lethal than the deadly shores and jungles of Africa. Moreover, European settlement in the West Indies was facilitated by the trade winds, which partially tempered the unrelenting heat of the tropics. The Caribbean also had easy access to cheap sources of provisions in North America, while the prevailing winds were helpful to oceanic commerce and to the powering of the sugar mills which processed the canes.[3] Indeed, such were the capacities in the islands to service the booming markets in Europe that some colonies became little more than vast sugar plantations. It was said, for instance of Antigua in 1751, that the land was 'improved to the utmost, there being hardly one Acre of Ground, even to the Top of the Mountains, fit for Sugar Canes and other necessary Produce, but what is taken and cultivated'.[4]

These were also 'slave societies', in the sense of human communities which depended above all else on unfree, forced labour for their very existence. Without the slave, the sugar economies of the Caribbean would have been impossible. By 1750 Africans and those of African descent comprised about 85 per cent of the population of the British West Indies. It was scarcely surprising that the contemporary commentator Malachy Postlethwayt, writing in 1745 in *The African Trade, the Great Pillar and Support of the British Plantation Trade in America*, asserted that the nation's transatlantic commercial empire ultimately depended on an African foundation. Slaves outnumbered whites by six to one in

1748 and by twelve to one in 1815. They were sourced by British vessels from several regions in western Africa, particularly Senegambia, Sierra Leone, the Gold Coast, the Bight of Benin, the Bight of Biafra and west-central Africa. The trauma of the enslaved removed from these districts began long before their arrival in the colonies. William Wilberforce, in a speech on the slave trade to the House of Commons in 1789, reckoned that over 12 per cent died during the notorious and terrible Middle Passage from Africa to the Americas, and 5 per cent at seizure, on forced marches to the coast, incarceration there and final deportation. Another third, he suggested, would perish in the Caribbean itself during the initial period of 'seasoning' or acclimatising. During the transatlantic crossing male slaves were commonly chained two-by-two below decks for long periods to minimise the threat of disorder during the voyage. It was said that as a result the stench from slave ships could be picked up by other vessels from several miles away downwind.

The 'free coloured' populations of the Caribbean, sometimes of Scots descent, should also be recorded as part of the labour force. They were a larger group than the whites and in several islands were essential to the operation of the plantations as managers and overseers, so helping to make large-scale absenteeism of white owners possible. The children of Scots migrants and both enslaved and 'free coloured' women are also therefore an important legacy of Scotland and slavery. Most whites were transients, hoping to make a quick fortune and return home as quickly as possible with their gains, though, despite the fabled riches of the Caribbean, few actually managed to do so. But one consequence was that in the British West Indies the sojourners failed to develop 'inte-grated, locally rooted societies, comparable with the North American colonies'.[5] Scots did not establish schools or churches on the Caribbean islands where they settled in the manner familiar in other parts of the Empire. Janet Schaw visited Antigua in 1775 in the course of her travels from Scotland to the West Indies and North Carolina between 1774 and 1778. She was the daughter of a family of gentleman farmers near Edinburgh and was accompanying her brother to St Kitts, where he was to take up an appointment as a customs official. Schaw noted in her letters home how most planters left their families behind and those who did not do so usually sent their children back to Scotland to be educated. As there was no Presbyterian church on the island, she herself had to attend Anglican services on the Sabbath.

This was not the only point of difference between the two colonial systems. Another was in the stark contrast of the treatment of blacks. Not for nothing was the Caribbean known as the graveyard of the slaves.

Even by the arduous conditions of unfree labour in the North American plantation colonies for tobacco and rice cultivation, the suffering of the blacks in the West Indies was especially horrendous. About 1830, crude death rates in the USA and Jamaica were 20 and 26 per thousand respectively. The differences in birth rates were even more dramatic – 50 and 23 per thousand respectively. It was reckoned in the 1750s that a quarter of all slaves died within three years of arrival, though mortality rates could often be significantly higher than that. On the Codrington plantations in Barbados between 1741 and 1746, for instance, 43 per cent of all Africans died within three years of arrival. It should be remembered, of course, that slave mortality on the islands was also very much influenced by Africans picking up diseases on the Atlantic crossing and on the forced marches to the African coast. Partly high death rates were also based on an inhuman calculation. Planters generally believed until the later eighteenth century that buying 'salt-water' blacks, straight off the slave ships, was 'cheaper' than encouraging family life and reproduction of the existing 'stock'. Thus, it was common practice then for plantations to buy slaves at crop time and set them to work with little or no time spent on seasoning. By definition also, slavery was an oppressive regime where work was only done under threat of punishment. Some scholars have suggested that coercion reached especially rigorous and exacting levels in the Caribbean because the grossly skewed ratios of whites and blacks generated rancorous fear and paranoia among British planters about the menace of slave rebellions. Sir Hans Sloane saw the responses in Jamaica:

> The Punishments for Crimes of Slaves, are usually for Rebellions burning them, by nailing them down on the ground with crooked Sticks on every Limb, and then applying the Fire by degrees from the Feet and Hands, burning them gradually up to the Head, whereby their pains are extravagant.[6]

Crimes of a lesser nature were dealt with by 'Gelding, or chopping off half of the Foot with an Ax [sic], while for trying to escape the slave was burdened with iron rings, chains, pottocks and spurs'.[7]

Essentially, however, the high levels of slave mortality were caused to a significant extent by the unrelenting nature of the plantation regime. The slave gangs on the sugar estates toiled from dawn to dusk in land preparation, in harvesting the canes and in sugar-boiling. In the Caribbean about 90 per cent of the slaves worked in these tasks. One scholar estimates that it was 'probably one of the highest labour participation rates anywhere in the world'. Janet Schaw observed the regime in St Kitts. She noted that every ten slaves had a driver, who walked behind them holding a long and a short whip in his hand. Both men and women were naked 'down to the girdle' and so she was able to make out the marks left by the use of the lash. Each slave had a basket which was carried up the hill filled with manure and then brought back with sugar canes for the mills: 'They go up at a trot, and return at a gallop, and did you not know the cruel necessity of this alertness, you would believe them the merriest people in the world.'[8] Schaw accepted that 'humane Europeans' would be appalled at this treatment but asserted that such reactions were misconceived:

> When one becomes better acquainted with the nature of the negroes, the horrour [sic] of it must wear off. It is the suffering of the human mind that constitutes the greatest misery of punishment, but with them it is merely corporal. As to the brutes it inflicts no wounds on their mind, whose Natures seem made to bear it and whose sufferings are not attended with shame or pain beyond the present.

The arduous toil helps to explain why about half the slave women in the British West Indies never bore a child in the mid-eighteenth century. On the American mainland there was never the same intensity of work on a single crop. Tobacco cultivation, tending farms, cutting timber and domestic service were just some of the varied range of tasks undertaken. Recent work on slave skeletal remains in Barbados burial grounds by nutritionists and anthropologists has added a new dimension to an understanding of slave mortality in the Caribbean. These results point unambiguously to malnutrition as a vital factor reducing the immunity of the black population to the epidemic diseases which infested the low-lying plantations and their malignant environments.[9]

Nor should the human factor be neglected in this account. The Caribbean was notorious for planter absenteeism, especially near the end of slavery. In 1832, 540 (84 per cent) of a total of 646 sugar estates were owned by absentees or minors. Proprietors were often keen to escape home from the tropics as soon as they had managed to make enough for leisured living in Britain. By 1800 it was often their attorneys, managers and overseers who actually ran most plantations in the West Indies. This class was committed to maximising production, not simply to satisfy the expectations of their masters, but because they also were determined to make money quickly and return to spend their last years in more congenial surroundings at home. The pervasive culture of avarice engendered a regime of unrelenting rigour on the slave plantations. Untold numbers of blacks were quite literally worked to death.

It is hardly surprising, therefore, that modern scholarship has identified the islands of the British West Indies as the location of the most deadly and destructive systems of slavery in the New World. Only in the later decades of the eighteenth century did the policy on most estates alter in favour of encouraging new generations of slaves to be born in the Caribbean itself rather than simply purchasing 'salt-water' blacks off the ships from West Africa. As a result, the trend towards some amelioration came to be established on the plantations.

III

As Stuart Nisbet shows in Chapter 3, Scotland's sugar trade with the Caribbean goes back to the middle decades of the seventeenth century. During and after the American War of Independence one hundred years later, however, the business rapidly became the dominant sector in Scottish overseas commerce, assuming the position that the tobacco trade had long occupied over previous decades. By 1815, 65 per cent of all goods exported from Scotland were destined for the West Indies, the country's biggest overseas market by far at the time. The enormous increase in cargoes of cotton wool from the islands also became of strategic significance as the raw material of the first stages in the Scottish Industrial Revolution. Some of the nation's most powerful and wealthiest merchant houses were now trading to the region and young Scots in increasing numbers became engaged in the management of plantations. The Caribbean connection may have been long forgotten nowadays, but in the eighteenth and early nineteenth centuries it was of central importance in the economic history of Scotland.

Two old myths about that relationship have been demolished by modern historical research.[10] The first was the belief that the relationship did not flourish until after the Anglo-Scottish Union of 1707 because only from then were Scottish merchants able to trade on a legitimate basis with the former English, now British, colonies across the Atlantic. However, there was no legal constraint on the actual settlement of Scots in the islands of the Caribbean before 1707 and so by the later seventeenth century they were to be found there in some numbers, a motley group of indentured servants, small traders, planters, prisoners of war banished by Cromwell, Covenanters forced into exile by Charles II and James VII, criminals and vagabonds transported to the plantations and even survivors from the ill-fated Darien expedition of the 1690s. A total of 4,000 to 5,000 Scottish settlers have been identified in the West Indies for the period 1660 to 1700.

Also, Scots were indeed legally prohibited from direct trading with the English transatlantic colonies for much of the period before 1707. But they found numerous ways of circumventing the official controls by smuggling, employment of English vessels as covers, trading from English ports and the use of counterfeit papers. So by 1700 a substantial Scottish interest in the Caribbean was well established. It was a local variant of Scotland's growing orientation to the Atlantic world as the ancient commercial links with Europe began to stagnate and decline in comparative terms from the middle decades of the seventeenth century, only then to be powerfully reinforced and energised again after the Union by the re-export trade to continental countries in imported colonial tobacco and sugar. Darien may have failed spectacularly but that ambitious project nevertheless signified the intention of the Scottish governing class to commit the economic future of the nation to seizing commercial opportunities across the ocean in the western hemisphere.

The second myth was that only after the American War of Independence and the collapse of the tobacco trade at that time did Scottish involvement in the West Indies really take off. It is correct to argue that from the 1770s there was a dramatic strengthening of the relationship, not simply because of diversification by the tobacco lords but as a result of the demand of the new Scottish textile mills for West Indian 'sea island' cotton and the growing popular appetite for sugar as national population and real incomes continued to rise. Yet, as the chapters which follow confirm in detail, Scots were flooding into the region long before 1783, especially after the British victories of the Seven Years War (1756–63) which released several former French Caribbean islands for plantation ownership and business exploitation. Indeed, to distinguish the sugar and tobacco trades one from the other before the American War is essentially to draw a false dichotomy. Several leading Clyde merchants had fingers in both pies, and transfer of capital from the much more extensive American enterprise became an important influence fuelling expansion in West Indian commerce in the eighteenth century.

Certainly also the Union was a necessary precondition for Scottish success across the Atlantic. Only the lethal force of the Royal Navy could provide effective protection to the British merchant fleets which sailed the seas during a century of endemic conflict with France and other continental powers for global supremacy. An independent Scotland did not have anything like the naval or military muscle to stand alone in this world of aggressive martial giants. Immediately before the Union, the Scottish 'navy' comprised only three or four vessels.

Nevertheless, 1707 cannot in itself be considered a sufficient explanation for the advance of Scottish enterprise in the West Indies and the over-representation of Scots in some islands as they often were elsewhere in the British imperial world. To understand that, it is essential firstly to take a long view of Scottish overseas ventures before 1700 and then secondly to probe those aspects of the society and culture of eighteenth-century Scotland which might account for a disproportionate Scottish presence in the Caribbean. The movement en masse of Scots into Jamaica, the Ceded Islands and Demerara/Berbice /Essequibo (later British Guiana) in the second half of the eighteenth century was a regional variant of their penetration elsewhere in the Empire. For centuries, as pedlars, soldiers, clerics and scholars, the Scots had been a nomadic people. Scotland was a country where emigration was the norm rather than the exception, with a widely developed culture of long-distance mobility. From long experience of trading in central and northern Europe since medieval times, they traditionally tended to avoid areas where competition was entrenched and instead struck out into fresh frontier territories which presented potential opportunities, as well as considerable risks, for bold interlopers and adventurers. It was that strategy which had led to earlier Scottish successes in Poland-Lithuania in the sixteenth and seventeenth centuries and especially across the hinterland of the great river Vistula. Smuggling, a brazen disregard for commercial regulations and the habit of trading in close kin-based networks in order to minimise risks and squeeze out competitors were also familiar traditional practices.

These old methods of doing business in alien and volatile markets were transferred en bloc, first across the Atlantic and then eventually to Asia as the British Empire in the west and east experienced massive territorial expansion after a succession of colonial victories over European powers. Indeed, on occasion, the new connections were forged not from Scottish ports but from Scottish mercantile colonies in continental centres such as Amsterdam and Rotterdam. Enhanced intervention by Scots in the West Indies ran in parallel with the business of the Glasgow tobacco houses with the small planter class in the back country of the Chesapeake, away from the London-dominated tidewater areas; the Nor'West Company's vigorous engagement in the Canadian fur trade in the Arctic wastes, eventually threatening the hegemony and then the very survival of the mighty Hudson Bay Company itself; and the 'private trade', anchored originally among Scots servants of the East India Company and then spreading across south-east Asia to China and Japan in the early nineteenth century. In the Caribbean, for example,

Scots adventurers were always under-represented in Barbados, a colony long settled by the English since the early seventeenth century; they made instead for other islands where unreclaimed land and limited existing settlement promised richer future pickings. Classic examples were their rapid penetration of the former French islands after 1763 and annexed Dutch colonies on the South American mainland in the 1790s and after.

Those who emerged in this period as plantation owners, merchants and professionals in the West Indies were often the kindred of the small laird and urban mercantile-professional classes of Scottish society. They were seduced by the reputation of the slave colonies for making quick and easy money despite the lethal threat to life from tropical diseases. Janet Schaw in her letters home, for instance, reckoned that at times these could kill as many as four out of five new arrivals in their first year before their 'seasoning' was completed.

Given the choice, these migrants might very well have preferred to try to make their fortunes in healthier climes south of the Border. After all, Scots had long found success in London and established Scottish trading communities had flourished there for several generations by the eighteenth century. Nevertheless, for many young neophytes, breaking into the opportunities and riches of the capital with its long-established patronage connections and metropolitan networks was often challenging. Even the professionals, such as physicians and surgeons trained in the famous Scottish medical schools, had difficulty because of the refusal of the London colleges to accept their qualifications. More typical therefore of the movement of younger Scots traders to London, who did not already have family or personal connections there, was to seek some success overseas before attempting to obtain a foothold in the capital, as Eric Graham describes in Chapter 4. Posts and jobs in imperial territories, often avoided by the progeny of English elites because of the risks to health in far-off lands, were easier to access by Celtic adventurers. This was especially so where Scottish family, regional and local connections were already embedded by the middle decades of the eighteenth century and capable of offering support to new arrivals.

In her travels, Janet Schaw noted the Scottishness of the island of Antigua. She landed 'at a Wharf belonging to a Scotch Gentleman' and soon met with many Duncans, Millikens, Blairs, Bairds, Hallidays, Mackinnons and Malcolms. She noted that 'many Scotch names' were inscribed on the tombstones of the local graveyards and in St Kitts there were 'many fine plantations belonging to Scotch people who do not reside in them'. She observed too that resident Scots gave their business primarily to Scottish merchant houses. Clanship may have been in its death throes at home but neo-clanship (based on kindred ties and with profit-making rather than tribal security and martial purpose the new rationale) flourished in overseas territories. By the later eighteenth century, for example, a veritable plantation empire of Campbells of Argyll bestrode the western areas of Jamaica (see Chapter 4). Successful ethnic networks like these aroused a degree of Scotophobia among other whites in the slave colonies. Time and again the correspondence of the English in the plantations is peppered with dismissive remarks about 'the Scotch' as clannish, ubiquitous and doing very well for themselves.

This theme of the influence of Scottish networks on the promotion of business success is pursued again in several of the chapters which follow. Yet care must be taken. Scots were not alone at the time in employing family and personal connections for commercial ends. Only future comparative study can really tell us how distinctive and advantageous their networking was in relation to that of other ethnicities within the Empire.

Scots had also long been over-represented among the officer class of the British army even before 1707. From their loyal ranks, accustomed to unquestioning military obedience and to the enforcement of authority as determined by the state, were often recruited the governors and lower functionaries who administered the new colonies annexed during and after the series of eighteenth-century imperial wars. So it was that a number of Scottish governors were to be found in the Ceded Islands after 1763, the Leewards in earlier decades and, most importantly of all, in Jamaica when Alexander Lindsay, Earl of Balcarres, became not only the most important British grandee in the West Indies in the 1790s but one of the most powerful throughout the Empire. Once again, ethnic interest, clientage and influence in the Caribbean were likely to increase through the power of these Scottish colonial elites, though it would be an exaggeration to suggest that each and every one of them always and inevitably were keen to favour the interests of their fellow countrymen.

Closely related to the issue of opportunity abroad were conditions at home. While many of the nation's elites prospered, the later eighteenth century was also a time of increasingly acute economic and demographic challenge for a number of the Scottish laird classes and their cadet branches. On the one hand, the number of non-inheriting younger sons was increasing rapidly because of the significant rise in population at the time and the steep fall in infantile mortality which was one of its causes. Quite simply, there were now many more male offspring surviving well into adulthood than ever before. Genealogies show that it was not uncommon for some gentry families to have as many as six, eight, ten or even more surviving adult children by the early nineteenth century.

Because of the legal tradition of primogeniture, excluding all but the eldest son from the inheritance to family estates, remaining male siblings had to find alternative careers to avoid the threat of downward social mobility into the depths of genteel penury. An inherent difficulty was the tiny size of the Scottish civil administration, which meant that public posts available through patronage and family networking were few and far between at home. Annuities, pensions and dowries (in Scotland, tochers) needed also to be funded for the women of the family. Since they tended on average to outlive men, a pressing problem in eighteenth-century elite society was how to provide for the potential legions of surviving spinsters, widows and their dependants. Significantly, no less than 40 per cent of claims for compensation at the end of slavery in 1833 in Britain were made on behalf of pensioner females who were at least partly dependent on accruals from slave property for a regular income from mortgages on Caribbean plantations (see Chapter 8).

At the same time, confirmation of social rank in the eighteenth century was now more than ever being determined in the public sphere by display – material consumption, fashionable clothing, rich furnishing, trains of servants, domestic refurbishment and the building of houses which were designed to impress. Later in the century the increasing value of rent rolls on many estates did much to offset these costs. Earlier, however, and until around the 1770s, agricultural rents in Scotland were mainly static or only showed modest increases. A rise in indebtedness, often on a very significant scale, became therefore an anxious fact of life for many old landed families. In the Western Highlands and Islands, for instance, where these problems were often most critical, over two-thirds of estates changed hands (sometimes, ironically, to returning imperial adventurers who had been born and raised in Gaeldom) after c. 1800, as hereditary owners were squeezed out by overwhelming debt, encumbered lands and, for some, final bankruptcy and sequestration. That the influences were also Scotland-wide is illustrated by the fall in the number of smaller estates throughout the Lowlands as richer aristocratic magnates bought up more and more of the properties of less fortunate families.

Imperial opportunities in trade, the army, navy, administration and the professions often became one of the few routes of escape from the inexorably contracting vice of these twin financial pressures. Indeed, the availability of places in the expanding Empire came like a godsend to numerous impoverished but genteel kindreds the length and breadth of Scotland. A great exodus of young men, for the most part little older than fifteen or sixteen years of age, was propelled to the furthest reaches of the Empire, not only to satisfy personal ambition and access careers but also to buttress decaying family fortunes through remittances sent back by those who managed to achieve some success in distant lands. Even those destined to succeed to the family property in due course as eldest sons went abroad when younger, such were the financial imperatives of the time. Unlike the Catholic gentry of Ireland, these Scots did not face discrimination on religious grounds, as their rights as Presbyterian subjects of the Crown were affirmed and protected by the Treaty of Union of 1707. The frontiers of this British world were always porous. Siblings of the same family settled in different colonies and often travelled between different territories across the oceans during the course of their lives. The complex connections of kindred and influence stretched from North America to the Caribbean to India and well beyond.

It is also important to remember, however, that the economic constraints on many families did not entirely negate the possibility of modest funds being made available by some, either on credit or on landed security or via kindred networks, to provide younger sons with some 'start-up' funds. The Glasgow merchant community may not have been representative but it had the tradition of reserving some capital to those male progeny who were unlikely to inherit family lands to enable them to gain an initial foothold in alternative careers. How widespread this practice was is a question which can only be resolved by future research. If it was at all common, some young adventurers would have been given yet another advantage in the imperial job market.

What added to the migration at a lower social level was the impact of the agrarian revolution throughout rural Scotland. As improvement gathered pace in the Lowlands and southern and eastern Highlands during the last quarter of the eighteenth century, so consolidation of smaller single and multiple tenancies into compact individual farms progressed inexorably. The practice became one of embedding impartible inheritance as the number of tenant holdings started to shrink to a greater or lesser extent across the country, just as the number of surviving offspring in tenant families began to rise. Also in the western Highlands and Islands, the expansion of single-croft tenancies held directly from landowners caused the contraction and eventual disappearance of the old 'tacksman' class of middling tenantry. Once again, as with elite families, the search was on for opportunities elsewhere among the young men of middle rank and artisan class in the countryside who were now failing to gain an expected position in a rapidly changing world. Because of the Scottish schooling tradition they were usually proficient in basic reading, writing and arithmetic and often much more, skills in great demand in the counting houses of merchant companies trading overseas and the expanding imperial bureaucracies.

No one has yet worked out what became of these Scottish migrants in the mass during their sojourns in the West Indies. All we can say at this stage of knowledge is that many died soon after arrival, others, almost certainly a small minority, became rich, and the majority probably had relatively routine careers. Those who made their fortunes are remembered in the books and have left family archives for posterity to explore and help recount their successful activities. But the Caribbean, despite its legendary allure, was not always an easy route to material success. This was especially so in the crisis years between 1799 and 1807. It is reckoned that in Jamaica alone during that time, 65 plantations were abandoned, 32 sold for debts and 115 others had law suits pending against them. The many challenges included the volatility of climate and crops (there were three disastrous growing seasons, for instance, from 1789 to 1791), the continuing struggle between French and British forces until 1815, and the increasing incidence of slave revolt as in Grenada and St Vincent in 1795. The years 1793–4 were marked by the bankruptcy of numerous British merchant houses trading to the Caribbean and even the greatest enterprises were not immune from failure, as when the doyen of the Scottish sugar trade, the giant firm of Alexander Houston & Co., faced imminent bankruptcy with such potentially grave consequences that government itself had to step in to provide support to the partnership.

Uncertainties also applied to the more educated cadre of professional Scots. By 1800 Scotland had six universities (if the Andersonian, later Strathclyde, in Glasgow, founded in 1796, is included) compared to England's two and was reckoned to have more places in higher education per head of population by that date than any country in Europe. The orientation of the system had been reformed and transformed from an entire teaching dependency on classical languages, philosophy and theology to an additional focus on law, medicine, history and science. These were modern centres of learning, equipping their students with 'useful knowledge', to use the phrase of the time, for modern careers. But huge imbalances soon built up between limited opportunities in Scotland and increasing numbers of the trained and educated, especially when the products of the town grammar and better parish schools were also added to the growing pool of aspirants. Large-scale intellectual migration to all parts of the Empire became an inevitable consequence. Remarkably, therefore, it is estimated that between 1680 and 1780 as many as a third of the university-educated men who went to the American colonies from Britain and western Europe had studied in only three Scottish centres of learning: Aberdeen, Edinburgh and Glasgow. In the Caribbean, for instance, the diaspora of physicians trained in Scotland was especially noted. They included those who used their medical earnings from working on the slave ships and treating the enslaved on the plantations to buy their way into the trade itself. The Scottish universities produced as many as 10,000 medical graduates between 1750 and 1850. Only a minority of this army of physicians could hope to obtain posts in the UK, in part because the major London institutions would only employ those with qualifications awarded by the London Royal Colleges. The majority made their careers throughout and beyond the Empire, including, for a time, the West Indies. By 1800 the evidence suggests that even there the medical job market was threatened with a glut as would-be physicians desperately fought for fewer openings than the numbers arriving in the islands warranted.

This, then, is the general background to the story of Scotland and Caribbean slavery. The chapters which follow explore several of the themes already briefly described in more depth and detail.

NOTES

1. Adam Smith, *Wealth of Nations* (1776; London, 1937 edition), p. 366.
2. J. R. Ward, 'The British West Indies in the Age of Abolition, 1748–1815', in P. J. Marshall (ed.), *The Oxford History of the British Empire, Vol. II. The Eighteenth Century* (Oxford: Oxford University Press, 1998), p. 427. See generally, Nuala Zahedieh, *The Capital and the Colonies. London and the Atlantic Economy,1660–1700* (Cambridge: Cambridge University Press, 2010). For the relationship between the growing taste for all things sweet and the expansion of slavery discussed below, see Sydney W. Mintz, *Sweetness and Power: The Place of Sugar in Modern History* (New York: Viking, 1985) and Elizabeth Abbott, *Sugar: A Bittersweet History* (New York: Overlook Press, 2010).
3. Ward, 'British West Indies', pp. 127–8.
4. Quoted in R. B. Sheridan, 'The Formation of Caribbean Plantation Society, 1689–1748', in Marshall (ed.), *Oxford History*, p. 402.
5. Ward, 'British West Indies', p. 433.
6. Quoted in Richard B. Sheridan, *Doctors and Slaves: A Medical and Demographic History of Slavery in British West Indies, 1680–1834* (Cambridge: Cambridge University Press, 1985), p. 190.
7. Ibid.
8. Philip D. Morgan, 'The Black Experience in the British Empire, 1680–1810', in Marshall (ed.), *Oxford History*, p. 470. All references to Janet

Schaw's diary come from *The Journal of a Lady of Quality being the Narrative of a Journey from Scotland to the West Indies, North Carolina and Portugal in the years 1774 to 1778*, edited by E. W. Andrews and C. McL. Andrews (New Haven: Yale University Press, 1939), pp. 19–143, 259–76.

9. See, *inter alia*, Michael Craton, *Testing the Chains: Resistance to Slavery in the British West Indies* (Ithaca: Cornell University Press, 1982); Elsa V. Goveia, *Slave Society in the British Leeward Islands at the End of the Eighteenth Century* (New Haven: Yale University Press, 1965); Jerome S. Handler and Frederick W. Lange, *Plantation Slavery in Barbados: An Archaeological and Historical Investigation* (Cambridge, MA: Harvard University Press, 1978); Sheridan, *Doctors and Slaves, passim*; Morgan, 'The Black Experience', pp. 467–73.

10. Full supporting references and more detail on the next two sections can be found in T. M. Devine, *The Transformation of Rural Scotland: Social Change and the Agrarian Economy 1660–1815* (Edinburgh: Edinburgh University Press, 1994, 1999), pp. 36–59, 111–35; Robert Dodgshon, 'The Clearances and the Transformation of the Scottish Countryside', in T. M. Devine and Jenny Wormald (eds), *The Oxford Handbook of Modern Scottish History* (Oxford: Oxford University Press, 2012), pp. 131–58; T. M. Devine, *Scotland's Empire, 1600–1815* (London: Penguin, Allen Lane, 2003), pp. 26–48, 221–49; T. M. Devine, *To the Ends of the Earth: Scotland's Global Diaspora, 1750–2010* (London: Allen Lane, 2011), pp. 1–31; John M. MacKenzie and T. M. Devine (eds), *Scotland and the British Empire* (Oxford: Oxford University Press, 2011), pp. 30–53; Herbert S. Klein, Stanley L. Engerman, Robin Haines and Ralph Shlomovitz, 'Transoceanic Mortality: The Slave Trade in Comparative Historical Perspective', *William and Mary Quarterly*, LVIII, no. 1 (January 2001), pp. 93–118. On Scottish networks, see Angela McCarthy (ed.), *A Global Clan: Scottish Migrant Networks and Identities since the Eighteenth Century* (London: Tauris Academic Studies, 2006).

1

Lost to History

T. M. Devine

I

THE RECORD OF THOSE Scots who helped achieve the abolition of the slave trade in 1807 and then slavery itself within the British Empire in 1833 has already been well recorded in books by C. Duncan Rice and Iain Whyte. Yet Scottish engagement in the slave system itself was either ignored or lost from both academic history and popular memory for generations until the early years of the present century. When amnesia started to take root is difficult to determine. Compensation to Scots slave owners after emancipation remained a live issue into the late 1830s as assessment of claims was not completed until 1837. However, a mere four decades later, on the fiftieth anniversary commemoration of abolition in 1883, the Glasgow West India Association felt able to publish a triumphalist statement in the *Glasgow Herald* newspaper:

> It is to Glasgow's lasting honour that while Bristol and Liverpool were up to their elbows in the slave trade, Glasgow kept out of it. The reproach can never be levelled at our city as it was at Liverpool that there was not a stone in her streets that was not cemented with the blood of a slave.[1]

This bold assertion was remarkable at several levels.

For a start, the claim was brazenly hypocritical. Just a generation before it was made, the city's West India Association had been one of the most vocal and powerful anti-abolition pressure groups in the United Kingdom, famed for its unyielding and unrelenting opposition to the liberation of slaves in the Empire. The statement is confined to slave trading alone and in isolation. As shown below, direct trafficking of slaves from Africa to the Americas by Scottish ships from Scottish ports was indeed on a minor scale compared to the enormous human trade conducted from the major English centres.[2] Hence, by ignoring Scottish involvement in the slave economies more generally, the Association was able to claim the moral high ground for Glasgow and the city's transatlantic business community.

Again, from the 1883 abolition commemorations, a new tradition was established then and in subsequent anniversaries: to ignore or marginalise the history of slavery itself and focus instead on celebration of the moral victory of emancipation. The change in approach was by no means unique to Scotland but a pan-British phenomenon. As the London-based *Morning Star* reported with pride at the time: 'Emancipation exalted this nation high above all the other civilised nations of the earth.' Ending the slave trade became a badge of national honour in Britain which for many served to mask the realities of the country's slavery past. A similar focus on the celebration of abolition, while eschewing the darker realities of its associated history, has also been identified in France, which itself had a long slaving tradition from the ports of Bordeaux, La Rochelle and Nantes.[3]

The emphasis on abolition went with the grain of Scottish political values in the second half of the nineteenth century, the great era of unrivalled Liberal hegemony in the country. The Conservatives won only seven seats in nine general elections between 1832 and 1868 and, in 1857, 1859 and 1865, not one successful Conservative candidate was returned. So overwhelming was Liberal dominance in the towns that only half the elections over that period were actually contested. Liberalism appealed to the Scottish electorate because the party was identified with the progressive virtues of reform and liberty in opposition to the forces of reaction and conservatism. These values both reflected and reinforced Scotland's image of itself as an abolitionist nation in the van of the crusade to destroy slavery, not simply in 1833 but through support for the cause of emancipation in the decades which followed in all corners of the world.[4] Michael Morris, in Chapter 2, also shows that Scottish literature after abolition avoided the history of Caribbean slavery altogether as a subject too shameful, malign and repellent for genteel Victorian tastes; better by far to recall and celebrate achievements rather than become embroiled in troubling aspects of the national past.

Perhaps it was also predictable against this background that the subject of the Scottish role in the slave system failed for a long time to attract much if any interest from modern academic historians north of the Border. In England, the publication of Eric Williams' controversial but influential *Capitalism and Slavery* in 1944 eventually generated much scholarly writing in response to his arguments.[5] From the 1960s in particular, a rich historiography emerged on the subject from the pens of such scholars as Howard Temperley, Roger Anstey, James Walvin, David Richardson, Joseph Inikori and several others. Indifference and silence, however, prevailed in Scotland. The single monograph of that period with a slavery focus was C. Duncan Rice's *The Scottish Abolitionists, 1833–1861* (1981), which explored the dynamics of the emancipation movement rather than the brutal realities of slavery history itself.

The first modern scholarly text to consider the role of Scots in the Empire, Gordon Donaldson's *The Scots Overseas* (1966), ignored Scottish settlement in the Caribbean entirely and made only a single reference to 'coloured labour'. My own work of that time, *The Tobacco Lords* (1975) and the article 'An Eighteenth-Century Business Elite: Glasgow West India Merchants' (1978), mentioned slaves but only briefly in the context of their employment as sources for labour for the plantation colonies.[6] The two path-breaking general histories of modern Scotland published in the 1960s, William Ferguson's *Scotland: 1689 to the Present* (1968) and T. C. Smout's *History of the Scottish People, 1560–1830* (1969), had no reference to slavery or the slave trade in either their text or indexes. Indeed, as late as 2001, the authoritative *Oxford Companion to Scottish History* made only one allusion to the West Indies, and this related to the sale of Scottish linens there. There was no index entry to 'slavery' and the single reference to 'slave trade' maintained the orthodox approach of focusing on abolitionism and emancipation. More understanding of the Scottish role in the slave colonies was in fact emerging before 2000 but that work was being done by American-based scholars such as David Hancock, Alan Karras and R. B. Sheridan as part of their more general research on slavery and colonial trade.[7]

II

Academic neglect was paralleled by popular amnesia. Here there were both comparisons and contrasts between the Scottish and English experiences. As has been noted, until the later twentieth century most English commentators at public events tended to ignore the realities of the history of black slavery and instead addressed their remarks to the achievements of the abolitionists. Typically, for instance, during the bicentenary commemorations of 1933–4, the Oxford historian of empire, Sir Reginald Coupland, in a lecture at William Wilberforce's birthplace of Hull, proclaimed that the abolition of slavery in the British Empire was 'a striking example – perhaps, he noted, the most striking example one can think of in modern history – of the power of pure idealism in a practical world'.[8]

The fact that Britain was the first country globally to end the slave trade in 1807 and then subsequently abolish slavery itself in 1833 came to be regarded as proof positive of the nation's claim to moral pre-eminence in the civilised world.

In both England and Scotland, an estimated 250 commemorative events took place between March 1933 and November 1934. North of the Border, in part because emancipation remembrance was so strongly supported by the Protestant churches, large meetings and services of thanksgiving were held in places as far apart as Edinburgh, Perth, Glasgow, Aberdeen, Lochgelly, Stepps, Airdrie, Girvan, Wigtown and elsewhere. But again the British record of involvement in the slave trade over many decades was rarely if ever mentioned. William Wilberforce's national reputation for selfless idealism was at the heart of the rituals of remembrance and came to embody the belief that the history of slavery demonstrated, not exploitation on an inhuman scale, but rather the depth of Christian concern of white Britons for their suffering African brethren.[9]

However, from the 1970s and 1980s, public remembrance of slavery in England was transformed. Black issues and black histories in general attained a much higher profile as a result of political controversies over non-white immigration to the United Kingdom from the 1950s, the launch of the Notting Hill Carnival in 1959 as a mass celebration of Afro-Caribbean culture, and the Brixton Riots (or Risings) of 1981. Black History Month grew directly out of these events and energised the campaign for more attention to be paid to slavery and the struggle against racism. National Lottery funding, available from 1994, enabled black and Asian groups to demand that these new resources should be used to the benefit of all ethnic communities, a message which chimed well with the new political narratives of multiculturalism and the need for more inclusive forms of 'Britishness'. A striking result was an expansion in the number of galleries and museums in England devoted to slavery and the slave trade, most especially with major developments in Liverpool, London and Bristol, often developed in full consultation with local black communities.[10]

The climax of the process of reinterpretation and recognition in England came with the bicentenary of the abolition of the slave trade in 2007. One of the country's most distinguished experts on the history of Britain and slavery, Professor James Walvin, reported of that year:

> The 200th anniversary of the abolition of the British slave trade was remembered by an astonishing number of commemorations in galleries, museums, libraries – indeed in most institutions from Parliament down to hundreds of

schools. Throughout, there was strong and influential political interest (and a plethora of accompanying government publications) along with substantial funding made available, on a competitive basis, to 150 different commemorative projects by the Heritage Lottery Fund. The outcome was the most pervasive and eye-catching public commemoration in recent years, even surpassing some of the more recent spectacular history commemorations, such as Trafalgar and D-Day for example.[11]

A range of programmes was presented on both BBC TV and radio, followed by a veritable blizzard of newspaper reports and an outpouring of scholarly and popular books, essays and commentaries. The decision was also made that the story of slavery and abolition should become part of the compulsory school curriculum in England from 2008. The then Prime Minister, Tony Blair, in introducing the year-long programme of commemorative events, concluded that 'The slave trade was a profoundly inhuman enterprise and the bicentenary provides us with an opportunity to express our sorrow that it happened.'[12]

In Scotland, by contrast, celebration of the commemoration was more muted. No popular breakthrough in black history had taken place of the kind which occurred in England in the 1980s and helped establish the long-term foundations for the events of 2007. Indeed, pioneering academic studies of Scotland and slavery had only just started to appear a few years before that date.[13] Jackie Kay, the poet and novelist of Nigerian and Scots parentage, penned a scathing critique in the *Guardian* in March 2007 on what she regarded as unacceptable indifference north of the Border:[14]

> Being African and Scottish, I'd taken comfort in the notion that Scotland was not nearly as implicated in the horrors of the slave trade as England. Scotland's self-image is one of a hard-done-to wee nation yet bonny and blithe. I once heard a Scottish woman proudly say: 'We don't have racism up here, that's an English thing that's down south'. Scotland is a canny nation when it comes to remembering and forgetting. The plantation owner is never wearing a kilt.

She then went on to assert that 'Glasgow does not readily admit its history in the way that other cities have done' and questioned the absence of major commemoration events of 1807:

> What's happening in Glasgow? – in the Gallery of Modern Art, for instance, which was originally the Cunninghame Mansion, built in 1778, the splendid townhouse [sic] of William Cunninghame, a tobacco baron? Or in Buchanan Street, the great shopping street, named after Andrew Buchanan, another tobacco lord, or in Jamaica Street, Tobago Street and Kingston Bridge?

Even more illuminating was the fate of the proposed 2007 commemorative booklet commissioned by the (then) Scottish Executive.
Two academic specialists in the field, Drs Eric Graham and Iain Whyte,
both contributors to this volume, were invited to write a *Historical
Review: Scotland's involvement in the Transatlantic Slave Trade and its
Abolition* (1807). However, the initial draft was coldly received by the
Equality Unit of the Executive, which requested a radical rewrite of the
text. That in turn provoked a robust response from the two scholars that
'the "dumbing down" of language and content was unnecessary in our
professional opinion, based on our experience as communicators and
educators, widely published authors and contributors to various history
radio and TV programmes'. After subsequent unproductive discussions,
Graham and Whyte had their contracts terminated for refusing to make
major amendments to the text. In their view the suggested changes 'compromised historical accuracy and our professional integrity'. The project
was finally awarded to an English-based educationalist whose publication focused more on the British rather than the Scottish experience.[15]

At the same time, the major Scottish museums were becoming more
interested in fuller depictions of slavery history, although the approach
was not yet on the same strategic or comprehensive level as their counterparts in England. The original exhibits in the prestigious Museum
of Scotland in Edinburgh, which opened in 1998, made no reference
to the nation's slavery past. Thus far (2014), the policy of National
Museums Scotland is one of careful adjustment of displays rather than
root-and-branch revisionism. Within the 'Scots in the Americas' part of
the 'Scotland in the World' gallery are now featured the following with
their descriptors:

1. Covered cup made by Charles Allan around 1750. Allan was a Scottish
   goldsmith who worked in Kingston, Jamaica, from 1742 to 1763.
2. Candlesticks by George Fenwick, Edinburgh, engraved with the arms
   of George Ferguson of Pitfour, a governor of Tobago and plantation
   owner. Fenwick emigrated to Tobago, where he died and was buried on
   Ferguson's estate in 1821.
3. Caribbean coins from the eighteenth century, a time when many Scottish
   merchants were involved in the Caribbean trade, and whose profits were
   dependent on slave labour.
4. Graphic –
   • Scots and slavery. Adam Smith (baptised 1723–90), the philosopher
     and economist, noted that the profits created from the production
     of sugar 'were generally much greater than those of any other
     cultivation'.

- *Edinburgh Advertiser*, 20 January 1769, advert for the sale of a slave.
- Plan of the slave ship, *Brookes*, from a petition for the abolition of the slave trade delivered before a Select Committee of the House of Commons in 1790.
- List of slaves for sale by auction at the Huntley Estate, Demerara, now in modern Guyana.[16]

In Glasgow's Kelvingrove Art Gallery and Museum, the subject is presented in a case as part of the 'How Glasgow Flourished' exhibition and elsewhere is 'integrated into an examination of five elements of the "Glasgow System" of business management: community, credit, cheap labour, slavery, products and stores'. Further developments are promised.[17]

To be fair, all modern museum displays based on scholarship and material culture crucially depend on the chance survival of artefacts and images from the past. Not surprisingly, given the record of national amnesia on slavery and the urge to forget and dissemble, these are not likely to be very common in Scotland. A long-lost story has yielded few remains apart from a rich archive of ledgers, plantation correspondence, accounts and the like, which are mainly the stock in trade of the historian rather than those who seek to understand the past through the prism of material evidence.

More influential to date, therefore, in awakening some consciousness of the slavery past than the public institutions have been events sponsored by Black History Month, occasional features in the national print and TV media, some educational websites for schools and a growing corpus of creative literature, described in Chapter 2 by Michael Morris and exemplified by James Robertson's successful novel *Joseph Knight*, published in 2004. Interest was further aroused during the Commonwealth Games held in Glasgow in the summer of 2014 with a series of high-profile lectures, discussions and theatrical performances on Scotland and black history, particularly under the auspices of the Empire Café project, expertly organised by Louise Welsh and Jude Barber.

The point is also often made by Professor Geoff Palmer, himself a descendant of Jamaican slaves, that the legacy of the Scots in the West Indies lived on through the centuries in the surnames of descendants of the enslaved – he estimates around 70 per cent of the names in current Jamaica telephone directories are of Scottish origin. In addition, throughout the islands, the scattered remains of ironwork, street furniture and plantation equipment stamped 'Made in Glasgow' can still be seen, a later part of the Scottish legacy perhaps, but still evidence of the historic connection. Scottish place names of former plantations also proliferate across the Caribbean.[18]

Thus, between the middle decades of the nineteenth century and the end of the twentieth, the central Scottish role in the transatlantic slave economies was mainly lost to the history of the nation at both academic and popular levels.

Why should this be?

III

A key element was that even before the abolition of the trade, the Scottish connection to slavery had limited public visibility within the country itself. To some extent this was because those active in the business abroad were careful not to publicise their activities at home. Indeed, cases are recorded of Scots in the West Indies writing to their families to advise careful discretion when referring to slavery, suggesting that friends and neighbours would not really 'understand' life on the plantations. As argued in Chapter 2, references to the slave plantations in Scottish literature of the time were also sometimes presented in coded and oblique terms, as with the Caribbean being referred to vaguely and ambiguously as 'yonder awa' in Sir Walter Scott's *Rob Roy* (1817), rather than directly by name.

The nature of the Scottish connection also helped to maintain much domestic ignorance. From the early seventeenth to the early nineteenth centuries, countless numbers of British ships sailing year after year from Liverpool, Bristol and London carried more than 3.4 million Africans into bondage across the Atlantic. But the role of Scottish merchantmen in that 'triangular trade' between Britain, Africa and the Americas was minuscule by comparison. Between 1707 and 1766, for instance, only twenty-seven slave voyages direct from Scottish ports have been recorded, with around 4,500 slaves eventually embarked. Glasgow's outports of Greenock and Port Glasgow accounted for twenty-one of these, while the remainder shipped out of Montrose and Leith. By the 1760s even this limited activity had come to an end.[19]

It was these small numbers which partly enabled Victorian commentators to claim the moral superiority for Scotland on slavery and on which some of the comforting myths described above were constructed. In fact, most Scottish slavers accounted for in recent research worked out from ports south of the Border or from the Caribbean itself where, as merchants and plantation owners, they engaged directly in the importation of blacks from Africa (Chapter 5). One example of the business was the enormous slaving enterprise of the Malcolms of Poltalloch from Argyllshire. They supplied Scottish planters from West Africa to Jamaica and across the Caribbean from Tobago to Honduras with slaves. By the 1770s they were repatriating profits in excess of £40,000 a year from a gross annual turnover of £115,000. Multiplication by 80 gives a rough idea of how these figures might be represented in 2015 values. The Malcolms invested these riches in landed estates in Argyll, London's West India docks, in Yorkshire shipbuilding and in shipping insurance in the South China seas.[20]

The limited direct role of Scottish ports in the forced migration of Africans was not, however, based on moral scruple. Indeed, the most famous Scottish attempt at colonisation in the Americas in the seventeenth century, the failed expeditions to Darien on the Isthmus of Panama in the 1690s, was managed by the 'Company of Scotland trading to Africa and the Indies'. As the title suggests, the original objective of the enterprise was not to establish a settlement in Central America, as later happened, but rather to pursue both commercial and slaving interests in West Africa and the lucrative trade in spices in the East via the Cape of Good Hope.

The more likely explanation for the lack of direct involvement from Scotland itself is to be found in economic realities. As the eighteenth-century Atlantic economy expanded, Jacob Price showed that a form of functional specialisation emerged among the major western British ports. Liverpool and Bristol had already become dominant from an early period of the seventeenth century in both sugar importation and slave trafficking. But, as indicated in the Introduction to this volume, the Scottish mercantile tradition had long been to seek out opportunities at the peripheries where commercial competition from entrenched rivals was weaker. Thus the merchants of the Clyde ports increasingly avoided slaving but instead built up business even before the Union in those tobacco areas of mainland America situated in the back country of Virginia and Maryland. Ironically, of course, these plantation economies could not themselves flourish without extensive purchases of African slave labour. The business techniques of the big Glasgow merchant houses ensured in time quite extraordinary levels of success and by the 1750s they were importing more tobacco leaf by value and volume than London and all the English outports combined. Withdrawing from modest activity in the slave trade in which rival ports had long pre-eminence was therefore simply an acknowledgement that Scottish comparative advantage was best achieved in other sectors of the Atlantic economy.[21]

Probably also unremarked was the contemporary presence of numerous Scots expatriates who were active in English slaving ports, not just at the margins but frequently in a dominant role. Studies of the Scottish diaspora have significantly increased in recent years but systematic progress has been slower on researching the migration of Scots to England. Nevertheless, from the limited details currently available, a substantial Scottish presence in the slave trade south of the Border has already been identified. In Liverpool, Scots managed at least five firms, and of the 128 slaving captains who sailed from the port in the later eighteenth century whose origins have been documented, twenty-five were Scots, as were no fewer than 136 ships' surgeons.[22] Suzanne Schwarz's findings on Scots in Liverpool in Chapter 7 add even more substance to this evidence. One of the most powerful merchant dynasties in the north of Scotland, the Baillies of Dochfour, near Inverness, was partially founded on the profits of slave trading from Bristol.[23] In London, one in ten of the capital's African traders was Scots-born in the 1750s, a proportion which increased in later decades. They were heavily involved in the activities of the Company of Merchants trading to Africa.[24] London-based Scots, led by Richard Oswald and the Grant and Boyd families, founded the notorious slave 'castle' on the Sierra Leone river at Bance Island which was linked to a dozen 'out factories' or slave-gathering centres in the mainland interior. Between 1748 and 1784 the business shipped nearly 13,000 Africans across the Atlantic, many of them delivered to Scots plantation owners in the Caribbean.[25] Nicholas Draper's analysis of the compensation records after emancipation in 1833 in Chapter 8 not only provides further detail on expatriate activity in England but shows that some of the biggest slaving houses there were either Scottish-owned at the end of slavery or had been founded by Scots merchant syndicates in earlier years.

The campaigns for and against abolition and emancipation were fought with passion by both sides in Scotland before the passage of the historic legislation in 1807 and 1833. Those opposed to slavery as a wicked moral evil, with the Church of Scotland in the vanguard of the movement, were faced by powerful vested interests and well-organised hostility from anti-abolitionists. This was hardly surprising given the enormous economic stake the country had in the sugar islands of the West Indies. As Iain Whyte and Douglas Hamilton have shown, both anti-abolition petitions as well as pro-abolition counterparts flooded in from all parts of Scotland during those times of acrimonious and passionate debate. The Glasgow West India Association, founded in 1807, became, as indicated above, one of the most aggressive pro-slavery pressure groups in Britain, and the organisation was aided and abetted energetically by a leading newspaper in the city, the *Glasgow Courier*. And, as confirmed in Catherine Hall's chapter in this book, not all the country's influential public voices were necessarily abolitionist in their enthusiasms, even after the passage of the legislation of 1833.

Much of the anti-abolitionist pressure was applied behind the scenes. As members of Britain's ruling elites, wealthy Scots West India merchants, some of whom, like William McDowall of the giant house of Alexander Houston & Co. or James Baillie of the Baillies of Bristol, were also Members of Parliament, often had direct personal access to Government ministers. One of the most powerful of these was Henry Dundas, the 'uncrowned King of Scotland', whose parliamentary intervention in 1792 arguing for gradual abolition of the slave trade effectively killed off reform for a generation. Not surprisingly, he received grateful thanks from influential members of the West India interest for his support for their cause.

But from the 1840s the flames of bitter controversy over slavery died down and a new mainstream narrative became established which enshrined Scotland as a leading abolitionist nation where memory of the nation's slavery history and the last-ditch stand by the anti-abolitionist lobby gradually faded and then disappeared altogether from public awareness. Ironically, the Glasgow West India Association itself eventually metamorphosed into an anti-slavery organisation, making donations to the Anti-Slavery Society and publicly supporting preferential tariffs for British West India sugar grown by free labour rather than that produced by slaves from Brazil and Cuba. J. R. Oldfield concluded after examining the 1884 Commemorations throughout Britain, 'by the 1880s a new consensus had emerged ... that celebrated the nation's moral leadership in emancipating the slaves'.[26] Even the issue of the £20 million paid in compensation to colonial planters for their enslaved property after 1833, which had so embarrassed abolitionists at the time, was forgotten. Future commemorative celebrations in 1907 and 1933 were uncritical and enthusiastic tributes to abolitionist success with little reference to the horrors of the slave trade or the brutal experience of chattel slavery in the plantations.[27]

Four additional factors in the specific context of Scotland contributed to amnesia by the end of the nineteenth century.

First, the commercial connection with the West Indies, once so central both in terms of imports and exports to the Scottish economy and the Clyde ports in particular before the 1830s, faded into history from the second half of the nineteenth century. Sugar did continue to arrive in vast bulk but increasingly it came from Cuba and Brazil rather than the British Caribbean.[28] By 1861, only 4 per cent of the merchant tonnage entering Clyde ports originated in the West Indies.[29]

Second, by the mid-Victorian era Scotland had become a global economic force with burgeoning markets in Asia, Africa, Europe, the United States and Latin America as well as in the old Empire.[30] Merchant houses which had previously specialised in the Caribbean trades diversified in new directions, particularly into banking, cotton manufacturing, railways and overseas investment. The younger generations of these families were now more likely to seek careers and fortunes in the East India Company and the imperial professions of soldiering, medicine, accounting, banking, law and other pursuits.[31] Recent research on the West Indian merchant cohort who died in the period 1834 to 1877 has shown that they had more varied business interests and fewer residential ties with Glasgow and the West of Scotland than the previous generation.[32] Those that remained, as Stephen Mullen argues in Chapter 6, became among the most illustrious members of the city's social elite, the origins of their fortunes lost to history as they played to the full ostentatious public roles as provosts, town councillors, deans of guilds, university rectors, members of parliament and generous benefactors of good causes in Glasgow and beyond. By holding positions of high status in the hierarchical and deferential elite society of Victorian times, they were usually protected from public censure for the questionable foundational wealth of their families.

But perhaps even they were not always immune from the muted criticism of local gossip. There was, for instance, the interesting case of James Ewing (1775–1853), one of the very wealthiest of the West Indian sugar princes, who owned great estates in Jamaica and left a huge fortune of over £262,000 at his death at the age of seventy-eight. It was reported in one obituary that he was 'a major mercantile figure in Glasgow *who was apparently disliked by some because of his connection with slaves in the Caribbean*' (my italics). Ewing had of course lived into old age when slavery and then abolition remained live issues. Nevertheless, such minor public censure did not stop him from reaching some of the loftiest offices in the city as Chairman of the Glasgow Chamber of Commerce, Member of Parliament, Lord Provost and the recipient of an honorary doctorate from the University.[33]

Third, by the later nineteenth century, Glasgow was a city of world status, keen to celebrate its past and present achievements with civic pride and splendid ceremonial, most notably in the formal opening by Queen Victoria of the grandiose City Chambers in George Square in 1888, followed a few years later by the hosting of the Second International Exhibition in Kelvingrove, the largest public event ever held in Britain to that time and eventually attracting more than 11.5 million visitors from across the United Kingdom.[34] This celebratory mood encouraged the publication of a stream of books devoted to recording the deeds of the heroic mercantile figures of the age of tobacco and sugar whose commercial elan had transformed the city from a small provincial town to an urban colossus with a global reach. They included J. Maclehose, *The Old Country Houses of the Old Glasgow Gentry* (1870); J. O. Mitchell, *Old Glasgow Essays* (1905); Senex (J. M. Reid), *Glasgow Past and Present*, three volumes (1884); George Stewart, *Progress of Glasgow* (1883) and *Curiosities of Glasgow Citizenship* (1881); and J. Maclehose, *Memories and Portraits of 100 Glasgow Men*, two volumes (1886).

These works all contained impressive historical information and so have been much quarried by later scholars. Yet, in the final analysis, they were essentially uncritical hagiographies, silent on the slavery roots of much of the city's economic eminence and the role of the merchant adventurers whose profits, derived in large measure from the slave-based transatlantic economies, had caused Glasgow to flourish. It was an ambitious exercise in the invention of a certain type of glorious tradition which survived inviolate almost to the present day.

Fourth, the iconic influence of David Livingstone, the most famous Scot of the nineteenth century and the nation's 'Protestant saint', did much to further embed Scotland's self-image as an abolitionist, anti-slavery country without reference to the darker context of the past. Livingstone achieved distinction as an explorer and missionary but his crusade against African slavery was central to his fame, not least because his promotion of 'Commerce and Christianity' as the solution to the eradication of slavery had powerful appeal to both the material and spiritual elements of the Victorian mind. It is difficult now to grasp the extent to which Livingstone was lionised as the Victorian hero of the Scots. His remarkable impact was illustrated by the endless outpouring of biographies, pamphlets and press articles which kept his name and fame before the public, not only during much of his life, but well after his death. The Scottish National Memorial to him at Blantyre was considered by its leading promoter as 'a place of pilgrimage, a shrine' and attracted countless visitors for much of the twentieth century while, until the 1960s, books about Livingstone were the most commonly favoured prizes for able pupils in Scottish schools.[35]

Livingstone's mass appeal perhaps also represented something deeper – a passionate sense of moral outrage about slavery which was rooted in the greater intensity of middle-class evangelical religion in nineteenth-century Scotland exemplified above all by the Disruption of 1843, the emergence of the Free Church at that point, philanthropic support for numerous good causes at home and the flowering of Scottish Presbyterian missions across the globe in the Victorian era. Christianity and slavery were now deemed to be utterly incompatible and that the evil continued to survive became an unacceptable affront to the Kingdom of God on earth. This represented an ethical transformation from the moral ambiguities of the eighteenth century and earlier. 1807 and 1833 were the anchors of this new sensibility, persuading God-fearing people of Britain's glorious victories over slavery while avoiding mention of the sins of the past.

The question remains, however, why the Scots took longer than the English in the later twentieth century to start to come to terms with their slavery past. One explanation lies in the low profile of Afro-Caribbean culture in Scotland until very recent years. Much of the drive for public commemorations of the history of slavery in England came from the descendants of West Indian immigrants. The rise of a powerful, articulate and increasingly assertive English Caribbean community forced the pace in politics, education and culture, supported by a number of gifted writers of Caribbean descent such as David Dabydeen, Andrea Levy, Caryl Phillips and Zadie Smith. Their influence has combined to demand a new kind of history and cultural thinking south of the Border. By contrast, Scotland never experienced migration from the West Indies in the second half of last century on anything like the same scale as England. In London alone, the black population in 2007 numbered 820,000.[36] By contrast, in Scotland it totalled 6,546, or only around 0.1 per cent of the national population at the census of 2011. Scottish historians have published widely on immigrant groups but predictably their focus is mainly on the much more numerous Irish, English, Italians, Lithuanians and Jews, and on related topics such as religious sectarianism.[37]

Interest in the Empire and the related issue of slavery in Scottish academic history also lagged far behind England. The first book since the 1930s devoted to Scotland's role in Empire was not published until 2000. Indeed, by the late 1960s most Scots seemed to have lost interest in their imperial past as the Empire on which the sun had never set disappeared with such astonishing speed. During the 1950s the General Assembly of the Church of Scotland (the stateless nation's so-called 'surrogate Parliament') and the Scottish Trades Union Congress had vociferously condemned imperialism and championed the cause of freedom for subject peoples in Africa and elsewhere. A decade later, empire seems quickly to have become a subject of indifference and perhaps even embarrassment, an unwelcome relic from a history now best forgotten.

For a time, though, some public remnants of the old imperial order did linger on outside the pages of the empire-supporting *Scottish Daily Express*. In 1967, for instance, the Argyll and Sutherland Highlanders, led by the redoubtable Lieutenant Colonel Colin 'Mad Mitch' Mitchell, reoccupied the Crater district in the British colony of Aden. In a famous exploit which produced many headlines at home, the Jocks summarily evicted a group of insurgents who had earlier seized control of the area. The resolute operation stirred patriotic pride at home and came to be dubbed the 'Last Battle of the British Empire'. Yet even this demonstration of the old Scottish martial spirit awakened little in the way of imperial nostalgia. Three decades later the pipes and drums of the Black Watch took centre stage in the ceremonials which brought British rule in the last major crown colony, Hong Kong, to an end. The famous kilted regiment now performed a different role as the pallbearer rather than a spearhead of Empire.

Undeniably, the national political mood was also changing. The Scottish Unionist Party (Conservatives only from 1965), which retained some imperial sympathies and had dominated Scottish elections for much of the twentieth century, began an irreversible decline in popularity and eventual irrelevance even before the Thatcher years of the 1980s. Scotland moved to the left in electoral terms. The scene was now set for successive decades of Labour Party hegemony at national and local level. Even nationalism, long asleep, also began to stir and started to exert a more alluring appeal than at any time since the foundation of the Scottish National Party in the 1930s.

Many now came to see Scotland as a victimised country when the economy started to falter and then experience acute difficulties after the postwar boom finally came to an end. The celebrated dirge, *Flower of Scotland*, recalling the struggles of the medieval Wars of Independence with the plaintive line 'they fought and died for their wee bit hill and glen', was composed in 1967 and caught the temper of the times. Significantly, too, the histories which had most popular appeal were those written by the Anglo-Canadian John Prebble, who saw the Scottish past mainly through a lens of loss and tragedy as he successively (and profitably) chronicled such lamented episodes in the nation's history as the Darien Disaster, Glencoe, Culloden and the Highland Clearances.[38]

This mood of pessimism, and with it the coming of the so-called 'Scottish cringe', or crisis in national confidence, was self-evidently not one which could easily relate to the Scots' history as active slavers and aggressive imperialists. It was more likely anyway that ignorance and myopia about the more controversial aspects of the nation's past would prevail because the teaching of Scottish history in the schools of that time was notoriously erratic, dated and pedestrian, as anyone who was a pupil in secondary education in Scotland then can confirm. It was a rare history graduate from the ancient universities who entered the teaching profession during that period who had studied even a modicum of modern Scottish history as part of their degree course in the broader discipline.

Nor were professional historians in the universities yet equipped to come to the rescue. Modern Scottish academic history was underdeveloped for most of the twentieth century until a historiographical revolution was triggered from the later 1960s and 1970s. There were only around fifteen research scholars in the subject in the 1950s and most of them worked on the history of the independent nation before 1707. As late as 1966 a mere three doctorates in Scottish history were completed in the UK as a whole. Indeed, when J. D. Hargreaves delivered his inaugural lecture as the new Burnett-Fletcher Professor at Aberdeen in 1964, he famously claimed that the history of Scotland since 1707 was less studied than the history of Yorkshire.[39] Remarkably, William Ferguson's *Scotland: 1689 to the Present*, published in 1968, was the first-ever general study of the previous three hundred years of Scottish history written by an academic historian.

When the subject did grow dramatically from then on in the number of scholars, graduate students, seminal publications and methodological sophistication, it was inevitable that the vast areas of ignorance in the modern domestic history of the nation would receive first attention. The publisher for many of the important new monographs was the Edinburgh-based house of John Donald. Hardly any of its books from that period, or those of the successor Tuckwell Press, focused on the record of the Scottish experience overseas. Only latterly, from the early years of the new century, did important work on Empire and then slavery begin to be published. These contributions have now helped to provide the foundation and inspiration for several of the chapters in this book.[40]

Perhaps, therefore, and at long last, Scotland's slavery past may now indeed be recovered to history.[41]

NOTES

1. *Glasgow Herald*, 1 June 1883.
2. M. Duffill, 'The African Trade from the Ports of Scotland, 1700–66', *Slavery and Abolition*, 24 (December, 2004), pp. 102–22.

3. Quoted in J. B. Oldfield, *'Chords of Freedom': Commemoration, Ritual and British Transatlantic Slavery* (Manchester: Manchester University Press, 2001), p. 89; Nicola Frith, '"Working through Slavery": The Limits of Shared Memories in Contemporary France', *Irish Journal of Francophone Studies*, 12 (2013), pp. 17–39. I am grateful to Dr Firth for sending me a copy of her essay.

4. T. M. Devine, *The Scottish Nation: A Modern History* (London: Penguin, 2012), pp. 281–2.

5. B. Solow and S. Engerman (eds), *British Capitalism and Caribbean Slavery: The Legacy of Eric Williams* (Cambridge: Cambridge University Press, 1987).

6. The latter in *Scottish Historical Review*, vol. 57 (1970), pp. 40–67.

7. A. L. Karras, *Sojourners in the Sun: Scottish Migrants in Jamaica and the Chesapeake 1740–1800* (Ithaca: Cornell University Press, 1992); David Hancock, *Citizens of the World: London Merchants and the Integration of the British Atlantic Community, 1735–1785* (Cambridge: Cambridge University Press, 1995); R. B. Sheridan, *Sugar and Slavery: An Economic History of British West Indies, 1623–1775* (Barbados: Caribbean Universities Press, 1974); Richard Sheridan, 'The Role of the Scots in the Economy and Society of the West Indies', in V. Rubin and A. Tuden (eds), *Comparative Perspectives on Slavery in New World Plantation Societies* (New York: New York Academy of Sciences, 1977); R. B. Sheridan, *Doctors and Slaves: A Medical and Demographic History of Slavery in British West Indies, 1680–1834* (Cambridge: Cambridge University Press, 1985).

8. Quoted in Oldfield, *'Chords of Freedom'*, p. 1.

9. Ibid., pp. 90, 96, 98, 109.

10. John G. Beech, 'The Marketing of Slavery Heritage in the United Kingdom', *International Journal of Hospitality and Tourism and Administration*, 2 (2001), pp. 100–3.

11. Email message, James Walvin to T. M. Devine, 13 November 2007. I am grateful to Professor Walvin for this information.

12. A message from the Prime Minister. 2007 Bicentenary of the Abolition of the Slave Trade Act. Calendar of Events, HM Government (2007).

13. The books appearing between 2001 and 2007 included: T. M. Devine, *Scotland's Empire 1600–1815* (2003); Douglas Hamilton, *Scotland, the Caribbean and the Atlantic World, 1750–1820* (2005); Iain Whyte, *Scotland and the Abolition of Black Slavery, 1756–1838* (2006) – though focusing on abolition, Chapter 2 of the book contained an overview of the Scottish role in Caribbean slavery. Specialist articles in periodicals and essay collections had also been written by John W. Cairns, Mark Duffill, Eric Graham and David Hancock.

14. Jackie Kay, 'Missing Faces', *The Guardian*, 24 March 2007.

15. Email message from Eric J. Graham to T. M. Devine, 6 December 2013.

The version which was eventually published can be found at www.scotland.
gov.uk/Publications/2007/03/23121622/0 (accessed 19 November 2014). I
am grateful to Dr Graham for sending me details of this affair.

16. Email message from David S. Forsyth, Principal Curator, Medieval-Early
    Modern Collections, National Museums Scotland to T. M. Devine, 12
    August 2014. I am grateful to Mr Forsyth for this information.

17. Email message from Dr Anthony Lewis, Curator of Scottish History,
    Glasgow Museums to T. M. Devine, 12 August 2014. I am grateful to Dr
    Lewis for this information.

18. Geoff Palmer, 'Jamaican Scottish Connections', in Afe Adogame and
    Andrew Lawrence (eds), *Africa in Scotland, Scotland in Africa: Historical
    Legacies and Contemporary Hybridities* (Leiden and Boston: Brill, 2014),
    p. 351. Scottish audiences were also struck and intrigued by the number of
    Scots surnames of West Indian competitors at the Commonwealth Games.
    The point about Scottish material remains came in an email message from
    Dr Stuart Nisbet to T. M. Devine, 6 January 2015. For the reference to
    place names, see Chapter 5, pp. 104, 106.

19. Duffill, 'African Trade', pp. 102–22. Slaves were known in eighteenth-
    century Scotland. Black boy pages, footmen and servants were sought
    after as trophy employees in elite households, especially those which had
    a commercial connection to the Americas. John Cairns's examination of
    the relevant sources estimates there were around one hundred of them
    between 1740 and 1800, though he suggests the real numbers were prob-
    ably higher. Though unfree, their lives were of course far removed from the
    brutalised labour of field slaves in the Caribbean plantations; yet several
    ran away from their masters, suggesting that the experience was not always
    acceptable. John W. Cairns, 'Slaves and Slaveowners in Eighteenth-Century
    Scotland', Paper presented at the Centre for Scottish and Celtic Studies
    Research Seminar, University of Glasgow, 20 November 2012.

20. Allan I. Macinnes, *Clanship, Commerce and the House of Stuart 1603–
    1788* (Edinburgh: Tuckwell Press, 1996), pp. 229–30.

21. Jacob M. Price, 'The Rise of Glasgow in the Chesapeake Tobacco Trade,
    1707–1775', reprinted in Peter L. Payne (ed.), *Studies in Scottish Business
    History* (London: Routledge, 1967), p. 306. See also T. M. Devine and
    Philippe R. Rössner, 'Scots in the Atlantic Economy, 1600–1800', in John
    M. MacKenzie and T. M. Devine (eds), *Scotland and the British Empire*
    (Oxford: Oxford University Press, 2011), pp. 30–53.

22. Eric Graham, 'Scots in the Liverpool Slave Trade', *History Scotland* (March
    2001).

23. Hamilton, *Scotland, the Caribbean and the Atlantic World*, pp. 88–92.

24. David Hancock, 'Scots in the Slave Trade', in Ned C. Landsman (ed.),
    *Nation and Province in the First British Empire: Scotland and the Americas,
    1600–1800* (London: Bucknell University Press, 2001), p. 63.

25. Ibid., pp. 63–83.

26. Oldfield, '*Chords of Freedom*', p. 90.
27. See, for instance, *The Scotsman*, 29 May, 30 June, 15 and 17 July, 28 August 1933.
28. Mitchell Library, Glasgow, Clyde Navigation Trust Shipping Returns, 1861–1911.
29. Ibid.
30. T. M. Devine, *To the Ends of the Earth: Scotland's Global Diaspora, 1750–2010* (London: Allen Lane, 2011), pp. 56–84.
31. Anthony Cooke, 'An Elite Revisited. Glasgow West India Merchants, 1783–1877', *Journal of Scottish Historical Studies*, vol. 32, no. 2 (2012), p. 152.
32. Ibid.; Emma Rothschild, *The Inner Life of Empires: An Eighteenth-Century History* (Princeton, NJ: Princeton University Press, 2011), pp. 121–53.
33. *Gentleman's Magazine*, 1854, I, p. 203; 'James Ewing, Banker and West India Merchant, Profile and Legacies Summary', www.ucl.ac.uk/lbs/ (accessed 19 November 2014).
34. Devine, *Scottish Nation: A Modern History*, p. 249.
35. John M. MacKenzie, 'David Livingstone: The Construction of a Myth', in G. Walker and T. Gallagher (eds), *Sermons and Battle Hymns* (Edinburgh: Edinburgh University Press, 1990), pp. 27–8; Andrew Ross, *David Livingstone. Mission and Empire* (London: Hambledon & London, 2002); James Macnair, *The Story of the Scottish National Memorial to David Livingstone* (Blantyre, 1945); Devine, *To the Ends of the Earth*, pp. 199–204.
36. *The African Community in London*, http://archives/museumoflondon.org.uk/RWWC/Themes/1078/ (accessed 2 September 2014).
37. *Scotland's Census 2011 – National Records of Scotland, Table KS201SC – Ethnic groups – Release 3A*. For an overview of recent research results on these immigrant groups, see Ben Braber, 'Immigrants', in T. M. Devine and J. Wormald (eds), *The Oxford Handbook of Modern Scottish History* (Oxford: Oxford University Press, 2012), pp. 491–509.
38. Tom Devine, 'The Scottish Sixties: A Historical Context', in Eleanor Bell and Linda Gunn (eds), *The Scottish Sixties. Reading, Rebellion, Revolution?* (Amsterdam: Editions Rodopi, 2013), pp. 14–46.
39. J. D. Hargreaves, 'Historical Study in Scotland', *Aberdeen University Review*, vol. xi (1964), pp. 237–50.
40. T. M. Devine and J. Wormald, 'Introduction: The Study of Modern Scottish History', in Devine and Wormald (eds), *Oxford Handbook of Modern Scottish History*, pp. 8–15.
41. Publications which have appeared since the 2007 bicentenary commemoration include Devine, *To The Ends of the Earth*; Nicholas Draper, *The Price of Emancipation: Slave Ownership, Compensation and British Society at the End of Slavery* (Cambridge: Cambridge University Press, 2010); E. Graham, *Burns and the Sugar Plantocracy of Ayrshire* (Ayr:

Ayrshire Archaeological and Natural History Society, 2009); Cooke, 'An Elite Revisited, 1783–1877', pp. 127–66; Stephen Mullen, 'A Glasgow-West India Merchant House and the Imperial Dividend, 1779–1867', *Journal of Scottish Historical Studies,* vol. 33, no. 2 (2013), pp. 196–233; Rothschild, *Inner Life of Empires*; Douglas Hamilton, '"Defending the Colonies against the Malicious Attacks of Philanthropy": Scottish Campaigns against the Abolition of the Slave Trade and Slavery', in A. I. Macinnes and D. H. Hamilton (eds), *Jacobitsm, Enlightenment and Empire,1660–1820* (London: Chatto & Windus, 2014).

2

Yonder Awa: Slavery and Distancing Strategies in Scottish Literature

Michael Morris

When the cloth was removed, Mr Jarvie compounded with his own hands a very small bowl of brandy-punch, the first which I had ever the fortune to see. 'The limes,' he assured us, 'were from his own little farm yonder-awa' (indicating the West Indies with a knowing shrug of his shoulders).

Walter Scott, *Rob Roy*, 1817

so it was that the rum came to be from yonder awa awa, and the black ants lifting heavy load in that heathen land became yonder awa awa. Til your memory grew awa awa . . . and the land had broad back – you forget, and the land dash you awa – you forget . . . look how you can't run awa awa from truth. look how you cant back chat this one awa awa.

Malika Booker, yonder awa awa, 2014

WALTER SCOTT'S HISTORICAL FICTION *Rob Roy*, written in 1817, is set around the Jacobite rebellion of 1715. The century between the time of action and the time of writing had seen the city of Glasgow become a major Atlantic port, the flourishing of the Enlightenment, the defeat of the Jacobite claim to the throne, the solidification of an apparently enduring political union with England, the expansion of the empire to west and east, and the defeat of Napoleon in 1815 which brought an apparently conclusive victory to almost constant war with an imperial rival. During this time, Britain became the leading slave-trading nation from Africa to the Americas, before latterly abolishing the trade; a feature intimately intertwined with the more familiar 'national story' in ways that are only beginning to be fully recognised. In the novel's narrative present, the union of 1707 still struggles for credibility, the restoration of the House of Stuart over the Hanoverian usurpers seems both achievable and urgent, and the rule of state law carries little weight over large areas where glamorous brigands like Rob

Roy roam. Into this landscape, the arrival of limes signifies a fresh new beginning. The 'exotic' green Caribbean citrus fruit mixes in the punch bowl with classical European brandy (not rum) creating a zesty transatlantic cocktail suggestive of the kinds of delights that the Union and Empire can bring to Scotland. The drinkers 'found the liquor exceedingly palatable'.[1]

Scott's English protagonist Frank Osbaldistone foretells the rise of Glasgow from a university and cathedral city to a trading powerhouse:

> An extensive and increasing trade with the West Indies and American colonies, has, if I am rightly informed, laid the foundation of wealth and prosperity, which, if carefully strengthened and built upon, may one day support an immense fabric of commercial prosperity. (p. 224)

Carla Sassi observes, 'what lies behind this prosperity remains unsaid – unspeakable'. Nicol Jarvie, the portentous voice of the Glasgow merchant class, who proudly presents the brandy punch with limes, 'is unable to even pronounce [the name of the West Indies] and recurs, twice to an embarrassed euphemism – "Yonder Awa"'.[2] The second occasion is in dispute with Andrew Fairservice, who decries the 'deteriorating influence of the Union'. Jarvie proclaims:

> Now, since St Mungo catched herrings in the Clyde, what was ever like to gar us flourish like the sugar and tobacco trade? Will onybody tell me that, and grumble at the treaty that opened us a road west-awa' yonder? (p. 322)

Fairservice is afforded a 'grumbling protest' in which the spoils of empire fail to compensate for the loss of national sovereignty:

> That it was an unco change to hae Scotland's laws made in England; and that, for his share, he wadna for a' the herring-barrels in Glasgow, and a' the tobacco-casks to boot, hae gien up the riding o' the Scots Parliament, or sent awa' our crown, and our sword, and our sceptre, and Mons Meg, to be keepit by thae English pock-puddings in the Tower o' Lunnon. (p. 322)

Missing from both Jarvie's pugnacious celebration of British Union and Empire, and Fairservice's Scottish national 'grumble', is the violence at the heart of empire: the genocide of the Amerindians and mass transportation of enslaved Africans, perpetrated by Scots, among others, yonder awa in the West Indies. Indeed, it appears that Jarvie's embarrassment may stem more from the recipe for punch being associated with 'auld Captain Coffinkey' and 'the Buccaniers' – the glamorous brigands of the Caribbean Sea – rather than slavery. Nonetheless, Scott appears to insert a coded reference to slavery in Jarvie's final platitude: '"But it's excellent liquor," said he, helping us round; "and good ware has aften come frae a wicked market"' (p. 299). Contemporary readers would be likely to hear the echo of the apology for slavery – the ends justify the means – only a decade after the abolition of the slave trade (1807). However, any explicit acknowledgement of slavery seems doubly suppressed here, forestalling any extended discussion of enslaved labour in the context of Scottish historical fiction. Slavery, then, hangs like a shadow over the scene, present only in the readers' knowledge of historical context.

In 2014, Louise Welsh and Jude Barber invited a number of Scottish, English and Caribbean writers to contribute poems reflecting more directly on Scotland and slavery to a collection which borrows for its title Nicol Jarvie's phrase – *Yonder Awa*.[3] In a striking example of a post-colonial intertextual exchange, Malika Booker's poetic re-visioning of the phrase 'yonder awa' foregrounds the enslaved labour of transported Africans on which the 'immense fabric of commercial prosperity' relied, and which is left shrouded in silence by Jarvie's 'embarrassed euphemism'. Booker's poetry is profoundly concerned with social justice and identity, concerns shaped by her early upbringing in Guyana by her Grenadian mother and Guyanese father, before she moved to the UK the day after 'the Brixton uprising'. The poem's epigraph from Exodus 2.22 – 'have been a stranger in a strange land' – both suggests the New World as a meeting point of exiles, and taps into the abolitionist tradition which contested Biblical justifications of slavery by referring to Pharoah's enslavement and tyranny over the Hebrews.[4] The role of Scots here is akin to that of the Egyptians. Booker borrows Jarvie's euphemism and riffs on it, enveloping his Scottish expression in a sonorous Caribbean English rhythm and phrasing, bending its original meaning and function, and filling in its silences. She provides a new glossary of the Scottish phrase of vague and immense distance:

> yonder awa awa (yon.der.awa.awa) to enact
> a sense of amnesia. a place your mind forgot.
> a gap in history, death.
> as in, to provide distance from un-confessed
> sins committed in righteousness for the
> gaining of wealth's sake.[5]

Set in the land of yonder awa, Booker offers three figures (three wise men?) of the Scottish imperial project: the transported prisoner of war (the Duncan rebel); the victim of disease (Uncle Colin who 'caught fever so his mind run awa'); and the missionary (Father Calum 'run go fling words like scotch bonnet by cane fields and start baptise sinners in local muddy waters'). More figures would be possible: the Scottish slave trader, master, indentured servant, overseer, book keeper or attorney, for example. Scots permeated every level of the administration which upheld Atlantic slavery, yet the West Indies became removed from the mainstream of Scottish cultural memory, rendered peripheral as the ocean (sea journey) created a geographic distance that placed the goods (rum, sugar, tobacco) and the enslaved (black ants) at a moral distance.

This intertextual exchange between Malika Booker and Walter Scott introduces some of the themes of this chapter: distance and proximity, silence and voicing, and the role of language and literature in recovering the memory of Atlantic slavery. Pioneering historical research, as highlighted in this volume, has begun to introduce slavery more fully into the way that Scottish history is written and understood. The recognition of slavery has the potential to be transformative not only for historical research, but also for Scotland's self-conception of its current place in the world, impacting more broadly on Scottish narratives of identity in the present. As seen in the exchange above, literature is doubly implicated in the project to recover the memory of slavery: it is at least partly responsible for the euphemism, elision and misrepresentation that enabled slavery to be forgotten, as well as a key medium through which historical memory might be recovered. Therefore, this chapter has three main angles. Firstly, it addresses the paradigms around the professional study of Scottish literature which continue to contribute in important ways to the 'collective amnesia' in Scotland around empire and slavery. Secondly, it surveys the problematic appearance and disappearance of slavery in a selection of Scottish literature since the seventeenth century. It concludes with a discussion of the presence of Scotland and Scots in Caribbean writing, as well as the emergence of a Scottish-Caribbean cultural memory, which draws on historical research, but takes the conversation into areas that historiographical tools may have more difficulty reaching. Given the perceived distance between Atlantic slavery and Scottish narratives of identity, it will be the combination of a variety of modes of thinking, speaking, writing and performing that will most effectively narrow this gap.

A recent theoretical approach to literature and slavery has emphasised the need for greater comparative practice to conceptualise African chattel slavery not 'as a unique manifestation of historical evil but to place it in a longer historical trajectory of a global history where slavery was ubiquitous'.

> This contextualisation does not diminish the extreme manifestation of race-based chattel slavery in the Atlantic world; rather, it allows us to recognize that chattel slavery was part of a continuum of human oppression that many readers could access through different descriptions in literature.[6]

This 'holistic approach' brings into the picture Ottoman and African slaveries, as well as the question of how 'racialized systems of slavery in the New World interlocked with and depended on the subjugation of a class of poor English, Scottish and Irish indentured servants and transported criminals who were essentially slaves themselves'.[7] This suggestive approach poses two challenges for this collection: why focus specifically on chattel slavery, and what place indentured servants? Firstly, even bearing the comparative context in mind, there is a particular amnesia around chattel slavery, in which Scots were among the perpetrators, for which specific treatment is long overdue. Secondly, not to recognise that there is a relationship between indentured servitude and chattel slavery is just as inadequate as to conflate these conditions entirely is disastrous. Moreover, recognising this relationship can work, as Theodore W. Allen emphasises, in the service of 'a politics whereby all oppressed peoples join together to fight for their common interests'.[8] However, recent efforts to remember slavery in Scotland have been opposed to a troubling extent with invocations of indentured servants; these serve not a politics of liberation, but function instead as what Laurajane Smith terms a 'distancing strategy'.[9] Here, the suffering of indentured servants eclipses that of the enslaved, and Scots may retreat to a safe distance from any sense of responsibility or consequence. But T. M Devine's words in the Introduction to this volume alert the reader to the profound differences between the two systems of bondage (see above, pp. 1, 5). Thus, this survey of literary amnesia remains cognisant of multiple slaveries even as it explores the crucial specifics of chattel slavery; and it remembers the continuum of labour exploitation and oppression in the broad interests of social justice in the present.

Sassi's pioneering work on Scottish-Caribbean literary relations takes amnesia as a central organising metaphor. Her study implies a broad periodisation: the age before abolition stretching from the seventeenth century up to the later eighteenth century; and the period of intense slavery debates from the founding of the Society for Effecting the Abolition of the Slave Trade in Clapham in 1787, through the abolition of the slave trade in 1807, to emancipation in 1834. This was followed by a long period of (un)willed amnesia stretching roughly from 1834 to the late 1990s. The nineteenth century saw a glorification of British anti-slavery which overshadowed discussion of the slavery past, and celebrated the empire of free-trade capitalism and wage slavery. This long-standing national-imperial amnesia persisted over the surges in support for Scottish nationalism and socialism in Scotland until the late twentieth century. In recent years imaginative work including Maud Sulter's oeuvre (1989), Robbie Kydd's *The Quiet Stranger* (1991), Jackie Kay's oeuvre including *The Lamplighter* (2007), Zoë Wicomb's *David's Story* (2001), James Robertson's *Joseph Knight* (2003), Andrew O. Lyndsey's *Illustrious Exile* (2006), Iain Heggie's play *The Tobacco Merchant's Lawyer* (2008), Chris Dolan's *Redlegs* (2012) and Lou Prendergast's plays *Fifty Shades of Black* (2013) and *Blood Lines* (2014) signal a greater desire to 'inquire into the country's involvement in West Indian slavery and to assume historical responsibility'.[10]

Such long-standing amnesia has both external and internal contributing factors. Firstly, studies of slavery in American and 'English' literature often pay scant attention to the Scottish context, or exclude Scotland entirely. For example, John Richardson's skilful account of slavery in Augustan literature questions how much 'people in England' knew about slavery generally: 'Since the slave trade was a predominantly English exercise, it is appropriate to ask this question about England rather than Britain ...'[11] It would be more appropriate to note the British-wide involvement in slavery; Richardson's theoretical framing, despite the presence of Jonathan Swift, remains profoundly 'Anglo'. This is unfortunate because his acute observations are generalisable; he opposes the notion that prior to 1787 there was ignorance or indifference to slavery, offering instead the concept of 'managed discomfort'. Richardson describes the 'mental distance and moral levity ... made easy by the physical distance of Africa and the Caribbean, and by the language and silence surrounding them [which] ... in some of its slippery semantics, included the potential for denial and dishonesty'.[12] This description countenances more modern 'distancing strategies', of which at least two continue to bear influence even north of the Tweed. The first rehabilitates a broadly liberal 'civilising-enlightenment' line which minimises the violence of empire; the second related angle suggests that Scots tend to engage sympathetically with the natives whom they are colonising, both in reality and in literary representations. (Of course, both represent Caledonian versions of the myth of the Liberal British Empire, simply substituting Scottish for British.) Such 'distancing strategies' create a conflicted approach to empire, for which the 2011 edition, *Scotland and the British Empire*, a part of The Oxford History of the British Empire Companion Series, will serve as an example. The opening chapter by T. M. Devine and Phillip Rossner emphasises Caribbean slavery as a 'factor in Scotland's "great leap forward" of the eighteenth century. The islands provided markets for Scottish linen, raw material for the country's booming textile manufacture, and the sojourners who returned home with their profits put much of their capital into Scottish industry and landownership.'[13]

However, Cairns Craig's contribution, titled 'Empire of Intellect', severs this economic vision from social, intellectual and institutional life. This chapter identifies a continuation whereby nineteenth-century intellectuals developed and disseminated the work of their luminous predecessors. It therefore strikes a celebratory chord throughout, as it lists the 'impact' of notable migrants who founded masonic lodges, schools and universities, missions and churches; who promoted Scottish philosophy, medicine, political economy and literature to create 'the Scotland of a cultural and spiritual empire'.[14]

> The power across the globe of institutions founded on Scottish models, and the influence of Scottish ideas and Scottish writings in so many different territories, might, by the end of the nineteenth century, have suggested that the country had indeed established 'a dominion over the minds of men' at least as effective as the military and political power which kept the empire together. Building on its great eighteenth-century achievements, Scotland's 'empire of intellect' had given the nation a truly global significance.[15]

The language of empire is present – power, influence and dominion across the globe – yet it is a sanitised narrative of a cultural empire, void of any critique of the kinds of 'military and political power' that facilitated this intellectual expansion. Given Craig's previous use of Frantz Fanon to describe the subordination of Scottish culture within the United Kingdom, it is strange that there is no link from Fanon's theory of the ingrained 'inferiorism' felt by the colonised, to the 'impact' of just this 'spiritual and cultural empire' in which Scots forged a 'dominion over the minds of men'.[16]

In the same vein, the current academic fashion for studying imperial 'networks' – and the oft-noted 'clannishness' of the Scots – can risk repeating some of the rhythms of an older imperial history. This details the networks of the powerful (always more plentiful in the archives) with a diminished attention to those they overpowered. Angela McCarthy's chapter in *Scotland and the British Empire* emphasises a Scottish identity promoted by such networks of associational culture in the Empire (to the practical exclusion of any sense of Britishness). Turning to 'migrant-indigenous relations', she distinguishes between

Scottish sympathy and affiliation with the Maori in New Zealand, and 'Scottish attitudes towards Aborigines in Australia' in which 'Scots demonstrated an overarching British assumption of cultural superiority and desire to civilize'.[17] In a linguistic sleight of hand, sympathy is Scottish, antipathy is British (read English), and a certain distance from the violence of empire is maintained. Murray Pittock has developed the concept of 'fratriotism' – linking fraternity and patriotism – which selects and exaggerates sympathetic colonial encounters as representative of the Scottish (and Irish) approach to empire.[18] Sassi identifies this notion of Scots performing a 'transference of sympathy'[19] as a 'master narrative' of 'Scottish representations of the colonial enterprise in the late twentieth century'.[20] In the context of interactions between the Irish and Africans, Peter D. O'Neill and David Lloyd dismiss this 'sentimental framework': 'one shaped by a weak ethical desire that the Irish should have identified with another people who were undergoing dispossession, exploitation or racism – or indeed shown solidarity with oppressed peoples in general'.[21] In such approaches, selective quotations and selected writers (often Stevenson, even Buchan) are often advanced as compensation for, and even seem to outweigh, historical expropriation, at the same time as they obscure the ongoing depredations of Scoto-British financial capitalism and imperialist 'interventions'.

I might speculate briefly that this fantasy of moral distance persists given the inheritance of paradigms of Scottish literary criticism since the nineteenth century. Gerard Carruthers notes the founding influence of Matthew Arnold's construction of 'Celtic' literature as being closer to nature than the intellect. This form of Celticism overlaps with Orientalist discourse as analysed by Edward Said, and its influence may be considered a symptom of the provincialisation of Scotland in the nineteenth-century Union. The socialist and democratic urges of the twentieth century then informed 'the idea of Scottish culture as a small "no-nonsense" culture (at its best close to "the folk"), somewhat resistant to the metropolitan guile of the outside world, whether Rome or England'. Spellbound by ideologies of 'great tradition', Scottish 'generalist' approaches (from 1919 to the 1980s and beyond) either strove to rediscover a grand continuity, or despaired at Scotland's debilitating 'compromised authenticity and cultural split'.[22] Gregory Smith's 'Caledonian antisyzygy', itself a version of T. S. Eliot's 'disassociation of sensibility', became an influential concept in the 'nationing' of Scottish literature. Scotland's lack of national parliament, 'cultural bifurcation' and linguistic subordination removed it from the realm of great tradition (England and France), and distanced it from the cutting edge of world history. Yet Scottish literature was admirably distinct in other ways: more democratic, closer to the *volk*, 'even implicitly less crafted, than was the case in England'.[23] Scottish literature of empire, then, tends towards a sympathetic engagement with the colonised as an expression of ingrained national values. This was not helped by a 'first wave' of post-colonial treatments of Scottish literature from the 1990s. This was more interested in rephrasing Scotland's plight within the United Kingdom in the new terminology of post-colonial studies than in the self-critical reappraisal that a dominant European power like Scotland requires. This has been challenged more recently with a more subtle approach to Union, and a greater willingness to address both Scotland's historic and current role as an imperial force.[24]

It would be wrong, however, to posit instead a Scottish literature of 'unsympathy', with literature wedded directly to the economics of imperialism. Literature, as ever, opens a space where ideologies are contested, even as it bears the imprint of its social construction. Scottish literature of empire, I would argue, is both distinct and complex: complicit and supportive of empire even as it is shot through with critiques and anxieties around humanity and justice, as we have come to expect from the literature that emerges from any imperial power. That individual authors can bring humanity to their imaginative work speaks to the fact that the 'system' of imperialism is upheld by human beings, inconsistent and contradictory, who can be complicit in as well as suspicious of, or openly hostile to, different aspects of imperialism. Catherine Hall and Sonya Rose suggest a more flexible model of empire which opens up new understandings both of the Scottish position within the British Empire, and the full spectrum of shifting relations between Scots and those they colonised. They write:

> The British Empire with its complex mapping of difference across European, South Asian, African, Caribbean, Antipodean and North American territories never produced a stable set of dichotomies of coloniser and colonised, citizens and subjects: rather these were always matters of contestation . . . Since empires depended on some notion of common belonging, there was a constant process of drawing and redrawing lines of inclusion and exclusion. The British Empire was held together in part by the promise of inclusion, all British subjects were the same, while at the very same time being fractured by many exclusions.

Differences of biology or culture 'never could be fixed for they were neither natural nor self-evident'.[25] Scottish literature of empire emerges from a distinct national, religious, intellectual and political context in which Scots (and Gaels) were engaged in both drawing themselves inside and outside these lines of Britishness in shifting proportions, just as they were continually drawn and redrawn by others. Scottish literature cannot lay claim to being more anti-slavery than English literature: different aspects of the Scottish experience can inform an embrace of, an apology for or a critique of empire, as well as the many shades of ambiguity in between. Nationality is simply not a reliable indicator of how an individual will respond to empire or slavery. Scots were wrestling with the same questions of empire and resistance, profit and labour that circulated around the Atlantic world. In participating in this transnational exchange, the Caribbean was often imagined within a cultural framework which paid distinct attention to union and common belonging, Jacobitism, and language hierarchies. Caribbean slavery was imagined and excused in relation to bound labour conditions of Scottish colliers. Sympathetic literary representations, and perceived affiliations between African and Highland clan cultures, can be interpreted as a redrawing of these lines of inclusion and exclusion in order to 'do empire better'. It is time for Scottish literary criticism to eschew its variety of 'distancing strategies' and prevarications in order to redress its amnesia around the violence of empire and its relations with Atlantic slavery in particular.

Sassi notes that the Caribbean first appears in Scottish literature in seventeenth-century ballads which mourn the transportation or emigration of prisoners of war, criminals and indentured servants to this fearsome *pays de non-retour*. From the outset, the Caribbean was constructed as a site with a fundamental duality. On the one hand, a paradise of fecundity holding out the promise of luxury and rapid enrichment; on the other, a netherworld of disease and rapid death. In *Roderick Random* (1748), Tobias Smollet identified Jamaica as the 'fatal island' that was 'the grave of so many Europeans'; yet Roderick enjoys a sumptuous feast among a Scottish network on the island and, in the happy conclusion to the novel, he makes his fortune through slave trading from Guinea to the Americas.[26] The Caribbean's reputation as an 'inhospitable tropical region' extends to the 'larmoyant motif' of the off-stage West Indian death in novels like Henry Mackenzie's *The Man of Feeling* (1771) or Susan Ferrier's *Destiny: Or, The Chief's Daughter* (1831).[27] Such fleeting and marginal treatments of slave societies in literature represent a certain myopia which contributed to the later amnesia.

The long eighteenth century has been an important and closely scrutinised period of Scottish literary criticism, though slavery has only been faintly sketched into the picture. We might reconsider the fine scholarship on Anglo-Scottish relations, the deep concerns over language hierarchies, and the status and consequences of what later came to be called the Enlightenment more fully in an imperial context. Corey Andrews traces a long history of inchoate 'discomfort' and anti-slavery feeling, informed by Scottish Enlightenment sympathy and sentiment, from Robert Blair (1743), through Joseph Knight's advocate John MacLaurin (1760), James Beattie (1760), to Rev. John Jamieson (1789).[28] The abolitionist poetry of the soldier John Marjoribanks (1792) from Kelso, who travelled to the Caribbean, is notable for the immediacy of its invective which distinguishes it from the more abstract metropolitan poets.[29] Richardson notes that rhetorical opposition to political 'tyranny' and 'slavery' can be difficult to separate out from the issue of chattel slavery in the Americas. This is a symptom of the context of multiple slaveries in which British discourse about slavery could 'view the enslavement of Africans in the Americas as a necessary evil, consider the enslavement of Englishmen in the Mediterranean as an atrocity, and invoke metaphorical slavery to inveigh against the current socio-political state'.[30] Robert Burns' slippery engagement with the rhetoric of slavery, even in the midst of the abolitionist campaign, has been instructive in this regard.[31] Burns's intended emigration to Jamaica in 1786 to work as a 'poor negro-driver' remains troubling for modern Scotland, though it is counterweighed against the song *The Slave's Lament* (1792), which is often attributed, problematically, to Burns.[32] No matter the authorship, Marcus Wood has importantly critiqued the sentimental construction of enslaved persons, as found in this song, largely as passive, mournful victims. Despite the constant resistance to their condition performed in a variety of ways including marronage, abscondment, defiance, open rebellion, suicide, infanticide and theft, sentimental literature preferred them to be pitifully subject to 'the middle passage, domestic and plantation tortures, rape, [and] slave auction'.[33]

The central trunk of Scottish literature of slavery is shaped by just such sentimentalism, undergirded by an Enlightenment devotion to 'improvement'. Informed by Enlightenment approaches to sound estate management, the plantation ideal represents a mutually beneficial model of obedient, industrious subordinates devoted to an enlightened master, with both parties dedicated to gradual improvement, and with both parties secure in their station. This runs through James Grainger's long poem *The Sugar Cane: A West-India Georgic* (1764), and prose fiction such as Henry Mackenzie's *Julia de Roubigné* (1779), Hector MacNeill's *The Memoirs of Charles Macpherson* (1800) and the anonymous *Marly; or a Planter's Tale* (1828). Here, an enlightened master 'improves' his estate, and profits, at the same time as improving the character and conditions of the enslaved, without necessarily taking the 'extreme' and 'dangerous' step of removing their enslavement. At least, not yet: liberty, however desirable, was not the sort of thing that ought to be rushed. Such enlightened gradualism had two main consequences. Firstly, the soft image of benevolent masters guiding grateful slaves to civilisation was an extremely effective pro-slavery ideology which contributed to prolonging chattel slavery deep into the nineteenth century. Secondly, George Boulukos's study of the sentimental trope of the 'grateful slave' argues that the distinction between 'improved' European free labourers and 'improved' (or improvable) enslaved Africans was a key feature in the development of racism. In the emerging discourse of 'free labour ideology', the 'independent mind' and hardy spirit of the industrious freemen of the lower orders was much vaunted according to georgic ideals of estate management. While sentimental literature might castigate tyrannical masters, its vaunting of the 'grateful slave' trope is double-edged: it 'seems to call attention to the suffering and humanity of slaves, but it nonetheless works to imagine the problem of slavery solved by showing African slaves as capable of becoming devoted to their masters and even as embracing their condition'.[34]

By way of example, in *Julia de Roubigné*, Henry Mackenzie manages his discomfort by having his character Savillon immediately free his slaves only to find that they are more contented and work more efficiently bound voluntarily by gratitude: 'they work with the willingness of freedom, yet are mine with more than the obligation of slavery'.[35] Later, as the campaign to abolish slavery gained ground in the 1820s, *Marly* spins a tale of Scottish colonial success (with Jacobite undertones). The eponymous hero, and rightful master, ousts the dishonest attorney and is restored to his ancestral plantations on Jamaica. The enslaved gather to play the part of rejoicing peasants, paying 'homage' to 'their liege lord', with 'all the extravagancies of an uncivilized race, who were animated with joy, dancing in the African fashion, to the rude music, if it deserves such a name, of their favourite gumba [drum]'.[36] The delighted slaves assure Marly that they never desired their freedom in the first place, only a benevolent master. Boulukos argues that the sentimental promotion of Africans as more easily reconciled to paternalistic enslavement is a key factor in developing racial difference. It secured their position as shared humans with emotional capacities, yet it demoted them as childlike, in need of protection, and deficient in the moral and intellectual capacities with which brave European labourers would reject the bonds of enslavement and face the vicissitudes of freedom.

In the period following emancipation in 1834, grand sweeping narratives of Scottish historical fiction were all the vogue; however, slavery was not easily incorporated into (and would in fact fundamentally disrupt) the dialectic between romantic, backward Highlands and enlightened, progressive Lowlands. Sassi suggests that slavery represents a 'gap in the narrative' in nineteenth-century novels, suggesting that the generic demands of realism recoiled from representing slavery, which was 'too shameful an event, and the suffering of slaves too horrible a truth, to bear exposure and inquiry – paradoxically even by those who took part in anti-slavery movements'.[37] Scott, she notes, was always 'reticent' on slavery; while Stevenson's engagement with the Scottish-Atlantic focused more on pirates than the enslaved. Victorian gentlemanly euphemism, romantic Celticism and rural kailyard fiction did not lend themselves to tackling such a difficult and unflattering subject as slavery. Twentieth-century fiction excelled at imagining the changing landscape of rural and urban Scotland, and the baleful effects on the working classes. Neil Munro's historical novel *The New Road* (1914) treats the construction of General Wade's military road through the Highlands, revealing the changing face of early eighteenth-century Scotland. The New World plantations loom large as a dreaded site of banishment and toil. It is said of the Jacobite tyrant Simon Lovat that,

> To sell a lad to slavery would bother Sim no more than selling heifers at a fair ... The thing's against the law of course; he hasna got the right of transportation, but he drives a bargain –either transportation or the tree, and who would choose the tree?

The hero Aeneas has to be rescued from a ship bound for Virginia where he was tied to the mast, discovering the truth in the warning that any who cross Lovat would be found, 'his bones bleaching to the wind or cankering in the dungeon, or shivering to the lash in the plantations'.[38] In this re-inscription of the Caribbean's dreadful reputation the focus remains close to these shores, with the threat of transportation underlining the vulnerability of the Scottish lower orders at the hands of their callous ruling classes; African chattel slavery itself, however, continues to lurk in the shadows of the collective memory.

This amnesia is not matched in Caribbean and African-Caribbean diasporic autobiography and fiction, where Scottishness is a distinct and visible part of the fabric of the slavocracy. Giovanna Covi traces the perhaps surprisingly numerous 'footprints left in the sand' by 'Scottish and partly-Scottish characters' (as well as those simply with conspicuously red hair) in the fiction of a group of writers who are more often supposed

to be concerned with the primary division of black and white racial difference. Asking 'what does Scottishness imply in the Caribbean?', Covi
theorises that these 'often less than secondary characters'

> Implied a long-lived conflictual relationship in a shared space, one loaded
> with the overwhelmingly ambivalent significance of being a historical mark –
> certainly of perpetrated colonial racist exploitation, but in some cases also
> of a dissident, although collaborative, participation in imperial policy, and
> in others of suffered discrimination by English hegemony.[39]

Through discussions of the likes of Harlem Renaissance icon Claude
McKay (1889–1948), the Jamaican-Scottish poet Albinia Catherine
Hutton née MacKay (1894–?),[40] Marlene NourbeSe Philip's *Looking
for Livingstone* (1991) and Merle Collins' *The Colour of Forgetting*
(1995), Covi demonstrates that as Scottish literature of slavery is distinct
and complex, so is the representation of Scots in Caribbean literature.

This might be illustrated in the common association between Scotland
and imperialist military forces: 'sae famed in martial story'. In Derek
Walcott's *Omeros* (1990), the bagpipes signify the glorification and
horror of war. Major Dennis Plunkett, retired to a bar in St Lucia, is
haunted by the memories of his Second World War service in Africa,
being 'piped into Tobruk . . . I wept with pride'. In Walcott's hands, the
memories in the bar extend back further to wars between the British and
French in the Caribbean: 'We helped ourselves to these green islands
like olives from a saucer'. 'What was it all for?', he asks, 'the screech
of a bagpipe and a rag'.[41] Moreover, the complex history of maroons,
Africans who had escaped enslavement to establish independent communities throughout the Americas, is punctuated with encounters with
Scottish military aggression. For example, Robert Hunter (1664–1734)
was sought as Governor of Jamaica, largely it seems, to deal with the
'Maroon Problem'. Mavis Campbell notes that during his term from
1729 to his death in 1734, the Scot 'conducted the most energetic and
sustained campaign yet against the Maroons'.[42] Given his failure to
crush the Maroons, Hunter raised the idea of a treaty, which would
eventually be signed in 1738. This treaty guaranteed the Maroons their
freedom, on the condition that they return any runaway slaves they find
and help to quell slave uprisings; this bargain makes their smooth incorporation into modern grand narratives of liberation difficult to perform.

In 1977, the Jamaican Maroon writer Milton McFarlane penned a
little-known collection of stories celebrating the Maroon leader Cudjoe,
whose feats in fending off the attacks of the likes of Hunter are legendary. In a piece of romantic warrior fiction, McFarlane underlines

respect and compassion for your enemy in an honourable duel between Cudjoe and a Scottish soldier named Douglas MacGowan. Following Cudjoe's triumph, McFarlane generously provides a painful backstory for MacGowan. His diary reveals pressures of poverty and exile on the soldier who was 'stolen or shanghaied from south-east Scotland near Dundee by some English sailors who were part of a group called "spirits"'.

> A mere boy, no more than about fifteen years old, he was forcibly shipped to the West Indies along with many other equally unfortunate people from the British Isles, some of whom were hardened criminals; but others were political prisoners and the women among them mostly prostitutes or naïve and adventurous girls beguiled and then forcibly detained by 'spirits'.[43]

McFarlane's account of the Atlantic crossing clearly draws parallels with the Middle Passage, 'so that men and beasts lived alike, in that hot, mouldy, stinking hell of a hold in the ship that brought Douglas MacGowan from Scotland, against his will, to his death in the rugged mountains of Jamaica'. On arrival, they were 'sold outright in various ports for the highest prices obtainable', after which 'these bondsmen, were treated exactly like African slaves and worked side by side with them'.[44] This emphasis on the shared experience of transportation and labour of whites and blacks on the plantations speaks to the continuum of exploitation, which is perhaps unusual for 1970s narratives of slavery which had begun to be shaped by black nationalism. However, the feature which then distinguishes bondsmen from slaves is somewhat elided: MacGowan was able to pay off his indenture and join the army, a path which remained closed to the enslaved. In a final example, Fred D'Aguiar's 1991 play *A Jamaican Airman Foresees His Death* (inspired by Yeats's poem 'An Irish Airman Foresees His Death') reverses the military situation, placing four Jamaican men in Scotland for RAF training during the Second World War. D'Aguiar highlights the play's linguistic diversity where 'the English spoken was always on a continuum, with the Standard at one end and the Creole and Scots at the other, and the various characters swinging from one to the next'.[45] Scotland provides a mixed reception for the Jamaicans, who struggle against racial discrimination in the RAF. The protagonist Alvin is assailed in the dark by 'Four Scotsmen' who strip him in search of his tail, a shocking scene that harks back to Lord Monboddo's obsession with tails.[46] The romance between Alvin and a local woman, Kathleen, provides the redemptive heart of the play, though their relationship cannot survive its circumstances. Her parents, John and Mary Campbell, do not approve.

In bringing this chapter to a close, I would like to dwell on this theme of interracial sexual relations. The closing sentences of Malika Booker's poem run:

> Now you offspring play you haunted bagpipes awa awa. and seed does go awa, look how Duncan begat Duncan and Ross begat Ross, how McIntoshes begat McIntoshes and McIntyre begat McIntyre and red hair jump pon black skin people headtop yonder awa awa.

Although the prevalence of Scottish surnames in the Caribbean is sometimes whimsically invoked, Booker's language moves from the book of Exodus to Genesis to point towards the violence that took place yonder awa. (Although some surnames derive from enslaved persons adopting the names of their previous owners following emancipation.) The inspiring cultural theories around 'creolisation' – the creation of compound cultures in the Caribbean from a variety of African, European, American and Asian sources – do not, it should be remembered, have a happy genesis. Where it is usually the music of the lone piper that is haunting (or sounding the screech of war), here the Scottish icon is itself haunted by the memory of rape in the Caribbean. I subscribe to the argument that slavery exists on a spectrum of free and unfree labour, where parallels with working-class exploitation can be both enlightening and politically energising. However, feminist approaches have intervened in such a class–race approach to underline the ways in which colonialism and slavery itself were gendered institutions.[47] Although relations in the colonies would take a variety of forms, the concept of consent carried no weight in a society where a woman's body legally belonged to a master. Joan Anim-Addo notes,

> Atlantic slavery had instituted the most careless and irresponsible cohabitive practices . . . For the African-heritage males, the system held the advantages of the loosest polygamy possible and none of its responsibilities . . . black women's bodies were multiply colonised and often bore the offspring of the colonisers in a production/reproduction cycle.[48]

Rapes, and the threat of them, must have been a daily horror for women who laboured to produce profits. The destiny of any child they bore was at the mercy of the master who could choose to acknowledge and favour the child, use it to renew his enslaved labour force, or sell it on. It is the enormity of this feature which reminds us of the chasm that separates the lived experience of chattel slaves to other groups of oppressed. Given that so few of these cases make the written historical archive, and are so partial when they do, it seems that literature has a particular role to play here both in recovering the memory of such an experience, and in finding ways to overcome it.

Absentee (Scottish) fathers have been a feature of Caribbean writing, from Robert Wedderburn (1762?–1834?), who castigated his Scottish father, and Mary Seacole (1805–81), who venerated hers. Covi discusses the callous Scottish fathers in Jamaica Kincaid's *Autobiography of My Mother* (1996), as well as the predatory Scottish bookkeeper in Barbara Lalla's *Arch of Fire* (1998).[49] The final word, though, goes to Lou Prendergast who, through a series of plays, has explored her relations with her absentee Jamaican father (of African-Irish heritage) Harry Prendergast, who operated in the criminal underworld of 1960s Glasgow.[50] Prendergast draws on Scots-Caribbean experience to inform an interrogation of Scotland's imperial role; though her own ambivalent feelings about her father's 'dodgy dealings . . . which extended to prostitution' complicate any straightforward post-colonial championing of her father. At times touching, shocking or funny, *Fifty Shades of Black* (2013) is a play about power which interweaves the historical and the personal: Scotland's history of slavery, her strained relationship with her father, the racism she experienced herself growing up mixed-race in Clackmannanshire, up to modern-day exploitation and sexual politics including a dazzling rebuke to the misogyny of dancehall lyrics. In *Blood Lines* (2014), the stage was marked with a map of Jamaica showing Scottish place names. As Prendergast, her sister Sophie and other actors from Scotland's African-Caribbean community perform over the map, the geographical and moral distance between here and yonder awa is closed forever, and Prendergast's closing message that only in exposing this painful history can we reach reconciliation is confirmed:

> My father told my mother
> stories of how, back in Jamaica
> when women tried to flee their men
> they would catch them
> and lame them
> so they couldn't run again.
>
> Like *that's* not a hangover from slavery.
>
> Tough love.
> Rough land.
>
> Harry bore all the features
> Of that post-colonial male.
> King of his own castle
> And a black king

Can be every bit as wicked
As a white one.
No longer colonised by Britain
But still marginalised by her
None of this excuses
My father's treatment
Of the women in his life.
Our parents did their best
And Harry?
Well he did his worst.

But blame
Is just negative energy.
We learn.
We move forward.
And we forgive.

NOTES

1. Walter Scott, *Rob Roy* [1817] (London: Penguin, 1995) p. 299. All subsequent references to this edition.
2. Carla Sassi, 'Acts of (Un)Willed Amnesia: Dis/appearing Figurations of the Caribbean in Post-Union Scottish Literature', in Giovanna Covi, Joan Anim-Addo, Velma Pollard and Carla Sassi (eds), *Caribbean–Scottish Relations: Colonial and Contemporary Inscriptions in History, Language and Literature* (London: Mango Publishing, 2007), pp. 131–98, p. 147.
3. *Yonder Awa* (Glasgow: The Empire Café/Collective Architecture Ltd, 2014). Poets featured: Malika Booker, John Burnside, Vahni Capildeo, Jim Carruth, Fred D'Aguiar, Kwame Dawes, Etta Dunn, Vicki Feaver, Millicent A. A. Graham, Pippa Little, Aonghas MacNeacail, Richie McCaffrey, Kei Miller, Kathleen O'Rourke, Sasenarine Persaud, Tanya Shirley, Dorothea Smartt and Kathrine Sowerby.
4. See, for instance, Chapter 5 of Olaudah Equiano's *Interesting Narrative and Other Writings* [1789] (London: Penguin Classics, 2003).
5. Malika Booker, 'yonder awa awa', *Yonder Awa*, p. 33.
6. Adam R. Beach and Srividhya Swaminathan (eds), *Invoking Slavery in the Eighteenth-Century British Imagination* (Farnham: Ashgate, 2013), p. 13.
7. *Invoking Slavery*, p. 13.
8. *Invoking Slavery*, p. 14.
9. For a fuller discussion of 'distancing strategies' around slavery, see Laurajane Smith, '"Man's inhumanity to man" and other platitudes of avoidance and misrecognition: an analysis of visitor responses to exhibitions marking

the 1807 bicentenary', *Museum and Society*, November 2010, 8(3), pp. 193–214.

10. Sassi, 'Acts of (Un)Willed Amnesia', p. 187. The only non-Scottish writer here, the South African novelist Zoë Wicomb interweaves the story of the missing 'slave figure' in the Glassford Family Portrait into her novel of resistance to apartheid in *David's Story* (New York: The Feminist Press at City University of New York, 2001).

11. John Richardson, *Slavery and Augustan Literature, Swift, Pope and Gay* (London and New York: Routledge, 2004), p. 13.

12. Richardson, p. 37.

13. T. M. Devine and Philipp R. Rössner, 'Scots in the Atlantic Economy, 1600–1800', in John M. MacKenzie and T. M. Devine (eds), *Scotland and the British Empire*, The Oxford Companion to the British Empire Companion Series (Oxford and New York: Oxford University Press, 2011), p. 53.

14. Cairns Craig, 'Empire of Intellect: The Scottish Enlightenment and Scotland's Intellectual Migrants', in MacKenzie and Devine (eds), *Scotland and the British Empire*, pp. 84–117, p. 116.

15. Craig, 'Empire of Intellect', p. 112.

16. The rather forced comparison is between discrimination against Scottish speech and anti-black racism: 'It is not by our colour, of course, that we have stood to be recognized as incomplete within the British context, it is by the colour of our vowels . . .' Cairns Craig, *Out of History: Narrative Paradigms in Scottish and British Culture* (Edinburgh: Polygon, 1996), p. 2.

17. Angela McCarthy, 'Scottish Migrant Ethnic Identities in the British Empire since the Nineteenth Century', in MacKenzie and Devine (eds), *Scotland and the British Empire*, pp. 118–46, p. 140.

18. Murray Pittock, *Scottish and Irish Romanticism* (Oxford: Oxford University Press, 2008).

19. Honor Reiley, '"Wha sae base as be a slave?": Linguistic Spaces in Scottish Historical Fiction, and Where Slavery Doesn't Fit', Unpublished thesis, McGill University, 2011, p. 63.

20. Sassi, 'Acts of (Un)Willed Amnesia', p. 175.

21. Peter D. O'Neill and David Lloyd (eds), *The Black and Green Atlantic: Cross-Currents of the African and Irish Diasporas* (Basingstoke: Palgrave Macmillan, 2009), p. xvii.

22. Gerard Carruthers, *Scottish Literature*, Edinburgh Critical Guides (Edinburgh: Edinburgh University Press, 2009), p. 18.

23. Carruthers, p. 19.

24. Carla Sassi and Theo van Heijnsbergen (eds), *Within and Without Empire: Scotland Across the Postcolonial Borderline* (Newcastle: Cambridge Scholars Publishing, 2013).

25. 'Introduction', Catherine Hall and Sonya O. Rose (eds), *At Home With*

the Empire: Metropolitan Culture and the Imperial World (Cambridge: Cambridge University Press, 2006), p. 22.

26. Tobias Smollett, *The Adventures of Roderick Random* [1748] (Oxford: Oxford University Press, 1979), p. 207.

27. Sassi, p. 145.

28. Corey Andrews, '"Ev'ry Heart Can Feel": Scottish Poetic Responses to Slavery in the West Indies from Blair to Burns', *International Journal of Scottish Literature*, 4, Spring/Summer 2008.

29. Karina Williamson, 'The Anti-Slavery Poems of John Marjoribanks', *Enter Text*, 7.1 (Autumn, 2007).

30. *Invoking Slavery*, p. 1.

31. Nigel Leask, 'Burns and the Poetics of Abolition', in Gerard Carruthers (ed.), *Edinburgh Companion to Robert Burns* (Edinburgh: Edinburgh University Press, 2009); Murray Pittock, 'Slavery as a Political Metaphor in Scotland and Ireland in the Age of Burns', in Sharon Alker, Leith Davis and Holly Faith Nelson (eds), *Robert Burns and Transatlantic Culture* (Farnham and Burlington: Ashgate, 2012), pp. 19–31.

32. See my own 'Robert Burns: Recovering Scotland's Memory of the Black Atlantic', *Journal for Eighteenth Century Studies*, 2014, 37(3), pp. 343–59.

33. Marcus Wood, *The Poetry of Slavery: An Anglo-American Anthology* (Oxford: Oxford University Press, 2003), p. xvii.

34. George Boulukos, *The Grateful Slave: The Emergence of Race in Eighteenth-century British and American Culture* (Cambridge: Cambridge University Press, 2008), pp. 14–15.

35. Mackenzie, *Julia de Roubigné*, p. 100.

36. *Marly*, p. 318.

37. Sassi, p. 170.

38. Neil Munro [1914], *The New Road* (Edinburgh: B. & W. Publishing, 1994), p. 225, p. 133.

39. Giovanna Covi, 'Footprints in the Sand: Attorneys, Redlegs, and Red-Haired Women in African-Caribbean Stories', in *Caribbean–Scottish Relations*, pp. 12–45, pp. 13–14.

40. See also Carla Sassi, 'A Double Strangeness: Albinia Catherine Hutton's negotiation of home and exile identities between Scotland and Jamaica', in B. Bijon and Y. Clavaron (eds), *La production de l'étrangé dans les littératures postcoloniales* (Paris: Honoré Champion, 2009).

41. Derek Walcott, *Omeros* (London: Faber & Faber, 1990), Chapter V.i, pp. 24–7. Presumably the 'rag' refers to a flag.

42. Mavis C. Campbell, *The Maroons of Jamaica 1655–1796: A History of Resistance, Collaboration and Betrayal* (Trenton, NJ: Africa World Press, 1990), p. 57. Campbell notes that Hunter also opposed Irish immigrants: 'They are a lazy, useless sort of people who come cheap and serve for Deficiencies and their hearts are not with us', p. 85.

43. Milton McFarlane, *Cudjoe the Maroon* (London: Allison & Busby, 1977), p. 112.
44. McFarlane, p. 112.
45. Fred D'Aguiar, 'A Jamaican Airman Foresees His Death', in *Black Plays: Three* (London: Methuen Drama, 1995), p. 280. It was staged at Royal Court Theatre Upstairs in 1991.
46. D'Aguiar, p. 256.
47. Verene Shepherd, Bridget Brereton and Barbara Bailey (eds), *Engendering History: Caribbean Women in Historical Perspective* (Kingston: Ian Randle, 1995).
48. Joan Anim-Addo, 'A Brief History of Julianan Lily Mulzac of Union Island, Carriacou and Grenada: Creole Family Patterns and Scottish Disassociation', in *Caribbean–Scottish Relations*, p. 67.
49. Covi, 'Footprints in the Sand', pp. 37–9.
50. *Fifty Shades of Black*, Ankur Productions, Citizens Theatre, September 2013; *Blood Lines*, Arches Theatre, July 2014. Quotes are from unpublished scripts.

3

Early Scottish Sugar Planters in the Leeward Islands, c. 1660–1740

Stuart M. Nisbet

IN THE EARLY STAGES of Scottish transatlantic trade, the 1660s was a key decade, with the founding of Port Glasgow, the first Scottish sugar houses, and the first signs of the benefits of trade in Glasgow.[1] In the British Americas the 1660s was also the decade that black chattel slavery took hold.[2] Though separated by the Atlantic, these phenomena were hardly coincidental. Of the three stages of transatlantic commerce, namely: cultivation in the colonies; shipping across the Atlantic; and processing and marketing in Britain, it is really only the second and third stages which have received significant attention in Scotland.

In Scottish history the direct connection between the import of transatlantic staples and slave labour has rarely been made until recently. Yet the gradual increase in transatlantic trade could not occur without cultivation of the staples by the growing enslaved workforce. The rise in the use of enslaved Africans becomes of even greater interest to this volume if Scots were directly involved in their control and ownership. This chapter investigates the rise of Scots operating as planters in the Americas. It asks how deeply, and to what scale, Scots were involved in the ownership and control of enslaved Africans. As the leading staple in the pre-1740 period was sugar, the focus is on sugar plantations in one part of the British Caribbean.[3]

Although Caribbean sugar plantations in the study period are relatively well documented from an English perspective, it is important to ask why we should revisit the subject from a Scottish angle. The answer is primarily a question of balance: to balance the attention paid to transatlantic trade in Scotland; to balance the acknowledged role of Scots on various British Caribbean islands from the end of the study period; finally, to balance the enormous social success of sugar planters in Scotland.[4]

Building on the work of E. V. Goveia and L. J. Ragatz, the most prominent historian in the middle decades of the twentieth century to seriously consider slavery from the Caribbean side of the Atlantic was Eric Williams.[5] Although his views on slavery and economic growth remain controversial, Williams highlighted the centrality of the Caribbean sugar plantation to slavery.[6] He was also relatively rare in featuring Scotland in his work.[7]

The focus here is on Scottish planters who settled on two of the Leeward Islands, St Kitts (St Christopher) and Nevis.[8] Due to their diminutive size on an Atlantic scale, the islands are easy to ignore, especially compared to much larger colonies, whose strong Scottish presence post-dates the study period, from the much bigger Caribbean island of Jamaica, to mainland North America. The choice of islands is noteworthy. St Kitts and Nevis were 'by far the most important' of the four Leeward Islands in the seventeenth century, with St Kitts being the original 'Mother Colony' of the British Empire.[9] When the Port Glasgow customs accounts become available from the early 1740s, the Leewards were the main source of Atlantic imports, after American tobacco.[10] By the middle decades of the eighteenth century, in proportion to its extent, St Kitts was the richest colony in the British Empire.[11] At barely two miles apart, the islands can almost be treated as one. However, at different periods they had differing strengths and fortunes.

From the mid-seventeenth century, along with Barbados, Nevis was the first of the Leeward Islands to invest in sugar monoculture.[12] Comparison between the British sugar islands is difficult as they varied greatly in surface and cultivable area. At 36 square miles, Nevis is only a quarter the area of Barbados, an area which is further reduced by Nevis's more mountainous interior. It was a question of concentration as much as output. The largest British island, Jamaica, despite being more than 120 times the area of Nevis, had barely double its sugar production by 1686.[13]

Although recorded by Columbus on his initial voyages in the 1490s, the Leewards were virtually ignored by the Spanish, due to their small size, dense jungle down to the shore and lack of mineral resources. However, they served as watering holes for ships of many nations. Following initial English settlement from the 1620s, the native population, often relatively small, was either driven out or wiped out.[14] As the forests were cleared, white indentured servants, including many Scots, were brought voluntarily or involuntarily from Britain. From the mid-seventeenth century, when Nevis began to focus exclusively on sugar, the labour required became too intensive to be tolerated by free indentured servants, who were gradually replaced by chattel slaves brought forcibly from Africa.[15] Sugar monoculture would transform the economy and society of British Caribbean islands from small units of subsistence farming of a wide variety of staples, to large labour- and capital-intensive plantations specialising in the growing of sugar-cane and its processing into crude sugar and rum for the British market. In the early decades, virtually the whole island production was exported, making the society dependent on long-distance trade to carry off the crop and to bring in supplies, people and food.[16]

The emergence of a wealthy planter elite marked the sugar colonies as the first major successes in the British Atlantic world. In the early period it has been claimed that the most significant contribution of Scots was in 'populating rather than promoting'.[17] It is possible that some Scottish indentured servants rose gradually through the system to become overseers and planters. However, surviving evidence suggests that most were voluntary emigrants of higher social status seeking economic opportunities. Two early examples are William Wardrop and William Colhoun, who came to the Leewards as importers of sugar to Glasgow.[18] Wardrop was a partner in Glasgow's Wester Sugar Works, and a sugar planter on St Kitts by the 1680s.[19] More detail exists for Wardrop's partner Colhoun, who had business interests on both Nevis and St Kitts, where he was also a planter, for two decades from the 1660s.[20] By 1677 Colhoun was significant enough to be elected to the ruling island assembly, which was dominated by his fellow planters. By looking abroad, the experience of Scots in the seventeenth-century Caribbean was much more positive than at home. Despite perceived restrictions to Scottish trade by English Navigation Acts, the Acts provided little or no restrictions to Scottish settlers living and working in the colonies. When Scots planters did engage in trade, they were as likely to send their sugar to the leading English ports as to Scotland, simply because there they achieved the best market. Colhoun was described by a fellow English planter as, 'a Scotch merchant who hath dwelt upon the island ever since I knew it . . . a more intelligent person and more knowing of the state and interest of this and the neighbour islands cannot be found'.[21] When he retired to Scotland in the 1680s, Colhoun's experience was valued for wider colonial endeavours.[22]

Despite the early connections between Nevis and the Clyde, according to the 1677–8 Nevis census, Scots comprised less than 2 per cent of the white population (51 persons).[23] A further 20 per cent were Irish, the remainder being recorded as English. We can gauge the number of enslaved Africans owned by Colhoun from surviving data for his partner, William Freeman. From just 16 on his plantation in 1666, they grew steadily to 23 in 1673, and 51 in 1678.[24] In general in the 1670s, about 50 middling Nevis planters each owned from 20 to 60 enslaved Africans, the eight biggest planters averaging 100 each.[25] The growth of the enslaved population mirrors the rise of sugar monoculture. In 1672 the overall black population of Nevis was just over 1,700, and during the next six years the slave population of the Leewards more than doubled.[26] In this period Nevis was the most stable, best defended and most successful of the Leeward islands, suffering fewer hostilities from French and Dutch military forces than St Kitts. In 1678 the Governor of the Leewards reckoned that the output of Nevis was worth nearly £400,000, double the value of the other three Leewards combined.[27] From 1673 the Royal African Company based its Leeward Island traffic on Nevis and the island would be the springboard for more significant Scottish involvement in the early eighteenth century.[28]

It is in the generation after Colhoun's return to Scotland on which we have more specific information on slave ownership by Scots in the Leewards. Our specific interest in this paper is two of them, William McDowall and James Milliken.[29] In this early period the numbers of Scots involved as planters was relatively small. However, on their retirement to Scotland in later life, the influence of McDowall and Milliken was great, both socially and commercially, and also as founders of what was to become Glasgow's largest Caribbean merchant house, Alexander Houston & Co.[30] As will be demonstrated below, they also came to own and control very large numbers of enslaved Africans. Although their subsequent success was on St Kitts, both McDowall and Milliken started out on Nevis in the 1690s. Whether we accept Williams's claim that the pair were the 'missing link' in turning Glasgow into one of Britain's leading sugar ports, they were certainly among the earliest and most successful.[31] The period marked a growing awareness among the enlightened landed and mercantile classes in Scotland of the career opportunities for younger sons as trainee planters.[32] The sugar system provided the opportunity to rise to immense wealth beyond almost any other venture in this period.

Although William McDowall (1678–1748) came from a landed family with a range of military, political and ecclesiastical interests, his most significant connections were mercantile. His father was a burgess of Edinburgh, as was his grandfather James (c. 1610–61) who was also a customs associate of Thomas Tucker, the earliest and best-known commentator on Glasgow's trade with the Caribbean in 1656.[33] McDowall's friend, partner and subsequent relative by marriage, James Milliken

(1669–1741) had more direct links with the Glasgow sugar houses and was a kinsman of Hugh Montgomery, leading partner in Glasgow's Wester Sugar House, with Nevis planter William Wardrop.[34] Milliken also had maritime connections through the Ayrshire ports.[35] Both McDowall and Milliken's younger brothers, Captain David McDowall and Captain Thomas Milliken, would follow them out and captain some of their ships. Those who had the ambition, stamina and good fortune to survive the hard regime and tropical disease often returned to be among the wealthiest in their country and with the experience to found mercantile dynasties. Those who failed, such as three sons of Maxwell of Williamwood, sent out from Glasgow in the same decade as McDowall and Milliken, disappeared without trace.[36] Rather than going out as part of organised colonial schemes, the overall reason for venturing to the Leewards from the West of Scotland in the early 1690s was a loose conglomerate of kinship and mercantile awareness, partly through the early Scottish sugar houses. Recent research has identified a growing successful Scottish interest in clandestine trade throughout the Caribbean several decades before 'legitimate' Scottish commerce 'began' after 1707.[37] If there was any plan, it was what has been dubbed 'imperialism by stealth'.[38]

McDowall's correspondence reveals a great deal about the role of a young Scottish overseer on a late seventeenth-century Nevis sugar plantation. During his eleven-year period of apprenticeship he wrote that he was the only white on the plantation.[39] The sugar took about eighteen months to mature, during which time the labour force were forced to prepare, plant, tend, weed and care for numerous fields or cane 'pieces'. When the cane was ripe, it was harvested, crushed in mills, boiled in coppers and processed by boiling and crystallised into raw sugar. It was then barrelled and shipped to the main British ports, where it was further refined in sugar houses, to produce palatable sugar and rum.

McDowall's main challenge was the management of the enslaved workforce. He wrote that throughout his training, he had 'many indifferent negroes'.[40] To persuade them to work he had to rely on his own strength of character, through a hierarchy of gangmasters, backed by the island legal system. As sugar monoculture developed, and the number of enslaved Africans increased, each of the sugar islands developed a legal system to control and suppress the growing African majority. This functioned as an oligarchy, based upon a monopoly of political power in the hands of the white elite, and was two-pronged.[41] Firstly, it rested upon the concept of enslaved Africans as property, exactly the same as other purchasable items, including boiling coppers and cattle.[42] In the surviving

Figure 3.1 Sugar-boiling copper, William McDowall's Upper Canada Plantation, St Kitts

inventories of William McDowall, his slaves are listed along with his livestock. Secondly, although the enslaved may have been legally defined as property, they were also persons, with the faculty of free will. Several laws were established to regulate their conduct, entice them to work and reduce the chances of rebellion. The legal system on each British sugar island was essentially similar and new laws were added in reaction to specific events or concerns by the planters. The penalty for relatively minor crimes, such as theft, resulted in mutilation and death. On 29 January 1686, Nevis Council passed a law specifying the cutting off of ears for the first two offences of stealing sugar and 'for the third offence death'.[43] On most islands, including the Leewards, the legal system did not recognise that the wilful killing of a slave by a white planter was murder.

After eleven years on Nevis, William McDowall had ingratiated himself into the local planter network and had begun to build up a small plantation on St Kitts, owning thirteen enslaved Africans.[44] His friend Milliken, being several years older, had married the widow of a Nevis sugar planter in 1705. At the beginning of the global War of the Spanish Succession the following year, Milliken owned 112 enslaved Africans on his Nevis plantation, sixty males and fifty-two females.[45] By this time, Nevis had about one hundred large plantations, the largest having almost two hundred slaves. Sixty-four per cent were involved in fieldwork, 10 per cent in sugar works, 14 per cent in domestic chores, and the remaining 12 per cent as overseers, craftsmen and carters.[46] Milliken's initial term as a planter was short-lived as the French invasion virtually destroyed his plantation and Nevis never regained its position as a leading sugar producer. However, adjacent St Kitts changed from being half-French during the previous century to being wholly in British hands. As conflict drew to a close from 1710, former French sugar plantations were granted provisionally to those who were most influential on the islands. The process of paying the British Government for their plantations was drawn out for more than a decade, providing the opportunity to build up profits but with little outlay.

Around 20 per cent of the plantation grants went to a group, including McDowall and Milliken, who have traditionally been perceived as Scots.[47] As this was one of the first significant groupings of Scots planters in the Caribbean, it has been oft-repeated by historians. However, the group of 'Scots' also had family connections, or were born to Scottish parents, in Ireland, Germany, Holland and France.[48] This reflected a route to the Leewards through older ties with continental Europe as much as direct migration from Scotland itself.[49] Scots were just as likely to venture to the Leewards via Europe as direct from Scotland, and trade their produce with English ports. Success depended in merging among a group of planters, some of whom may have been primarily of Anglo-Irish origin, but all were multinational in form and outlook.

McDowall and Milliken received plantations after 1710 containing approximately 200 acres of cane land, each of which required the labour of about two hundred enslaved Africans, the rule of thumb by this time being one slave per acre. A group of 191 Africans are listed in an inventory for William McDowall's St Kitts plantation: 75 men, 71 women and 45 children.[50] Each is named, along with occupations and value in pounds sterling. Many of the given names were Scottish, including Glasgow, Arran, Gordon, Andrew, Jenny, Flora and Scotland.[51] The average value of active slaves was £32 and most were involved in fieldwork. However, the tasks were by no means all menial, and many also had skilled occupations, including craftsmen, carpenters, coopers and masons. Sugar-making was as much an art as a science and the most highly valued were those skilled in the sugar works, usually valued at more than £50 each, the most expensive being a sugar boiler named Edinburgh, valued at £80.

The legal system on the islands continued to evolve. In 1711 the St Kitts Assembly passed a law stating that if any 'slave oppose, struggle

Figure 3.2 Windmill, James Milliken's Monkey Hill Plantation, St Kitts

or strike any white person . . . the said Negro shall be publicly whipped; but in case such white person be hurt, the slave shall be sentenced to death'.[52] The penalty for the murder of a slave by a white was a nominal fine, paid to the owner of the murdered slave. As the African majority increased, and fear of revolt intensified, the laws increased in draconian severity of punishment. In 1722 William McDowall and two other St Kitts planters feared their workforce would run away to the mountains. The leading plotter was one of McDowall's most valuable Africans, 'Christopher'. To resolve the issue, McDowall became person-ally involved in setting up a new law, which claimed that the mutilation and torture which had been legally sanctioned had *'proved too mild and gentle* to curb and restrain' the slaves.[53] The proposed law preferred that the escapees should suffer 'the pains of death' when captured, allowing planters to kill *suspected* escapees out of hand, without trial, and be rewarded for doing so. McDowall's Law was put into practice in the summer of 1725, when two slaves involved in an attempted escape were captured, hanged and burned alive before a trial could be arranged.[54] A black gangmaster named Frank was implicated but absconded and McDowall's partner, James Milliken, was sent to recapture him.

The total number of enslaved Africans under their control soon multiplied. McDowall built up further slave gangs to work a second plantation on higher ground.[55] He and Milliken also became responsible for many more, as they took on additional roles as 'attorneys', with overall responsibility for adjacent plantations, whose owners had returned to Britain. McDowall acted as attorney for the Stapleton plantation on St Kitts (1717–22) and was followed in this role by Milliken (1722–9).[56] McDowall and Milliken were also joint attorneys for the Mead plantation (1722–8) and McDowall continued in this role with another Scottish planter, James Gordon (1728–33).[57] Thus, at any one time, between their own plantations and in the role of attorney, McDowall and Milliken were directly responsible for around a thousand African slaves.

Enslaved Africans were the planters' most expensive asset and so their deliberate maltreatment would be foolish. On the one hand, William McDowall wrote of taking 'great care' of his enslaved and directly attributed deaths to a 'want of care'.[58] The enslaved depended entirely on the planters and their overseers for sustenance, but saving costs meant that supplies of food and clothing shipped from home were minimised. A generation later, in the 1760s, William McDowall's family would own the 430-acre Mount Alexander sugar plantation on the Windward island of Grenada.[59] They also owned about 100 acres of adjacent 'provision land' there, to grow crops to feed the enslaved. However, in early eighteenth-century St Kitts, the intensity of sugar cultivation meant that little land was spared for either the planters or the labour force to grow food. Later visitors still described every acre of the island entirely planted with the sugar crop.[60] A large part of the plantation budget was spent in providing food rations for the enslaved, and profits could be maximised by the overseer or planter by shrewd budgeting, including minimising the spend on food.

William McDowall's character conformed to what is often considered a stereotype of the eighteenth-century colonial Scot on the make, mixing toughness and frugality with extreme ambition. His partner Milliken, older and perhaps even more ambitious, was also known for his ruthlessness. At the French invasion in 1706, Milliken had been among those who accepted the surrender, and he was later favoured to recapture escaped slaves and punish them.[61] Such qualities made good planters, but harsh managers of their workforce. These Scots may have operated their plantations on a fine line, between providing barely enough food to sustain hard work and starvation rations. For instance, during Milliken's term as attorney for a plantation owned by the Stapleton family on

St Kitts, the enslaved were described as being 'sickly and very bare of cloaths, and pinch'd in their bellies'.[62] Despite all the tropical diseases and ailments in the Caribbean, the biggest problem for the workforce was deliberate underfeeding, leading to malnutrition and starvation. Economic frugalism was a stronger motivation than the desire to care for the enslaved. Such a harsh policy may have increased profits in the short term, but was risky on tropical islands with a volatile climate. Any delay in the shipping of food from home through war or hurricane resulted quickly in increased mortality. In 1701 McDowall had to cope with a severe drought, when no canes were planted.[63] In another, in 1726, the situation on St Kitts and Nevis again descended into crisis.[64] Cattle began to die and it was not long before slaves inevitably followed.[65] Although deliberate cruelty is absent from McDowall's correspondence, deaths were often recorded and new slaves had therefore to be purchased. In addition to his own plantation, James Milliken managed another at the same time, as attorney, and wrote to the owner, 'I am sorry to tell your ladyship I never see the Island in so bad a condition as it is now in, dry weather has destroyed the next crops, and no canes planted as yet.'[66] A few months later, thirty to forty enslaved were sick and Milliken wrote, 'there is several of your negroes dead here, we must buy others'.[67]

The same policy of controlling costs was applied to clothing as to food. When it was hot, clothing protected the labour force from the direct sun. Wind and rain could also make them relatively cold. In 1724 Milliken's assistant wrote, 'I have suffered much uneasiness on account of your negroes' nakedness in a hard winter.'[68] The following year, Milliken wrote, 'I must desire you order clothing out for your negroes, we have had such cold weather this year that the like has not been seen for many years.'[69] Medical care and shelter had similar issues and the policy of rigorous cost control applied also to inadequate nursing of sick or dying slaves. Though many Scots later served as doctors in the Caribbean, in the early period medical care was rudimentary. McDowall himself favoured employing an old woman, rather than 'all the doctors in your country'.[70] At his newly developed upper plantation on St Kitts, William McDowall sited his slave village directly west of his sugar works. A later survey shows a schematic plan of this village with nearly two dozen 'Negro Houses' in an enclosure measuring about eight acres.[71] In the late 1720s, McDowall's manager petitioned to have these houses rebuilt, to improve living conditions, but McDowall wrote: 'I observe what you write about my negro houses . . . [but] as they have stood in the same place ever since I began the settlement without any ill consequence, I would by no means have them altered'.[72]

Overall, the deliberate policy of penny-pinching with food, clothing and shelter compounded the harsh treatment of the enslaved. Perhaps the most costly result of the combination of hard labour, limiting food and poor conditions was the inability of many enslaved women to reproduce, which inevitably increased the need to purchase new slaves to replace those who died.[73] Through most of the early British Caribbean in the late seventeenth and early eighteenth centuries, slave populations registered high rates of natural decrease.[74] In general, the earlier we look, the worse the conditions and the higher the death rate. Annual mortality around 1700 averaged 4 per cent a year.[75] However, this increased in times of scarcity and drought. In 1732 a Nevis clergyman and planter reckoned an annual mortality of nearly 7 per cent (1 in 15) in times of drought or when provisions were scarce.[76] This rate could double (to 1 in 7) when diseases such as smallpox were prevalent. The replacement of slaves who had died was the most costly task on the plantation. The inability of slaves to reproduce inevitably increased the need to purchase 'saltwater' slaves, those newly arrived off slave ships, who had to be 'seasoned' to acclimatise them to the hard labour regime. The seasoning process resulted in further loss of life and the need for even more replacements.[77] When managing Madam Mead's St Kitts plantation in 1724, McDowall managed a total of 150 enslaved Africans. That year sixteen new Africans were purchased: '6 Negro men at £27 and 10 Negro boys at £23 sterling'.[78]

Due to the cost of replacing slaves, it was inevitable that planters would consider dabbling in direct slave trading between Africa and the Caribbean. McDowall and Milliken were personally involved in slave trading from the Clyde as the Leeward agents for one of the earliest recorded Scottish slaving voyages, the *Hannover*, which left Port Glasgow in December 1719.[79] Of 134 slaves on board, a quarter died on the crossing. McDowall sold the remaining cargo of twenty-eight men, twenty-five women, eleven boys and four girls to his fellow St Kitts planters. Five years later McDowall and Milliken personally purchased a much larger slaver, with a capacity of 300. It was renamed the *Fair Parnelia* after Milliken's daughter. Like the *Hannover*, the voyage of the *Fair Parnelia* encountered trouble and was seemingly lost during the Atlantic crossing.[80] McDowall and Milliken initially discussed recovering their loss through insurance. However, five months later a sworn testament from the surviving Captain Gillespie of the vessel revealed that the *Fair Parnelia* sailed from Cape Coast Castle on 7 May 1726 with 120 enslaved Africans on board. Further slaves were purchased along the coast, making a total of 273 men, women and children.[81]

Tragedy struck on 8 June when, 482 leagues west from Cape Coast, the *Fair Parnelia* was struck by a whirlwind and overturned, drowning all but one of the Africans held below decks. Thomas Gillespie arrived in St Kitts the following February, via Africa, 'in a very weak condition'. After this terrible loss, no record survives of any further slaving voyages organised by McDowall and Milliken.

When McDowall returned to London in 1724, aged forty-six, to petition parliament to secure formal ownership of his provisionally granted St Kitts plantation, he initially intended to return to St Kitts, but then decided to retire to Britain. Following attempts to acquire a landed estate in southern England he decided that 'sugars will sell as well at Glasgow as in any other part of Britain'.[82] This marked the start of a gradual transfer of his business, property, sugar ships and refining from London and Bristol to Glasgow and Port Glasgow. He also began employing kinsmen and other young Scots as overseers and agents, including his cousins, William and Alexander Houston, latterly the leading partners in the family firm of Alexander Houston & Co., into his business.[83]

Africans were also purchased to ship home, for the use of friends and relatives. In 1727 McDowall requested 'a good handsome negro boy about ten years old' to be shipped to Scotland for his kinsman.[84] The following year he ordered two boys, one as a servant, and one to accompany his son Billy to school in Glasgow.[85] When his wife came home to Glasgow in 1728 she brought a retinue of servants including four black maids.[86] By this time McDowall also employed Africans on his newly purchased country estate, not just as servants, but as apprentice tradesmen. These were some of the earliest recorded cases of Africans brought to the West of Scotland from the Caribbean.[87] Little is known about their fate when they reached Glasgow, where they had to endure the cold climate and exposure to unfamiliar diseases. However, when McDowall's wife Mary and her sister, both born and raised on Nevis, and who spent their entire lives in the tropics, sailed to Glasgow in November 1728, both died of smallpox a few weeks after arrival. Along with Milliken's daughter, who had also died of smallpox the previous month, they were buried with ceremony in the choir of Glasgow Cathedral.[88] The resting place of Glasgow's enslaved Africans is unknown.

As the son of a landed family, whose father had several dozen farming tenants on his lands, William McDowall came from a colonial tradition familiar with treating those below his status with rigour. An experience of managing enslaved Africans for three decades also affected the treatment of his tenants at home. On his newly purchased Scottish estate in the late 1720s, McDowall believed that his tenants deliberately sought to obstruct his improvements. He claimed that 'the creatures here ... choose to live upon potatoes and oatmeal on their own dunghills', and considered them to be 'a parcel of unruly and barbarous people, who were enemies to the laudable spirit of improvement'.[89] It is unlikely that when first arriving on Nevis in the early 1690s, his attitude differed much from that of his contemporary and friend Azariah Pinney, who commented, 'I was shock'd at the first appearance of human flesh exposed to sale. But surely God ordained 'em for the use and benefit of us.'[90]

In Glasgow's history, McDowall and Milliken's roles as slave owners have been concealed for nearly three hundred years by tales of careers as soldiers and riches gained through 'fortunate marriage'. Their supposed military ranks, which benefited them greatly among the landed gentry in Scotland, were simply those of the island militia, bestowed on them by their planter peers.[91] In Glasgow, after his death in 1748, McDowall was described as a gentleman of fine character, the most popular man in Glasgow and the darling of the city, who did much to shape its social and human qualities.[92] In the Caribbean, through the second half of the eighteenth century, the family plantation empire expanded to other islands including Grenada. In Scotland, McDowall and Milliken and their sons and grandsons took leading social and political positions in city and country, as patrons of parish kirks, rectors of Glasgow University, MPs and city provosts.

Overall, the treatment of enslaved Africans by Scots was a double-edged sword. On the positive side, the fortunes of planters ultimately depended on the quality and quantity of sugar produced, through the labour and skill of their labour force. So Africans were of considerable economic value and McDowall wrote of the need to care for them.[93] Once home in Scotland he even entrusted a young African to be a companion for his son.[94] Another served as a personal footman, but McDowall's wife was jealous of their relationship and asked him to 'put the Negro away'. McDowall replied that 'he would not live without his favourite Negro and he was determined to separate from her', rather than be rid of him.[95] Although some such Africans who had been brought to Scotland may have been valued, for others life was intolerable. In 1748 one of McDowall's enslaved named Cato ran away from his master's country estate and an advertisement in the Glasgow press offered a reward for his recapture.[96]

The drive to produce sugar at maximum profit, and the legal systems of the British Caribbean which supported this aspiration, produced the harshest of environments, especially during the period surveyed in this chapter. McDowall's character may have made an effective planter, able to turn a good profit, but his regime had grave consequences for the enslaved. As chattels (or property) his Africans had no rights whatsoever and through the relentless quest for profit he limited both care and provisions for them. Effectively, for much of the time in the West Indies, he worked his slaves to untimely deaths.

From the beginnings of intensive sugar cultivation in the 1660s, growing numbers of Scots were involved in the ownership and management of enslaved Africans. Scots who succeeded despite perceived restrictions at home, and went out under their own initiative, rather than through organised colonial schemes; Scots whose sugar was sent to London, simply because the metropolis was the principal market for it; 'Scots' who were granted former French plantations from 1710, but whose identity and route to the Caribbean were just as likely to reflect earlier Scots connections with continental Europe; Scots whose success was achieved primarily as individuals, among a multinational plantocracy, with little collective identity beyond a few associates. If there was a turning point for Scottish planters in the Leewards, it was in the late 1720s, when the leading players began bringing out sons and associates as overseers and saw favour in switching their sugar business from London to the Clyde.

To date, the focus in Scotland on shipping and trade has masked the means of production of the trading staples in the Americas. The chattel slave system provided immense wealth, transforming planters into leading merchants and social figures on their return to Scotland. However, these achievements need to be balanced by how their success was achieved in the Caribbean. If Scots made fortunes through direct participation in the cultivation process, plantation slavery can hardly continue to be seen as something worthy of little attention. The conclusion of one observer in 1718 that 'The labour of negroes is the principal foundation of our riches from the plantations' can apply as much to Glasgow as to other British port cities.[97]

This chapter suggests that the lack of research until recent years in the personal involvement of Scots in sugar plantations has resulted in a grave imbalance in the traditional historiography. Whether we agree with Eric Williams that McDowall and Milliken provided a turning point in Glasgow's early mercantile success, the wealth they derived from sugar plantations made them leading merchants of their day, bringing contacts and experience back to Scotland.

At its most stark, and without raising moral issues which were irrelevant at the time, we can begin by measuring the success of these Scots

in the Caribbean by the number of enslaved Africans under their ownership or direct control. They rose steadily from a handful in the 1670s,
to 100 or more by 1705, to 200 by 1720 and to 1,000 by 1730. It is
not difficult to extend these figures to conclude that a middling Scottish
sugar planter, who owned a plantation for several decades, worked his
way through hundreds of enslaved African men, women and children.
For larger planters such as the McDowalls, Millikens and their subsequent partners and kinsmen, operating extensively as attorneys for
other planters, and expanding plantation ownership to other islands
through the eighteenth century, the tally of African lives is measured
in thousands. In the 1690s McDowall and Milliken were two of a relatively small number of pioneering Scots among a primarily Anglo-Irish
plantocracy. However, by their deaths in the 1740s, partly through
their influence, many more of their countrymen were venturing to the
Caribbean as overseers, doctors, attorneys and planters, with direct
personal control of the lives of enslaved Africans. From that time the
evidence for direct personal ownership and control of enslaved Africans
by Scots becomes overwhelming.

NOTES

1. I am grateful to Dr Douglas Hamilton of the University of Winchester for
   feedback on a draft of this paper. T. C. Smout, 'The Early Scottish Sugar
   Houses 1660–1720', *Economic History Review*, 14 (1962), pp. 240–53;
   Frank A. Walker, 'The Origins and First Growths', in Peter Reed, *Glasgow:
   The Forming of the City* (Edinburgh: Edinburgh University Press, 1999),
   p. 19.
2. Richard S. Dunn, *Sugar and Slaves – The Rise of the Planter Class in the
   English West Indies, 1624–1713* (University of Carolina Press, 1972), p. 123.
3. By 1700 sugar was 'the paramount tropical agricultural commodity enter-
   ing Europe from the New World': Richard B. Sheridan, 'The Formation of
   Caribbean Plantation Society, 1689–1748', in P. J. Marshall, *The Oxford
   History of the British Empire: Vol. II: The 18th Century* (Oxford: Oxford
   University Press, 1998), p. 399.
4. A. L. Karras, *Sojourners in the Sun, Scottish Migrants in Jamaica and
   the Chesapeake 1740–1800* (Ithaca and London: Cornell University Press,
   1992); Douglas J. Hamilton, *Scotland, the Caribbean and the Atlantic
   World 1750–1820* (Manchester University Press, 2005); T. M. Devine,
   'An Eighteenth-Century Business Elite: Glasgow-West India Merchants,
   c. 1750–1815', *Scottish Historical Review*, 67 (1978), pp. 40–67.
5. Kenneth Morgan, *Slavery, Atlantic Trade and the British Economy 1660–
   1800* (Cambridge: Cambridge University Press, 2000), p. 31; Richard B.

Sheridan, 'Eric Williams and Capitalism and Slavery', in Barbara L. Solow and Stanley L. Engerman (eds), *British Capitalism and Caribbean Slavery – The Legacy of Eric Williams* (Cambridge: Cambridge University Press, 1987).

6. Eric Williams, *The History of the Caribbean 1492–1969* (London: Vintage, 1970).

7. Eric Williams, *Capitalism and Slavery* (North Carolina, 1944), pp. 75, 91, 102; albeit the specific Scots mentioned were those who feature in traditional Glasgow publications.

8. At the time the Leewards consisted of four islands, Nevis, St Kitts, Antigua and Montserrat.

9. Dunn, *Sugar and Slaves,* p. 18.

10. National Records of Scotland (NRS) E504/28/1.

11. Sheridan, *Formation of Caribbean Plantation Society,* p. 402.

12. Ibid., p. 395.

13. Nuala Zahedieh, *The Capital and the Colonies* (Cambridge: Cambridge University Press, 2010), p. 200.

14. Brian Dyde, *Out of the Crowded Vagueness: A History of St Kitts, Nevis and Anguilla* (London: Macmillan Caribbean, 2005), p. 25.

15. There is also an argument that Africans became cheaper than white servants: H. Beckles, *A History of Barbados* (Cambridge: Cambridge University Press, 1990), pp. 30–1.

16. Philip Curtin, *The Rise and Fall of the Plantation Complex* (Cambridge: Cambridge University Press, 1998), p. 11.

17. Nicholas Canny, 'The Origins of Empire', in N. Canny (ed.), *The Oxford History of the British Empire Vol. 1: The Origins of Empire* (Oxford: Oxford University Press, 2001), p. 18.

18. For wider background and sources for the planters studied in this paper, see Stuart M. Nisbet, 'Clearing the Smokescreen of Early Scottish Mercantile Identity: From Leeward Sugar Plantations to Scottish Country Estates c. 1680–1730', in Allan I. Macinnes and Douglas J. Hamilton (eds), *Jacobitism, Enlightenment and Empire 1680–1820* (London: Pickering & Chatto, 2014), pp. 109–22; the spelling of Colhoun/Colquhoun has been standardised to that used in the seventeenth-century papers; NRS E8/40: Petition for Wm. Colhoun of Craigton and Walter Gibson merchant in Glasgow (1 July 1687); between 1666 and 1696 at least two or three boats arrived in the Clyde every year from the Caribbean with sugar: Smout, *Sugar Houses* p. 250.

19. Possibly a kinsman of the Wardrops of Dalmarnock near Glasgow. Wardrop's brothers James and Alexander were also involved in Caribbean trade.

20. J. C. Jeaffreson, *A Young Squire of the Seventeenth Century 1676–1686* (London: Hurst & Blackett, 1878), Vol. 1, pp. 244–9.

21. Ibid., p. 244.

22. 'Memorial Concerning the Scots Plantation to be Erected in Some Place of America', *Register of the Privy Council of Scotland*, 3rd series, Vol. vii, pp. 664–5.

23. Nevis Census 1677–8 in Vere Langford Oliver, *Caribbeana: Being Miscellaneous Papers Relating to the History, Genealogy, Topography and Antiquities of the British West Indies* (London: Mitchell, Hughes & Clarke 1909–19), Vol. 3, pp. 27–35, 70–80; it has been suggested that some Scots were omitted from the official figures: N. A. Zaced, *Settler Society in the English Leeward Islands 1670–1776* (Cambridge: Cambridge University Press, 2010), p. 59. In the St Kitts census of 1678 the proportion of Scots was not noted: *Caribbeana,* Vol. 2, pp. 66–77.

24. David Hancock, *The Letters of Wm. Freeman, London Merchant 1678–85* (London Records Society, 2002), p. xvi.

25. Nevis Census 1677–8, *Caribbeana*, Vol. 3, pp. 27–35, 70–80.

26. Dunn, *Sugar and Slaves,* pp. 123–5.

27. Ibid., p. 128.

28. Sheridan, *Plantation Society*, p. 162.

29. See Nisbet, *Clearing the Smokescreen*, pp. 109–22.

30. The principal sources used here for Col. Wm. McDowall's colonial career are: National Library of Scotland [NLS] 301/107 – Letterbook of Col. Wm. McDowall of Castle Semple (c. 1726–35); and National Records of Scotland [NRS] GD 237/12/35 – Letters of Capt. David McDowall (1728–33).

31. Williams, *Capital and Slavery*, p. 112.

32. Hancock, *Letters of Wm. Freeman*, p. viii.

33. M. D. Young (ed.), *The Parliaments of Scotland – Burgh & Shire Commissioners* (Edinburgh: Scottish Academic Press, 1993), Vol. 2, p. 450; C. B. B. Watson, *Roll of Edinburgh Burgesses and Guild Brethren 1406–1700* (Scottish Record Society 1929); F. D. D. Dow, *Cromwellian Scotland 1651–1660* (Edinburgh: John Donald, 1980), p. 169.

34. Douglas Watt, *The Price of Scotland* (Edinburgh: Luath Press, 2007), p. 53.

35. Tom Barclay and Eric Graham, *The Early Transatlantic Trade of Ayr 1640–1730* (Trowbridge: Cromwell Press, 2005), pp. 12–34.

36. NRS GD1/31/6 Maxwell of Williamwood Papers, Vol. 6.

37. Allan I. Macinnes, *Union and Empire: The Making of the United Kingdom in 1707* (Cambridge: Cambridge University Press, 2007), p. 149.

38. T. M. Devine, *Scotland's Empire* (London: Penguin, 2003), p. 4.

39. NLS 301/107 – Col. Wm. McDowall, Castle Semple, to Jas. Gordon, St Kitts (16 May 1732).

40. NLS 301/107 – Col. Wm. McDowall, London, to Jas. Gordon, St Kitts (9 July 1728).

41. E. V. Goveia, *Slave Society in the British Leeward Islands at the End of the Eighteenth Century* (New Haven: Yale University Press, 1965), pp. 152–4.

42. Acts of Assembly of Nevis 1689: Act for making Negroes, Coppers, Mills and Stills as Chattels.
43. Calendar of State Papers (CSP), Colonial Series, America and The West Indies, Vol. 12 No. 557 (29 January 1686).
44. St Kitts Census 1707–8 in Oliver, *Caribbeana*, Vol. 3, p. 136.
45. Public Record Office, London, CO 152/7: List of Inhabitants of Nevis (March 1708).
46. Richard Pares, *A West India Fortune* (London: Longmans, 1950), p. 24.
47. Richard B. Sheridan, *Sugar and Slavery: An Economic History of the British West Indies 1623–1775* (Baltimore: Johns Hopkins University Press, 1974), p. 156; Nisbet, *Clearing the Smokescreen*, pp. 119–20.
48. Ibid., pp. 119–20.
49. Allan I. Macinnes, 'Circumventing State Power – Scottish Mercantile Networks and the English Navigation Laws, 1660–1707', in *Water and State in Europe and Asia* (2008), p. 214.
50. W. Hector, *Selections from the Judicial Records of Renfrewshire* (Paisley, 1876), Vol. 2, pp. 67–9.
51. The use of Scots names for Africans was common: see NRS CS96/3102 for McDowall's friend and fellow St Kitts planter, Robert Cunningham, in the same period.
52. Act of Assembly of St Christopher, No. 2 (1711), *Act for the better Government of Negroes.*
53. Laws of the Island of St Christopher 1711–1791 (St Kitts, 1791), No. 52.
54. Ryland Stapleton Mss. (RSM), John Rylands University Library, Manchester, transcripts by Brian Littlewood: Thos. Butler, St Kitts, to Wm. Stapleton, London (21 November 1725).
55. NLS 301/107 – Col. Wm. McDowall, Castle Semple, to Robt. Cunyngham, London (3 September 1730).
56. RSM: Tim Tyrrell, Nevis, to Madam Stapleton, London (30 April 1722).
57. NRS GD 237/12/50: *Accounts, St Kitts plantation rented from Mrs. Penelope Mead by Wm. McDowall and Jas. Gordon* (1728–33).
58. NLS 301/107 – Col. Wm. McDowall, Glasgow to David Alexander, St Kitts (1 January 1729); Col. Wm. McDowall, London to Maj. Jas. Milliken, St Kitts (18 June 1726).
59. NAS GD 237/12/56; Stuart M. Nisbet, *Castle Semple Rediscovered* (Paisley, 2009), pp. 94–7.
60. E. W. Andrews, *Journal of a Lady of Quality 1774–76* (New Haven: Yale University Press, 1923), p. 130.
61. RSM, Jos. Herbert, Nevis, to Madam Stapleton, London (1 August 1729).
62. RSM, Jos. Herbert, St Kitts, to Madam Stapleton, London (23 December 1728).
63. RSM, M. Mills, Nevis, to Madam Stapleton, London (19 October 1701).
64. NLS 301/107 – Col. Wm. McDowall, London, to Jas. Gordon, St Kitts (20 June 1726).

65. RSM, Jas. Milliken, St Kitts, to Madam Stapleton, London (27 October 1726).
66. Ibid.
67. RSM, Jas. Milliken, St Kitts, to Madam Stapleton, London (8 February 1726).
68. RSM, Jos. Herbert, Nevis, to Madam Stapleton, London (April 1725).
69. RSM, Jas. Milliken, St Kitts, to Madam Stapleton, London (28 February 1726).
70. NLS 301/107 – Col. Wm. McDowall, London, to Jas. Gordon, St Kitts (30 July 1728).
71. Stuart M. Nisbet, 'Early Glasgow Sugar Planters in the Caribbean', *Scottish Archaeological Journal*, Vol. 31, 1–2 (2009), pp. 114–36.
72. NLS 301/107 – Col. Wm. McDowall, Castle Semple, to David Alexander, St Kitts (27 November 1733).
73. Philip D. Morgan, 'The Black Experience in the British Empire 1680–1810', in Marshall, *Oxford History of the British Empire: Vol. II*, p. 469.
74. Ibid., p. 467.
75. Sheridan, *Sugar and Slavery*, p. 246, Table 11.1.
76. Rev. Robert Robertson, *A Detection of the State and Situation of the Present Sugar Planters* (London, 1732), pp. 42–4.
77. Morgan, *Black Experience*, p. 469.
78. NRS GD 237/12/50, fo.5 (March 1724).
79. E. Graham and S. Mowat, 'The Slaving Voyage of the *Hannover* of Port Glasgow, 1719–20', *History Scotland*, 3/5 (2002), pp. 26–34.
80. For full details of loss of *The Fair Parnelia*, see Stuart M. Nisbet, 'A Glasgow Slaving Tragedy', *Scottish Local History*, No.82 (February 2012), pp. 42–4.
81. http://slavevoyages.org/tast/database/search.faces?yearFrom=1514&yearTo=1866&shipname=parnelia (last visited 14 July 2014).
82. NLS 301/107 – Col. Wm. McDowall, Glasgow, to Maj. Jas. Milliken, St Kitts (6 August 1728).
83. Ibid., Col. Wm. McDowall, Castle Semple, to David Alexander, St Kitts (25 September 1730).
84. Ibid., Col. Wm. McDowall, Edinburgh, to Maj. Jas. Milliken, St Kitts (8 December 1727).
85. Ibid., Col. Wm. McDowall, Glasgow, to Mrs McDowall, St Kitts (11 January 1728).
86. Ibid., Col. Wm. McDowall, Glasgow, to Maj. Jas. Milliken, St Kitts (11 January 1728).
87. Ibid., Col. Wm. McDowall, Diary entry (22 June 1727).
88. Ibid., Col. Wm. McDowall, Glasgow, to Maj. Jas. Milliken, St Kitts (18 November and 23 December 1728).
89. Ibid., Col. Wm. McDowall, Castle Semple, to Daniel Smith, St Kitts (12 May 1731).

90. Pares, *West India Fortune*, p. 121.
91. McDowall was a Captain in the St Kitts militia by 1718: CSP, Vol. 30, No. 736 (26 October 1718); and a Colonel by 1720: Vol. 32, No. 251 (29 September 1720); Milliken was a Captain in the Militia by 1706: Vol. 31, No. 204 (18 May 1720); and a Major before 1718: Vol. 30, No. 797 (19 December 1718).
92. J. McUre, *History of Glasgow* (Glasgow, 1830), p. 229; C. A. Oakley, *Second City* (Glasgow, 1946), p. 9; G. Eyre-Todd, *History of Glasgow Volume III* (Glasgow: Maclehose & Jackson, 1934), p. 151.
93. NLS 301/107 – Col. Wm. McDowall, Glasgow, to David Alexander, St Kitts (1 January 1729).
94. This African may have been an illegitimate child, thus a sibling of his son.
95. A. Crawfurd, *Cairn of Lochwinnoch Matters* (Paisley, 1827), Vol. 19, p. 81.
96. *Glasgow Journal* (25 January 1748).
97. William Wood, *A Survey of Trade* (London, 1718), pp. 179–93.

4

The Scots Penetration of the Jamaican Plantation Business

Eric J. Graham

There are few sights more impressive in the world than a Scotsman on the make.

J. M. Barrie

THE FIRST HISTORIAN OF Jamaica, Edward Long, writing on the eve of the American War of Independence, thought it necessary to dedicate a section in his *History of Jamaica* to the Scots as, 'Jamaica indeed is greatly indebted to North Britain as very near one third of the [white] inhabitants are either natives of that country or descendants from those who were'. If his calculation of the total white population on the island is correct, the number of Scots on the island in the mid-1770s numbered between 5,000 and 6,000. More followed with the exodus of loyalists from the rebellious American colonies, and the final wave of sojourners during the last two decades of the 'golden era' in sugar when most of the large trading houses of Glasgow switched their shipping resources from the American to the West Indies trades.

As an English-born colonial administrator, Long was plainly impressed, not only by their diligence but also by their clannishness and loyalty to the old homeland. He was certain that the social cohesion it engendered when abroad was the key to their survival on first arriving on Jamaica in the first half of the eighteenth century, and their rapid advancement thereafter:

> their young countrymen who come over to seek their fortunes are often beholden [to] the benevolence of these patrons who do not suffer them to fall into despondence for want of employment but [place] them under friendly protection and if they are well disposed are soon put into a way of doing something for themselves.[1]

Long, however, did not mention the haemorrhage of many of the new arrivals, wiped out by deadly diseases before they could become established. Succeeding in the Caribbean entailed many risks as well as opportunities, and the evidence of surviving wills and testaments lodged in Scottish courts suggests that those who achieved real wealth were very much in the minority. What follows focuses on the successful. Those who failed or died in the attempt would repay further study.

THE 'CLAN PATRIARCH' PATHWAY TO RICHES

In the vanguard of the Scots invasion, and the first notable Scottish patriarch on the island, was a veteran military officer from Argyllshire. His Jamaican tombstone epithet records his rise in the ranks of the island's elite:

> Here lies the Honorable John Campbell, born at Inverary in Argyleshire, North Britain, and descended of the Ancient family of Auchenbrock, when a youth he served several campaigns in Flanders. He went as Captain of the Troops sent to Darien, and on his return by this Island, in 1700, he married the daughter of Colonel Claiborne by whom he had several children. In 1718, he married Elizabeth (now alive) relict of Col. Garnes. He was many years member of the Assembly, Colonel and Custos of St Elizabeth. In 1722, he was made one of the Privy Council. He was the first Campbell who settled in this Island, and thro his extream generosity and assistance, many are now possessed of opulent fortunes. His temperance and great humanity have always been very remarkable. He died January 29, 1740. Aged 66 years. Universally lamented.[2]

In the time-honoured tradition, he became known back home as 'John of Black River' after his extensive Jamaican estate in the parish of St Elizabeth on the south-west side of the island. His success as a planter was secured (1712–16) during the governorship of Lord Archibald Hamilton, when he acquired the patent on 1,200 acres adjacent to his original property. John's elevation in Jamaican society followed on with his appointment as Colonel of the Militia, election as a Member of the Assembly and, in 1722, to the island's ruling Privy Council.

Soon afterwards, the four sons of his eldest brother Dugald of Kilmory – Peter, Colin, James and John – joined him in quest of advancement. To finance their careers as 'planter proprietors', 'Colonel John' (as they knew him) sold off his holdings back in Argyllshire to the son of Colin, his second brother, the Jacobite Archibald of Knockbuy. From the proceeds he was able to provide half of the mortgages on plantations for two of the nephews in the parish of Hanover. On taking possession, they took the names of their estates: 'James of Orange Bay' (1720) and 'Peter of Fish River' (1724). In 1739 Peter died on his estate, which then passed to his brother Patrick. With Peter's death, the next eldest brother, 'Colin of New Hope' (another new estate in the parish of St Elizabeth), was next in line to inherit the Black River plantation. This he did on his uncle's death at his estate of Hodges Pen in 1740.

Some ten years before, the children of Colonel John's sisters, Elizabeth and Bessie, had also arrived to learn the skills of management on the family estates. Elizabeth's son, Dugald, was helped into the planter class in 1732 by a £400 bond underwritten by his uncle. This was used to purchase the 400-acre 'Salt Spring' estate in the parish of Trelawney where Dugald died in 1746. His sister, Henrietta of Knockbuy, had followed him out to the island and married her cousin James of Orange Bay. Their son, Archibald, later acquired a plantation in the parish of St Anns, which he called 'Minard' after the family home on the banks of Loch Fyne. By then other members of the extended family had arrived from Argyllshire, including Archibald, son of 'Old Knockbuy', and yet another cousin, James, brother of Duncan of Kilduskland, as merchant and manager of Salem, a family holding in the parish of Hanover.

In this way a veritable empire of Campbells was entrenched in the western half of the island by the mid-century. The five cousins alone owned almost 21,000 acres across three parishes. Collectively they constituted the third-largest family holdings on the island, with each cousin in possession of an 'opulent fortune'.[3] It is impressive that virtually all of the first two waves of 'Jamaican Campbells' chose to be permanent residents developing their estates rather than sojourners returning to acquire Scottish properties – as became the norm in the second half of the century. This may have been due to the difficulties in remitting monies safely back to Scotland in the earlier period.

Those without the clan tie were last in the queue for preferment. As one would-be Scottish businessman, Thomas Ruddach, on the island remarked to a colleague back home in 1777: 'I believe I may give up all expectation of his [James II of Orange Bay] doing any thing for me as he has so much Business to remember such as me (as I am not a Campbell) when out of sight . . .'[4]

Not all Campbells arriving from Argyllshire, however, came with the right patriarchal connections to underwrite their success. The promises of free passage and six months' provisions made under a scheme promoted among the local tenantry of mid-Argyll (1739) by the 'n'er-do-good' Sir James Campbell of Auchinbreck (cousin of Colonel John) were strenuously denounced by the clan chief, John, 2nd Duke of Argyll. Writing from London to Archibald of Stonefield, the Sheriff Substitute at Inveraray, he declared that this 'knavish trick' was a trap for 'poor ignorant folk' as he was certain that Auchinbreck's intention was to sell 'the poor wretches as slaves' on landing in Jamaica.[5]

Some forty years later, Edward Long alluded to such unscrupulous methods of supplying white indentured servants:

> great numbers used formerly to be brought from Scotland where they were actually kidnapped by some man traders in or near Glasgow and shipped for this island to be sold for four or five years term of service. On their arrival they used to be ranged in a line like new Negroes for the planters to pick and chose [sic]. But this traffic has ceased for some years since the despotism of clanship was subdued and trade and industry drove out laziness and tyranny from the North of Scotland.[6]

Irrespective of the methods of their arrival, the Campbell presence was conspicuous in Jamaican society. As Edward Long reported, 'I have heard a computation made of no fewer than one hundred of the name of Campbell only resident in it all claiming alliance with the Argyle family.'[7]

Joining the Campbell contingent were their kinsmen and neighbours in Argyllshire, the Malcolms of Poltalloch. Dugald Malcolm (anglicised from MacCallum), a merchant and heir to Poltalloch, was first to join the Argyllshire conclave in the Hanover Parish of Jamaica around 1750.[8] He married well, acquiring a sugar plantation owned by the Clerks (anglicised from McClerich) of Braeleckan, yet another Argyllshire family who had come out in 1713.[9] It was, however, his cousin and heir Neill (I) who would build the family plantation empire in the parish. He arrived in Jamaica in 1760, having received mercantile training in Glasgow and set up a 'store system' – as he had witnessed the 'Tobacco Lords' do in Virginia and Maryland – selling goods on credit in advance of revenue from the future sale of the next season's sugar and rum production. Like the Campbells, he also acquired shipping interests. He stayed on the island for eleven years before moving to London in 1771. As with many Scottish entrepreneurs climbing the colonial commodities trade ladder, he eventually made London the centre of his business (1786) and died there in 1802.

His son, Neill (II), inherited the Argyllshire estates and a portfolio of seven sugar plantations – Argyle, Knockalva, Alexandria, New Paradise, Pell River, Blenheim and Retrieve Old Works – along with two large stock ranges – Argyle Pen and Retirement Pen. In 1835 he received compensation close to £40,000 following the emancipation of his 2,176 slaves.[10]

The same business acumen cannot be said of the third and fourth generation of Campbells inheriting Jamaican estates. By the end of slavery in the British Empire they had either sold up or surrendered their properties to their mortgage holders to pay their accrued debts when living in London as absentees or to service the over-generous annuities and bequeaths left in the wills of previous owners during the era of high sugar prices. One physical legacy left on the island by a Campbell was monumental 'Auchendown Castle' built in Westmoreland by Archibald, the third son of John of New Hope, to mark his link with Argyllshire. He died on the island in April 1833, aged fifty-two.[11]

THE PROFESSIONAL PATHWAY TO RICHES

Of the higher professions, Scots doctors were a readily discernible group in Jamaica, many of whom aspired to hold 'letters of attorney' over slave plantations as a stepping stone to proprietorship. In his seminal work, Richard Sheridan reckoned that during the American War of Independence period when demand for their services was high, as many as two-thirds of the doctors on the island were Scots.[12] Most needed to win multiple commissions attending the slave populations on a number of estates over a lengthy period to accumulate the necessary capital to buy into a fashionable practice in Kingston or Savannah la Mar, or to enter the slave-owning side of the business.[13] Their higher education and status in Jamaican society also often secured them an advantageous marriage to a widow or an heiress daughter of a planter.

In the first half of the eighteenth century, however, not all 'doctors' proved to be an asset in promoting the island's general health and economic well being. Long wrote a lengthy tirade on the barely qualified, disreputable 'quacks' who had been infesting the island 'killing off the population' during the earlier part of the century.

One possible candidate for this title was the seventeen-year-old Alexander Grant of Dalvey, who landed in Jamaica as a 'Practitioner of Physick & Chiurgery' in 1721, having undertaken a one-year correspondence course on apothecary with Aberdeen University.[14] His rise to planter status took him nine years, serving as a 'country doctor' in the western parishes before he acquired the 300-acre 'Spring Garden' estate in the parish of St Elizabeth. From such a slow beginning his fortunes rapidly increased when he switched to merchandising in Westmoreland, where he built a store house along with his business partner Peter

Beckford junior. After three years he moved to Kingston, where he married Catherine Cooke, the only daughter of a St Catherine's planter and sister of a local doctor.

Grant's fortunes soared when he quit Jamaica for London two years later. There he formed a partnership with a former Scottish Barbadian planter, Alexander Johnston, as wholesale druggists. By the time they dissolved their partnership in 1753, Grant was well on his way to creating an integrated shipping and merchandising empire, in partnership with a circle of London Scots led by Richard Oswald of Auchencruive, which handled sugar consignments on commission, traded in slaves and supplied rum to the Navy Board.

Once imbedded in the London Scots network, Grant's knowledge of and connections in Jamaica made him invaluable to his northern cousins seeking advancement in the Empire over the next thirty years. Indeed, it was he who assisted Sir Archibald of Monymusk to find that 'anything in the way of Jamaica' that was to prove so lucrative and financed Monymusk's rebuilding of his castle and his renowned agrarian improvements on his Aberdeenshire estate. All of which ingratiated Grant to his clan chief and his close associates.

Even as an absentee, Grant maintained his interest in planting in Jamaica, acquiring a patent on 1,000 acres in the 1740s, to which he added a further 1,000 acres purchased in 1752–3. Around the same time, 'Sir' Alexander (he had finally secured the baronetcy of Dalvey in 1752 from his reluctant clan chief) acquired a string of large sugar estates over which he had held letters of attorney and which his cousin and partner – Alexander of Achoynanie – had managed. These were secured by foreclosing on the loans he had advanced to the owners. In this way he took over the lease on the Charlemont estate in St Thomas in the Vale and the freehold of the Albion and Eden estates in St Mary's Parish. In the following decade he foreclosed on the mortgages of a further four properties – notably the Berwick estate – which increased his plantation portfolio to seven estates totalling 11,000 acres and valued at £96,000 at the time of his death in 1772.[15] Achoynanie had taken ownership of Eden on the flip of a coin in settlement at the end of their agreement. In 1834 compensation of around £16,000 was paid out for the loss of 1,200 slaves on four of these estates to his grandson, Sir Alexander Cray Grant.[16]

Doctors continued to arrive on the island from all over Scotland, notably from the South-West, after 1750. One who made it to planter proprietor was James Irving 'the elder' of Bonshaw, Annan. He arrived in Jamaica via a convoluted route which included a spell as a physician in St Petersburg, the Bahamas and South Carolina, where he married Elizabeth Motte, a member of a well-established Charleston family (1745). He moved his family to Jamaica in 1752–3. Soon after their arrival he made an unusual deal in swapping their small estate in South Carolina for a 900-acre plantation in the Martha Brae River area of the parish of Trelawney, which he renamed 'Irving Tower'. From this head start he built up his holdings over the next decade, acquiring three other large estates in the Parish of St James, which he named Ironshore, Hartfield and Bonshaw, and a smaller holding, 'the Crawle', all of which amounted to over 4,400 acres.[17] By 1767 he was a successful planter and was elected a Member of the Assembly, on which he served until his death during a sojourn to London in 1775. His grandson, John Beaufin Irving, claimed £5,250 in compensation for the 268 slaves then on Irving Tower, Ironshore and Hartfield in 1835.[18] His descendants continued to hold these working plantations after the emancipation of slaves.

The last quarter of the eighteenth and the early nineteenth centuries witnessed an upsurge in the number of young doctors eager to emulate the earlier success of the likes of Grant and Irving. The Scottish universities – Aberdeen, Edinburgh and Glasgow – were then producing more apothecaries, physicians and surgeons, of various qualifications, than were required by the home market. Edinburgh alone churned out 2,792 between 1776 and 1826.[19] By then the high esteem that Scottish university qualifications conferred was being negated by over-supply in the West Indies, particularly in the peacetime years when positions in the armed forces rapidly contracted. The expectation of the high fees that they once commanded vanished after the American War of Independence. As Charles Douglas, the would-be employer of the forlorn poet Robert Burns as a bookkeeper on his Ayr Mount plantation in Portland, remarked in a letter home to his brother Patrick in Ayrshire in 1786: 'Young doctors are very plenty here many of them much at a loss to get employment in that way.'[20]

Those without the large amount of money necessary to purchase an alternative position abroad, such as the East India Company, sometimes – like the Bell brothers of Langholm, Dumfriesshire – worked their way across the Atlantic as surgeons on slave ships. If they survived that experience, they had the advantage of arriving with their earnings from the 'trade' with which to purchase a small plantation or set up in business.[21]

It was not a one-way street though, as over two hundred Jamaicans (mainly white) matriculated to study medicine at Edinburgh University. The largest cohort (eighty-five) graduated during the years 1791–1830 when moves were afoot on the island to regulate practitioners.[22] One notable graduate of the class of 1813 was Charles Mackglashan of

Kingston, who ran a fashionable practice in the town and, along with his brother John, amassed a formidable number of compensation claims on slaves held in the immediate area.[23]

The planter class of Jamaica was noted as a highly litigious group, particularly in relation to land boundary disputes which Long blamed on the poor quality of the early land surveyors. Despite such obvious opportunities for enrichment, the presence of Scots in the island's legal profession was very small as the island operated under the English Bar system which did not recognise Scottish qualifications. Many, however, utilised their education and skills to secure government positions on the island; as with John Dunlop, formerly an advocate in Aberdeen, who became the Landing and Tide Surveyor of the port of Kingston.[24]

One who did use his time in London to study for the English Bar and ultimately reached the pinnacle of the Jamaican legal system was John Grant, the eldest son of Patrick Grant of Glenorchy, Speyside. Little is known of his early career on the island other than that he spent several years as a Member of the Assembly before becoming an Assistant Judge to the Supreme Court. In January 1783 he succeeded Thomas French as the Chief Lord Justice. He held that position until 1790, when he retired back to Scotland, acquiring the Kilgraston and Pitcaithly estates in Perthshire from the Murray and Craigie families. He died in Edinburgh in March 1793 and was succeeded by his brother Francis, who died in 1818 leaving his heirs to claim the compensation of c. £4,500 for the freed slaves on the Blackness estate in Westmoreland.[25]

THE MERCHANT PATHWAY TO RICHES

Chasing the same dream of securing a fortune in Jamaica sufficient to sustain a gentleman's lifestyle back home attracted many able young men with mercantile connections and training. All were well versed in the basic 'ABC' of overseas trade – 'Arithmetic, Bookkeeping & Cyphering' – and some with the added refinements of classics and languages.

The spectacular rise of the island-born Simon Taylor from merchant to attorney, described by Governor Nugent as 'by much the richest proprietor in the island, and in the habit of accumulating money', of which he left around a million sterling to his nephew on his death in 1813, was the role model for many. Taylor acknowledged his Scots descent by naming two of his pens 'Montrose' and 'Burrowfield' after his father's (Patrick Tailyour) properties back in Angus, Scotland.[26]

The career of Simon Taylor's cousin John serves to illuminate the pathway to success of a newly arrived Scottish adventurer. Born in

Kirkton House, Marykirk, six miles north of Montrose, he was apprenticed as a clerk to the Glasgow tobacco firm of George McCall & Co.,
eventually rising to be their factor in Virginia. He struggled to maintain
the business during the American War of Independence and turned to
supplying British prisoners of war held by the Americans. In 1782, at
the instigation of his cousin Simon, he left for Jamaica along with many
other Loyalists. Once he was established in Kingston, he anglicised his
surname from Tailyour to Taylor to capitalise on his association with
his wealthy cousin, and established his own import/export business,
McBean, Ballantine & Taylor, using his Glasgow connections to trade
in plantation goods, dry goods and an array of domestic items. The
company later came to specialise in the processing and selling of slave
cargoes landed in Jamaica. In 1792 James Fairlie joined the company,
which was renamed Taylor, Ballantine & Fairlie, and John was able to
retire back to Scotland the following year when his health was failing.
He left the firm in Kingston to be run by his former clerks John McCall
(son of George) and David Dick.

John left behind in Jamaica his concubine of many years, Polly
Graham, one of his cousin's slaves by whom he had four children. Prior
to his departure he pleaded with Simon to sell Polly and their children to
him, 'having now experienced her care & attention in sickness & health
I confess myself much attached to her . . . I feel more anxious to obtain
this Favour than I can describe.'[27] This was agreed and Polly and her
family were freed by manumission and provided for by his new partners
McCall and Dick.

Back in Scotland, John married George McCall's daughter, Mary, and
re-purchased his family's house and the substantial estate of Kirkton Hill.
In 1797 he sold out his share of the Kingston business to Fairlie. He then
had his three surviving children by Polly – James, John and Catherine –
sent to him in Scotland, where they were educated and helped into suitable positions. John lived comfortably with his ten legal children on the
proceeds from his Jamaican business until his death in 1815.[28]

Simon Taylor also acted benevolently towards John's brother, James,
while the latter was in Jamaica, and also helped a neighbour from the
home Montrose area, Hercules Ross. Ross was the son of the Excise
officer at Johnshaven seven miles up the coast from Montrose and had
come out to Jamaica as a sixteen-year-old in 1761. His first position was
as clerk to Andrew Murray, a relative of Taylor and the Naval Office
agent at Kingston. With Simon's help, Ross set up in business six years
later with Henry Hanbury, trading slaves to the French islands. During
the American War of Independence he rented out his own slaves to

raise fortifications to defend the island and ran a private fleet of four privateers while acting as the leading prize agent in Jamaica. In 1779 he was appointed Agent General, charged with organising transports for a military expedition against Spanish Nicaragua. All these projects were highly lucrative, which allowed him to buy the Bushy Park plantation where he installed his mistress, Elizabeth Foord – a quadroon (one-quarter of African ethnicity) – and their six children.[29]

Three years later he sold up his assets in Jamaica and retired to Scotland on board one of his armed merchant ships, by far the surest way of transferring his fortune. Back home, as a very wealthy man, he was made an honorary Burgess of the City of Glasgow. Two years later he metamorphosed into a landed gentleman with the purchase of Craig House and the surrounding great estate of Rossie in the hinterland of Montrose for £33,250. His success was completed with his marriage to Henrietta Parish, the heiress of a Scottish trader in Hamburg, in 1784. Thereafter, he immersed himself in local civil and military duties and the building of the neo-gothic 'Rossie Castle', which he and his expanding legal family moved into in 1800. Like John Taylor, he sent for his children in Jamaica to be educated in Scotland.

One unique development that separated him from the other returning Jamaican neighbours was his conversion to the abolitionist movement. In 1790 he had been approached by William Wilberforce to give evidence on the slave trade to a Select Committee. Despite his own recent involvement, he took up the cause. Later, he and his wife took up two £50 shares in the Sierra Leone Company, which aimed to resettle freed slaves back in Africa.[30]

Across the tidal basin from Ross's estate was another wealthy Jamaican returnee, George Ogilvy, who bought the Ecclesjohn estate in 1787 for £10,000 and renamed it 'Langley Park' after his plantation in the Jamaican parish of St Mary's. Three years later he enlarged this Angus estate when he purchased the adjacent land of Tayock. Unfortunately it is not known by which pathway he first came by his Jamaican wealth. He died soon afterwards (January 1790) leaving no issue or will. His Scottish estate was eventually sold to the 44-year-old newly married James Cruikshank.

James was the elder of four brothers from an old Banffshire family who had made very large fortunes in sugar estates on the island of St Vincent. In 1775 his brother Patrick had bought the grand estate of Stracathro (2,000 acres), near Edzell, Angus, which Alexander inherited and had rebuilt in the Palladian style (1824–7). The remaining brother, John, purchased the close by and more modest Keithock House.[31]

This pattern, notably in the last quarter of the eighteenth century, of return from the West Indies with an 'opulent fortune' sufficient to ensure elevation to the landed elite of Scotland can be readily found in other regions of Scotland. As acknowledged in the *Scots Magazine* review of the new Rossie Castle, 'It must afford a subject of exultation to the inhabitants of Scotland, to observe the splendour of many of the mansions recently erected by our nobility and gentry, on almost every county, within the last 15 years.'[32]

The Angus network was not exceptional in their success in the very tricky business of repatriating their Jamaican wealth to Scotland. Alexander Grant of Aberlour, a son of a local minister and described as 'a planter and merchant of Jamaica', returned to his home parish with wealth sufficient to build his seat – Aberlour House – endow his village and leave £300,000 to his heir.[33]

In south Ayrshire, the young merchant Robert Hamilton of Clongall near Ayr founded a dynastic line of landed gentry based on his Jamaican wealth. Central to his phenomenal success was his marriage to Jean Mitchell, a planter's widow with two large plantations, Rozelle in St Thomas in the East and Pemberton in St Mary's, within months of his arrival in Jamaica (1734). Ten years later he was in that most coveted position of being able to retire back to Ayrshire with his wife and four daughters, leaving his plantations in the hands of a succession of nephews. Two years after that he purchased the estate of Bourtrehill near Irvine. In 1752 he made his master-move by selling his Rozelle sugar plantation, which passed into the hands of his neighbours in south Ayrshire, the Fergussons of Kilkerran and the Hunter Blairs of Blairquhan, thereby sidestepping the problems of repatriation of funds. He reinvested this capital in a large land purchase in the parish of Alloway on which he built a new mansion which he named 'Rozelle'. From there he launched the highly successful social careers of his daughters, marrying the eldest to the 22nd Earl of Crawford and his youngest to the future Earl of Eglinton.[34] His nephews did the same, returning from their stint managing the family's remaining Pemberton Valley plantation with the funds to build their own gentleman's seats nearby at Pinmore & Bellisle and Sundrum Castle.

James Stirling was a manager of Robert Hamilton's while he was still on the island. He was one of a very large number of brothers in an extensive old Jacobite Perthshire family, the Stirlings of Keir & Cawder.[35] Four of the brothers followed their elder brother Archibald to Jamaica. They all had little in the way of capital or professional status other than their tight allegiance to Archibald, or 'Baldy', who had become the family patriarch. Their Jamaican estates of Frontier and Hampden feature largely in Alan Karras's study of the attorney Francis Grant and his 'web of patronage' along the north-shore parishes of the island.[36]

THE PLANTER ATTORNEY'S PATHWAY TO RICHES

Edward Long concluded that there were only around one hundred attorneys in Jamaica in the early 1770s. They came from a wide spectrum of backgrounds – merchants, doctors, lawyers and even indentured servants – and had risen to the top of the management of the plantation system by dint of their experience and expertise. Holding letters of attorney over an absentee's estate did not require a professional qualification, although competence in handling the legal and financial affairs of a working plantation was assumed.

This number of attorneys can safely be assumed to have risen considerably after Long's departure to Britain with ill health in 1769, in parallel with the upsurge in the number of landlords absenting themselves from the islands. At the time of the outbreak of the American War of Independence (1775) one-third of the estates on the island, producing 40 per cent of the sugar, were in the hands of managers acting under letters of attorney. This number soared after the outbreak of the bloody slave revolt on Saint Domingue (1791) and the maroon revolt on Jamaica (1795), which unnerved many of the island's plantocracy. By 1832 it was reckoned that over 80 per cent of the large sugar estates had non-residential proprietors. In this exodus, fortunes were to be made by attorneys prepared to acquire a string of estates and animal pens to administer and, from the high fees they charged, purchase their own plantations and pens while sugar prices still soared, doubling between 1775 and 1799.

The slide in sugar prices over the next two decades prompted many absentees to sell up, creating further opportunities for those confident enough to step up to plantation ownership or to extend their holdings. Not all of the top attorneys came from the professions or minor laird backgrounds. William Miller – the 'Prince of the attorneys' – was described by the Church of Scotland Missionary Society evangelist Masterton Waddell as having 'gone from Scotland in the lowest capacity, and had risen to almost the highest position in the colony'.

Once an agent had established his reputation as an attorney within a web of patronage it was commonplace for him to oversee numerous properties at the same time, as with Francis Graham, an established planting attorney in the parish of St Catherine. When asked in November 1815 by a committee of the Honourable House of the Assembly of Jamaica, 'what is your present situation, and the nature of your connection with the island of Jamaica?' he replied that he

> represents solely and in part forty-nine sugar-estates, nineteen pens, and ten other plantations, on which there are about thirteen thousand negroes; that he possesses a sugar-estate, called Tulloch, with about four hundred and fifty negroes, and holds jointly with Lord Carrington the Farm Pen, with about two hundred and fifty negroes.[37]

He was then a Member of the Assembly and sat on the committee for the building of roads and bridges in the Jamaican county of Middlesex along with his fellow Scots, Hector Mackay, George Mackay, George William Hamilton, Malcolm McLeod and Alexander McInnes.[38]

How Graham, a forty-two-year-old entrepreneur from Dingwall on the Black Isle in the county of Ross & Cromarty, came to be so deeply imbedded in the island's establishment attests to the strength of the Scots networks at home, in his case mostly from the North and North-East of Scotland. He was the son of Alexander Graham of Drynie, Black Isle, and arrived in Jamaica in 1796. He came out to the island at the behest of his uncle, Charles Graham, who was then in partnership with Donald Davidson, heir to Tulloch Castle in Dingwall and the senior partner, since 1779, of their London counting house of Davidson & Graham of Fenchurch Buildings. Despite its London location, it was a very northern Scottish firm. On his uncle's death aged fifty, in 1801, a new partner, Aeneas Barkly of Cromarty (later laird of Mounteagle, Black Isle), joined the firm. On the death of Donald, Francis Graham was entered as a partner, along with Donald's son Henry. The firm would eventually own or hold the mortgages on a plantation empire of twenty-six properties located in British Guyana, Grenada, St Vincent, Trinidad and Jamaica. At the time of emancipation of slaves in the British Empire these estates were worked by over 1,800 slaves.[39]

One of the plantations Graham managed as attorney (1805–20) was the Georgia estate in the parish of St Thomas in the East, which was the property of the absentee heiress Rose Milles.[40] His close reliance on his fellow Scots in the Assembly is evident by his choice of replacement manager of the estate during his short absence from the island when he returned home to Scotland (1812–13) in order to marry Jemima Charlotte in Edinburgh Castle (February 1813). She was the third daughter of Lieutenant Colonel Colin Dundas Graham of the Scots Brigade and governor of St Mawes Castle, Cornwall.[41] His replacement on the Georgia estate was his fellow committee member George William

Hamilton, the son of John Hamilton of North Park, Glasgow. Hamilton again assumed the role when Graham fell fatally ill in 1820.[42] This preferment system was prevalent among the Scots on the island.

Prior to his death, Graham was in a position to display his wealth and status as one of the island's elite. Rich enough to bring his wife to the island, he hosted, in 1816, the society wedding of his sister-in-law Margaret to Michael Benignus Clare, Physician General of Jamaica, at his fine mansion of Williamsfield Park on the outskirts of Spanish Town.[43] It was considered a risky business bringing out a legal wife to such a lethal climate. A fellow planter attorney, William Lambie of Aberdeen, did the same, marrying Elizabeth, the daughter of Patrick Crichton of Gayfield Square, Edinburgh, who died giving birth in Kingston within a year of her arrival at the age of twenty-three. The twenty-nine-year-old Margaret, only daughter of Duncan Gardner of Irvine, was dead within eleven days of marrying the Scots attorney Duncan McCallum on the island. He buried her on the estate he was managing. Most chose to maintain a black or mulatto mistress (or a string of them, as in the case of Simon Taylor) and only to marry legally on return to the homeland. Observers of this way of life often commented on the ironic unswerving loyalty of the black and mulatto women *in their 'marriage' as they call it* to their white partners.[44]

CONCLUSION

The arrival and progress of the Scots in Jamaica was markedly different to those later investing in plantations on the 'Ceded Islands' from the mid-1760s and British Guyana from the 1790s. As one of the oldest English settled islands, Jamaica shared with Barbados an early trade in indentured servants and banished miscreants from Scotland which extended beyond the Act of Union. But unlike Barbados, which was largely taken up by small-holding cultivation early on, Jamaica offered the option of purchasing large tracts of cheap undeveloped land by Crown patent. The result was the average Jamaican plantation was 900 acres, three times that initially permitted by Crown agents on the Ceded Islands. In the former Dutch colonies of Berbice, Essequibo and Demerara, entry was invariably by purchase of a previously developed plantation.

Long's assertion that the Scots constituted one-third of the Europeans on Jamaica by the 1770s (when they were only 10 per cent of the mainland United Kingdom population) speaks volumes for the allure of this island to successive waves of business adventurers. Many were the younger sons of lairds pushed abroad to seek their fortunes by the practice of land inheritance by primogeniture. With them clanship and patronage was paramount and engendered a willingness to risk all to acquire the means to rejoin the landed gentry at home.

Then there was the sheer scale of opportunities available on Jamaica which was, by far, the largest and wealthiest of the sugar islands, holding over half the slave population in the British Caribbean. Indeed, on that island the minority of Scots who achieved success often became permanent or long-term residents rather than sojourners, rising through the ranks of the planter class to serve in the island's political establishment.

This Scots-Jamaican network connected the kinsmen of Scottish lesser and greater landowning families and extended to London. As the epicentre for their colonial business empires based on integrated shipping and commodity trading, the capital later became the preferred location for retirement. Even so, the deep-seated urge to demonstrate their success in the homeland resulted in the spate of estate acquisition, large-house building and 'improvements' which are still very much evident in the Scottish landscape today.

NOTES

1. Edward Long, *History of Jamaica; or General Survey of the antient and modern state of that island* (London, 1774), Vol. II, pp. 286–93.
2. His father was Rev. Patrick Campbell of Glenary, Torbhlaren in mid-Argyll. Marion Campbell (ed.), *Letters by the Packet: Family Correspondence 1728–1861* (Dunoon: Argyll & Bute Library Service, 2004), pp. 13–118.
3. Peter Dickson, '*A Villainous tribe of Fiddlers and Fixers' Campbell of Auchinbreck, Jamaica schemes 1712–1776*: http://www.jamaicanfamily search.com/Members/CampbellofAuchinbreck.htm
4. Letter from Thomas Ruddach to Charles Steuart, 5 January 1777, NLS, MS 5030, p. 8.
5. Letter from John, 2nd Duke of Argyll to Archibald Campbell of Stonefield, 22 March 1740, NRS GD 14/12.
6. Long, *History of Jamaica*, p. 288.
7. Ibid., p. 286.
8. Allan I. Macinnes, 'Commercial Landlordism and Clearances in the Scottish Highlands; the case of Arichonan', in Juan Pan-Montojo and Frederick Pedersen (eds), *Communities in European History: Representations, Jurisdictions, Conflicts* (Pisa: University of Pisa, 2007), pp. 47–64.
9. The Clerks of Braeleckan were close neighbours to the Campbells of Auchinbreck on the west shore of Loch Fyne.
10. *Legacies of British Slave Ownership* database, University College London, T71/872, 872, 915.

11. Philip Wright, *Monumental Inscriptions of Jamaica* (London: Society of Genealogists, 1966), Inscription No. 3056.

12. Richard B. Sheridan, *Doctors & Slaves: A Medical and Demographic History of Slavery in the British West Indies, 1680–1834* (Cambridge: Cambridge University Press, 1985). pp. 44, 372.

13. The average retaining fee for treating a slave per year was five shillings during the second half of the century.

14. David Hancock, *Citizens of the World* (Cambridge University Press: Cambridge, 1995), p. 50.

15. Ibid., p. 148.

16. *Legacies,* St Elizabeth claim 1018, St Mary's claim 260, St Thomas in the Vale claims 19177 and 296.

17. Aemilius Irving, *James Irving of Ironshore* (Toronto: College Press, 1918)

18. *Legacies,* T71/ 549 (A&B), 550 (A, B& C), 381 (A & B).

19. Sheridan, *Doctors & Slaves*, p. 58.

20. As quoted in Eric J. Graham, *Burns & the Sugar Plantocracy of Ayrshire* (Musselburgh: MDP&D, 2014), p. 1.

21. Eric J. Graham, 'Letters from the Bell brothers, Scottish Surgeons in the Slave Trade', *Scottish Local History* (December, 2014), pp. 22–8.

22. *The Edinburgh Medical & Surgical Journal*, Vol. 9 (Edinburgh: A. & C. Black, 1813), p. 499.

23. Ibid., pp. 56–61.

24. Probate of Will, Edinburgh Sheriff Court, 6 November 1819, NAS SC 70/1/20.

25. *Legacies*, T71/871.

26. The most recent appraisal is by B. W. Higman, *Plantation Jamaica* (Kingston: University of West Indies, 2005), pp. 137–51.

27. Letter from John to Simon, 3 January 1790, Simon Taylor papers, Institute of Commonwealth Studies, London.

28. See Tailyour family papers catalogue, William L. Clements Library, The University of Michigan.

29. He put up the young Horatio Nelson at his estate when he was struck down with fever.

30. Amanda Briant-Evans, 'A Portrait of the Rossie Estate and its Owners', *Flowing Past: More Historical Highlights from Montrose Basin* (Brechin: Print Matters, 2008), pp. 68–100. This article was largely based on the unpublished thesis by Agnes Butterfield, *Hercules Ross of Kingston Jamaica and Rossie, Forfar 1745–1816* (1982).

31. Amanda Briant-Evans, 'West Indian Fortunes at Langley Park', *Ebb and Flow: Aspects of the History of Montrose Basin* (Forfar: Pinkfoot Press, 2004), pp. 88–102.

32. *Scots Magazine*, September 1807, Vol. 69, p. 643.

33. *Legacies*, 'Profile & Legacies', Alexander Grant.

34. Graham, *Burns & the Sugar Plantocracy of Ayrshire,* Chapter 1.

35. William Fraser, *Stirlings of Keir and their family papers* (Edinburgh, 1858).
36. Allan Karras, *Sojourners in the Sun* (London: Cornell University Press, 1992), pp. 137–54.
37. *Further Proceedings of the Honourable House of Assembly of Jamaica relative to a bill introduced into the House of Commons for effectually preventing the unlawful importation of slaves . . .* Alexander Aikman (Kingston, 1816).
38. *The Laws of Jamaica*, Vol. 6, p. 336. Hector Mackay was then owner of Airy Mount estate in St Thomas in the East. The compensation was later awarded to 'Aeneas Barkly with the concurrence of H. Davidson and Wm Davidson, mortgagees in fee for £12,898 with interest from 31 May 1835' for 172 slaves, *Legacies* claim T71/855. Razamount plantation, claim T71/855. George Mackay is possibly George William Mackay of the 'Worcester estate' claim T71/852.
39. *Legacies*, 'Profile & Legacies', Henry Davidson and Francis Graham.
40. *Letter books & Accounts, Georgia Estate*, St Thomas in the East, 1805–35, National Library of Jamaica, Kingston, as quoted in Higman, *Plantation Jamaica*, p.116.
41. *The Scots Magazine & Edinburgh Literary Miscellancy* (Edinburgh: Constable, 1813) Vol. 75, p. 238.
42. His father was three times Lord Provost of Glasgow. After 1822 Hamilton was replaced by John McKenzie, originating from Perthshire: Higman, *Plantation Jamaica*, p. 116.
43. Sylvanus Urban, *The Gentleman's Magazine & Historical Chronicle* (London, 1817) Vol. LXXXVII, p. 465.
44. Samuel Robinson, *The Experiences of a Boy Sailor aboard a Slave Ship* (Hamilton: Naismith, 1867), pp. 119–54.

5

'The habits of these creatures in clinging one to the other': Enslaved Africans, Scots and the Plantations of Guyana

David Alston

ALONG THE MUDDY COAST of Demerara, on the north coast of the South American continent, some of the slaves whose forced labour made others rich could earn a little cash for themselves and their families by catching large prawns. These were hawked around the scattered plantations houses and in the only larger settlement, Georgetown. Today we might call these shellfish Norway lobsters, Dublin Bay prawns or *langoustines* but the slaves, with what one imagines was a bitter irony, noted 'the habits of these creatures in clinging one to the other' and called them 'Scotchmen'.[1]

There was a large Scottish presence in Demerara, and in neighbouring Essequibo and Berbice, which had all been Dutch possessions until they were surrendered to British forces in 1796. The three colonies were not formally ceded by the Netherlands until 1814/15, later united in 1831 to become British Guiana, and now form the Republic of Guyana. They have received even less attention than the islands of the British Caribbean in accounts of Scotland's role in the British Empire, despite being the only British colonies in South America. Indeed, they often seem to be glimpsed only in peripheral vision, unexpectedly not islands although part of the West Indies and in the Caribbean.

Research led by Nicholas Draper on the records of compensation awarded to slave owners at emancipation in 1834 now clearly demonstrates the importance of British Guiana at the end of colonial slavery, when there were 84,075 enslaved people held there. This was an eighth of the 655,780 enslaved in the colonies of the West Indies but, as a result of the demand for labour in the sugar plantations, these slaves were valued disproportionally highly at £4.28m, amounting to more than a quarter of the total compensation subsequently paid by the British Government. The equivalent value of this sum, expressed as comparative purchasing power in 2015, is £367.7 million. Other means of calculating comparative value would give a higher sum.[2] In both the number of enslaved at the time of emancipation and in the amount of compensation paid, British Guiana was second only to the long-established colony of Jamaica.[3]

The importance of Guyana to Scotland can be inferred from the compensation awarded to merchants and other individuals in Glasgow, who received more for slaves held there than in any other colony, including Jamaica. The 3,591 enslaved people held in British Guiana (approximately a quarter of the total owned by Glasgow merchants and numerically more than in any other colony) were valued at £193,991. This was 42 per cent of the total compensation they received and in today's terms can be expressed as the equivalent of £16.7 million (comparative purchasing power). As elsewhere in Britain, the payments were intended to ensure that Glasgow, which had flourished through the ruthless exploitation of hundreds of thousands of Africans and their descendants, would continue to thrive.[4]

Although the high value of slaves in Guyana reflected the importance of its sugar production, which had eclipsed cotton from about 1810, the large number of enslaved people was a consequence of the earlier and remarkably rapid development of cotton plantations after the Dutch capitulation and before the abolition of the colonial slave trade in 1807. In this period more than 22 per cent of newly enslaved Africans taken to the Caribbean in British ships were sent to Guyana, with the enslaved population of Demerara increasing from 29,473 in 1795 to 80,915 in 1807, and that of Berbice from 8,232 to 28,480 in the same period. Because a sand bar made it difficult for large vessels to enter the river Berbice, all but a few slaving ships disembarked their human cargoes at Stabroek (later named Georgetown) at the mouth of the Demerary.

Between 1780 and 1796 only eighteen slave ships had landed but the numbers then soared, with a further 246 before the end of 1807. In 1801 alone, a year in which Scots flocked to Guyana, fifty-two ships with 12,532 enslaved Africans docked at Stabroek. Over 1,300 others had died during the voyages from Africa.[5]

This, in the final years of the trade in human beings, was exploitation of enslaved labour as intense as in any other period and, indeed, it was here that the plantation system was pushed to its limits. Across the Caribbean islands in 1810, slaves outnumbered whites in proportions varying from roughly eight to one in the old colonies to twenty-three to one in the new colonies of the southern Caribbean. This was an increase from a ratio of roughly six to one in British colonies in 1748. But in

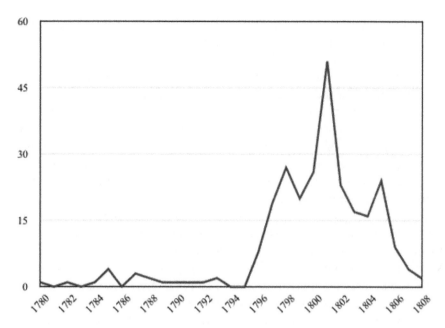

Figure 5.1 Number of slave ships landing in Demerara, 1780–1808. Source: data in David Eltis, Stephen Behrendt, David Richardson and Herbert Klein (eds), *The Trans-Atlantic Slave Trade: A Database on CD-ROM* (Cambridge: Cambridge University Press, 2000)

Demerara and Berbice these proportions were thirty-five to one and fifty-six to one respectively, higher than anywhere else and regarded as a serious risk by the authorities in these colonies.[6] Managers of plantations in Berbice struggled to maintain even the minimum ratio of one white to every seventy-nine slaves required by the colony's governor.[7]

In summary, Guyana is worth studying, firstly because of its economic importance to Scotland, as a producer of cotton until about 1810 and then as a producer of sugar; secondly, because of the particularly strong Scottish presence in the colony; and thirdly, because these Scots operated at the edge of empire, in colonies on what Kit Candlin has termed 'the last Caribbean frontier', a wild frontier land where the system was being pushed to breaking point in pursuit of profit.[8]

SCOTTISH COLONISTS AND COTTON

Although Berbice was the oldest Dutch settlement, there was a notorious suspicion of outsiders until the late 1780s, when it opened itself to new colonists.[9] In Essequibo, by contrast, the Dutch governor built Fort

Zeelandia in 1744, closer to the coast than earlier settlements, and then both encouraged established Dutch planters to relocate from upriver and opened the colony to British planters from the West Indies. The colony of Demerara was established the following year and grew in importance as the fertility of the soils of Essequibo became depleted. Initially settlement was along the banks of the river Demerary and this brought many sugar planters of British origin, mainly from Barbados, attracted by the availability of fresh land and by a ten-year tax remission. By the 1760s they formed the majority of the white population of this Dutch colony.[10] A crucial subsequent development, from the mid-1780s, was the creation of new plantations along the coast for the cultivation of cotton, created by the same techniques used to create polders in the Netherlands and consequently known as 'impoldered' land. From 1791, new grants of land were also made on the Berbice coast by its governor.[11]

Cotton from Guyana, and neighbouring Surinam, was reckoned to be among the finest available, securing a price in 1793 25 to 30 per cent higher than cotton from Jamaica.[12] Coffee was also an important crop and by 1800 Demerara and Berbice were the leading colonial producers of both these commodities.[13] Berbice was especially committed to cotton and in 1810 there were only four sugar plantations in the colony, insufficient to produce even enough rum for domestic consumption.[14]

Henry Bolinbroke, a young clerk who worked in Stabroek from 1799, noted that in only a few years 'all the uncultivated lots between the Demerary and Berbice were bought up with an avidity never before equalled', while by 1800 the chief of clan Mackenzie, Lord Seaforth, a Highland landowner who invested heavily in Berbice, was already of the view that 'since the period of us taking possession, the influx of English, and still more of Scots, adventurers was truly astonishing'.[15] Dr Henry Dalton, writing in 1855, held that Scots had been in the majority among the European settlers and had been more successful in business than the English or Irish. He also referred to a 'recklessness' in their conduct, which he regarded as 'characteristic . . . of the Gaelic race' but which might be interpreted as a greater appetite for risk, contributing to their success in this frontier land.[16] The rest of this section evidences the extent of that Scottish presence in Guyana and demonstrates a particularly strong connection with northern and Highland Scotland. But behind individuals from the North were the merchant houses of Glasgow, Liverpool, London and Bristol, into whose hands most of the estates and slaves would fall, as sugar replaced cotton.

The first Scots-owned plantation had probably been Weilburg, on the river Demerary, acquired before 1762 by James Douglas, of

Springwood Park near Kelso. Although the white population at the time was tiny, it was deeply divided and these factions made management difficult.[17] Altogether more successful was Thomas Cuming (1739/40–1815) from the parish of Dallas (Moray). Cuming spent over fifty years in Demerara and married into a Dutch family, which was very much part of the establishment in the colony, and this integration may account for his success. He arrived in the early 1760s and by the late 1790s owned four plantations, producing sugar and coffee. He became a member of the governing Court of Policy of the colony under Dutch rule and, paradoxically, was one of the six members who signed the formal surrender to British forces in 1796. He did not become involved in the rush to develop cotton-planting but laid out one of his estates to expand the town of Stabroek, creating what became known as Cumingsburg. At his death in 1815 he was described as the colony's 'patriarch' and 'the principal promoter of its prosperity and wealth'.[18]

He was a point of contact in the colony for new arrivals when Demerara 'was still in an infant state' and had been joined before 1791 by his cousin, Lachlan Cuming, who later played a part in establishing the first Scots kirk in the colony.[19] In 1790 another northern Scot, James Fraser younger of Belladrum (Inverness-shire), was reported to have purchased 'a good estate [in Demerara] that is likely to turn out to great advantage'[20] and he too became an influential figure in the colony, where he was joined by his brothers Evan and Simon. Both Lachlan Cuming and Simon Fraser also married Dutch women but, after the death of his Dutch wife, Thomas Cuming came to Scotland in 1798 to marry the Belladrums' sister, Isabella, returning to Demerara after her early death in 1800.

By 1798 there were, on the evidence of the names of the proprietors, at least six Scots-owned plantations on the river Demerary and sixteen on the coast (see Table 5.1). The predominance of owners who were of northern or Highland origin is striking. This was even more so in Berbice (see Table 5.2), where new cotton plantations were first laid out on the west sea-coast and, by 1801, on the east sea-coast and along the river Canje. In 1801 a consortium was formed, led by Lord Seaforth in Scotland and James Fraser of Belladrum in Guyana, to purchase lots owned by the Dutch Berbice Society, thus acquiring, after subsequent divisions, an additional eighteen plantations.[21]

The tables below identify twenty-five individual Scots across the two colonies, at least seventeen of whom were resident, and for almost all the absentee owners there were one or more family members in Guyana.

Table 5.1 Scottish plantation owners in Demerara, 1798

	Name	Place of origin	Resident or absentee	No.	Notes
1	Thomas Cuming	Dallas (Moray)	Resident	4	Cousin of Lachlan Cuming.
2	Lachlan Cuming	Moray	Resident	1	Cousin of Thomas Cuming.
3	James Fraser	Belladrum (Inverness-shire)	Resident	1	Brothers Simon and Evan also resident.
4	James Baillie	Dochfour (Inverness-shire)	Absentee	3	Established West India merchant and slave trader.
5	Daniel Stewart	Not known	Not known	1	Plantation named Dunoon.
6	Thomas Campbell	Inverawe (Argyll)	Resident	3	Uncle of Duncan, below.
7	Duncan Campbell	Inverawe (Argyll)	Absentee?	1	Nephew of Thomas, above.
8	George Inglis	Inverness	Resident to c. 1798	2	After 1798 managed by cousin, Hugh B. Inglis.
9	Dr William Munro	Easter Ross	Resident	1	
10	Kenneth Francis Mackenzie	Edinburgh/Redcastle (Ross-shire)	Absentee	2	Lawyer in Edinburgh. Uncle of John Wilson (see Berbice).
11	William Grant	Strathspey	Resident	1	
12	Alexander Macrae	Inverinate (Wester Ross)	Resident	1	Brothers Farquhar and Colin also resident.
13	Spencer Mackay	London	Resident until c. 1800	1	Father was William Mackay from Sutherland.

Sources: Friederich von Bouchenröder, *Carte genérale & particulière de la Colonie d'Essequebe & Demerarie* (1798); for details of individuals see the author's website *Slaves & Highlanders* available at http://www.spanglefish.com/slavesandhighlanders.

From this very Highland base the involvement of Scots in Demerara and Berbice grew rapidly. In a remarkable replication of place names from the northern Highlands, along the eighty miles of the Berbice coast were plantations named Borlum, Kingillie, Belladrum, Alness, Kiltearn, Edderton, Lemlair, Fyrish, Foulis, Culcairn, Brahan, Kintail, Kilcoy, Tarlogie, Glastullich, Fearn, Geanies, Ankerville, Nigg, Tain,

Table 5.2 Scottish plantation owners in Berbice, 1802

	Name	Place of origin	Resident or absentee	No.	Notes
	James Fraser	Belladrum (Inverness-shire)	Resident	4	One owned in partnership with Anthony Somersall.
14	James Fraser	Pitcalzean (Ross-shire)	Resident	2	His widow owner from 1801.
15	Thomas Fraser	Not known	Resident	1	In partnership with Alfred Bartrum.
16	William Innes	Moray	Resident	1	
17	Hector Mackenzie	Clyne (Sutherland)	Resident	1	
	Spencer Mackay	London	Resident until c. 1800	2	Born London. Father was William Mackay from Sutherland.
	Dr William Munro	Easter Ross	Resident	1	
18	John Ross	Nigg (Ross-shire)	Resident	1	
19	John Wilson	Scotland	Resident	4	Nephew of K. F. Mackenzie (see Demerara) and later partner of John Gladstone.
	Berbice consortium:			18	Also included Anthony Somersall, from a family of English origin resident in Demerara since 1750s.
20	Lord Seaforth	Brahan (Ross-shire)	Absentee		Managed by Peter Fairbairn, formerly his secretary at Brahan.
	James Fraser (Belladrum)	See above			
21	Edward Fraser	Reelig (Inverness-shire)	Absentee		Sons James and Edward in Berbice.
22	Archibald Alves	Inverness/ London	Absentee		Son of Dr John Alves of Shipland, Inverness. Managed by relation, Thomas Alves.
	Dr William Munro	See above			

Table 5.2 (*Continued*)

	Name	Place of origin	Resident or absentee	No.	Notes
	Fraser & Alves:			2	
	James Fraser (Belladrum)	See above			
	Archibald Alves	See above			
	Macdonald & Co.:			3	
23	Allan Macdonald	Scotland	Resident		
24	Gavin Fullarton	Dalry (Ayrshire)	Resident?		Brother John in
	Munro & Douglas:			2	colony.
	Dr William Munro	See above			
25	Douglas	Kiltearn (Ross-shire)?	Not known		Tentative identification as Gilbert Douglas, of Balcony (Kiltearn).

Sources: Friederich von Bouchenröder, *Kaart van de Colonie de Berbice* (Amsterdam, 1802); for details of individuals see the author's website *Slaves & Highlanders* available at http://www.spanglefish.com/slavesandhighlanders.

Ross, Cromarty, Golspie, Dunrobin, Rosehall and Kildonan. There were also plantations named Lochaber, Auchlyne, Balcraig, East Lothian and Scotland. To place this in some comparative context, the Berbice slave registers from 1817 to 1822 refer to twenty-two plantations with Highland place names, two with other Scottish place names, two with Irish place names, and twenty-two with English place names, but with no clustering of these in any one part of England. This suggests that the Highland Scots had the opportunity to form closer networks than other whites in the colony and had, as the slaves observed, the habit of 'clinging one to the other'.

It is impossible to give an entirely accurate figure of the number of Scots in Guyana during this period of growth. For Berbice, the more Scottish of the two colonies whose white population, excluding soldiers, did not exceed 500, an estimate of c. 200 by the end of the first decade of the nineteenth century is reasonable, with the proviso that this cohort would have needed a significant number of new recruits each year because of the very high death rate from fevers. Demerara and Essequibo had a white population of less than 2,500, of whom a third might have been Scots, and so the total Scots population of Guyana by 1810 may have been c. 1,000 of a total white population of less than

3,000. It is likely that as many again had died in the course of the previous fourteen years.[22]

There was also a vitally important 'free coloured' population, without which the colonies could not have functioned. Some 'free coloured' men worked as plantation managers and overseers but 'free coloured' women, some of whom came from other Caribbean colonies, outnumbered the men. Many of these women advanced themselves, and their families, by entering into sexual relationships with Europeans.[23]

In both colonies the intention of most Europeans, and almost all Scots, was to make money and return home. Communication of information within the scattered white population was, therefore, of prime importance because of the need to know what land was being bought and sold, what goods were being shipped in and out, what was for sale, when ships were due to arrive or depart, who was leaving and who had arrived, when newly enslaved Africans were to be auctioned, what runaway slaves had been recaptured, and so on. A weekly newspaper was published in Demerara from 1796, twice weekly from 1803, while Berbice had a weekly newspaper from 1806.[24] Isolation on the coastal plantations led to frequent correspondence with families, friends and business associates in Scotland; the tiny population meant that all Scots knew, or at least knew of, each other and gossip abounded; the common origin of many from the North of Scotland meant that there were many existing kin relationships; and, with frequent deaths, there was personal news to be conveyed and many wills, distributing real or imagined fortunes and making provision for both family and friends at home and for enslaved or 'free coloured' women, with their children, in Guyana. As a result, this body of Scots who in number amounted to little more than the equivalent of a village, left an abundance of richly textured archival material.

THE ALLURE OF GUYANA

The settlement of Guyana was in many ways like a gold rush sparked by talk of 'very rapid and splendid fortunes', with those who struck it lucky enticing others to follow, and those who died in the attempt, or simply failed, being quickly forgotten. It was, however, never portrayed in this way by those who hoped for success, for that would have been to downplay their own contribution. Both the peer, Lord Seaforth, and the relatively humble clerk, Henry Bolinbroke, used remarkably similar terms. Seaforth, in 1800, was insistent that 'the sudden accumulation of fortunes was . . . built . . . on the energy of British Capital and British Industry', and in 1807 Bolinbroke reflected that 'British capital, industry, and perseverance, had accomplished in eight years, what would not have been done by other means in half a century'.[25]

The wealth generated for a few of the early Highland adventurers was displayed in the donations made from the colonies in response to calls for support for schools, hospitals and other projects in the North. In 1798, when fundraising began to establish the Northern Infirmary in Inverness, £1164 3s (over 25 per cent of the total value of subscriptions) came from Demerara; between 1800 and 1810, £636 for the new Tain Academy (over 15 per cent of the total value of funds raised) originated in Berbice and Demerara; in 1810 donations of £285 10s were subscribed for Inverness Academy from Demerara; and in 1822 inhabitants of the two colonies gave over £200 towards the publication of a *Dictionary of the Gaelic Language* by the Highland Society of Scotland.[26]

A further indication of the extensive involvement of northern Scots in Guyana is that in 1800 more than one in six of the parish ministers in the North of Scotland had, or would soon have, a close family member who had gone to Guyana, and in some cases all the sons in the family sought their fortune there.[27] This is a remarkable figure since it relates only to Guyana and to it can be added family members in other Caribbean colonies. But the allure of Guyana extended to many other ranks in society and the perceived opportunities were frequently communicated to friends and relations at home. Donald Mackintosh, who had become insolvent about 1790 attempting to establish a bleach-field at Dunain, outside Inverness, had come to Berbice where he managed Belladrum's plantation Golden Fleece. In 1796 he wrote back to Inverness saying, 'I believe there is hardly any place where money may be made with more facility than here, the great difficulty is once to have a little; but when that little is in hand it can be increased by a rapid progression.'[28]

Since most buildings were wooden, there was a particular demand for carpenters and so advertisements appeared in newspapers, such as the *Aberdeen Journal*, which in early 1801 carried a notice seeking 'two or three young men, bred house carpenters, to go out to Berbice', with applications to be made to the minister of Cullen.[29] Other trades were also in demand and later in the same year Donald McRae wrote from Demerara to Simon Fraser, a shoemaker in Inverness: 'I wrote you apurpose that you might come out . . . and . . . if you came bring a young man with you the trade is so good that you can make the two together twenty or thirty shillings per day.'[30] And when Peter Fairbairn, Seaforth's manager in Berbice, needed overseers he wrote to Brahan in Ross-shire seeking 'two lads . . . if bred to gardening so much the better . . . they should not be younger than 18 to 20, and be able to read, write tolerably and know the common rules of Arithmetic'.[31]

A key facet in Guyana's allure was that, in the early days of the development of coastal cotton plantations, there was a potential route to a fortune, even for those of modest means. Donald Mackay is an example of one of the few who successfully reached this destination.[32] He arrived in Demerara from Inverness in 1801 with only his education and letters of recommendation from provost James Grant of Inverness, a cousin of the Belladrum Frasers, which gave him access to Thomas Cuming and to Robert Gordon, a fellow Invernessian. Mackay accepted a position with Gordon but soon left for a clerkship with the Highland-born merchants William Mackenzie and James Craufurd Macleod (of Geanies, Ross-shire). This was at a higher salary of £300 but more importantly he was allowed substantial credit on the purchase of slaves, which were sold by Mackenzie & Co. as agents for the slave trader George Baillie. Mackay hired out his slaves to a 'task gang' run by someone he trusted, Patrick Grant, also from Inverness, and gradually added to their number so that by 1806, when Grant died of fever, Mackay was earning more from the hire of his slaves than from his employment. When Mackenzie & Co. failed in 1808, he moved on and in 1811 bought a sugar estate in Essequibo, in partnership with George Mackenzie from Fodderty (Ross-shire), with credit of £25,000 from Robert and William Pulseford of London, to whom they shipped their sugar until the debt was paid off. Mackay returned to England in 1815, married, and put a nephew from Inverness in charge of the plantation. He subsequently received compensation of over £24,000 for 467 slaves and died as a country gentleman in Hertfordshire, very much part of English society. Along the way he had successfully brushed off requests for substantial support from a number of 'wretched relations' in Scotland, and in his dealings in the affairs of others in Demerara was said to be someone who could not 'but put a person in mind of the cruelties of Nero'.[33] However, Mackay had been aware that his own path to success had been closed off by the abolition of the colonial slave trade in 1807 and that ownership of slaves was the key to success: 'To . . . overseers, clerks & tradesmen, it [the Slave Trade Act] is a check on their industry; for their only encouragement to live in so baneful a climate was the benefit derived from owning some Negroes, their wages being barely sufficient for the necessities of existence.'

SCOTS, SLAVERY AND SLAVE RESISTANCE IN GUYANA

Although it is recognised that no Scottish port had any major, *direct* role in the slave trade, it is equally clear that expatriate Scots were active both in the merchant networks which pursued the trade from Liverpool and Bristol, and in the merchant houses which promoted and financed it.[34] The prominent role of the Baillies of Dochfour, and their cousin George Baillie, is well documented.[35] There were also Scots merchants who, as partners and agents of the slave traders, set up businesses in the colonies which included running slave auctions and selling to plantation owners the Africans who had survived the horrors of the Middle Passage.

In Demerara, where almost all slave ships for Guyana landed, advertisements in the local newspaper from November 1803 to December 1806 offered for sale, at auctions in or near Stabroek, a total of 8,637 newly enslaved Africans.[36] The sale of 23 per cent of these slaves was in the hands of Scots merchants, namely Colin Macrae & Co., of the Inverinate family in Wester Ross (10 per cent), William Mackenzie & Co. (8 per cent) described above, and McInroy, Sandbach, McBean & Co. (5 per cent), described below. The bulk of the sales were by English and Irish merchants backed by houses in London and Liverpool but Scots in Berbice, on the evidence of their surviving correspondence, seemed to prefer dealing with William Mackenzie and James Craufurd Macleod in Stabroek or with James Fraser, John Ross and John Sinclair in New Amsterdam (Berbice), who were all from the northern Highlands.

There is no convincing evidence to suggest that Scottish and other British slave owners were more humane than others, although there was a general trend towards improved conditions after 1807, if only to promote successful 'breeding' of a new generation of slaves. Despite this, in Berbice until 1826 the '11 O'clock Flog' was commonly administered to those men and women who, towards the end of the morning, had fallen behind on the task set for the day,[37] and in 1828 still a quarter of the working slave population had been physically punished in the first half of the year.[38]

Given the high ratio of enslaved to whites, it is unsurprising that in the early 1800s the most common form of resistance by newly enslaved Africans was escape into the savannah, the bush land behind the plantations, and then to the rain forest. To combat this, plantation owners organised expeditions to hunt down 'runaways', also known as 'bush negroes' or maroons, usually led by Charles Edmonstone, later of Cardross Park (Dunbartonshire). Edmonstone's wife, Helen Reid, was the daughter of a Scot and an Amerindian woman of high status. This was similar to the way in which Scots formed relationships with native Americans in Canada in furtherance of the fur trade.[39] Edmonstone's link to the Amerindians gave him access to the rain forest and he was an important source of specimens for naturalists in Britain, but he also made more sinister use of this connection. Edmonstone engaged Arawak men whose knowledge of the forest and tracking skills led to the capture or killing of many fugitive Africans, with a bounty paid for those captured alive or for the severed right hand of those killed. In the largest of these expeditions, in January 1810, seventy-six Africans were captured and twenty-six killed, wiping out a maroon settlement which had survived for a number of years. Edmonstone was repeatedly honoured by his fellow colonists with exemption from taxes, the presentation of inscribed swords in 1807 and 1809, the position of 'Protector of Indians', and when he left for Scotland in 1817 after thirty-seven years' residence, a piece of silver plate whose inscription recorded that 'his prudence and humanity, entitled him to the command of repeated expeditions, against the revolted negroes of Guiana, and his courage always ensured success'.[40]

Sexual abuse of slaves in the colony was endemic and, although some women and their children were made free, by 1819 around one in fifty of the enslaved population in Berbice was the child, or grandchild, of a white European. Abused females included very young women and children, as for example the enslaved girl Susannah, who was no more than twelve years old when, in 1808, she gave birth to the first of three children fathered by George Munro from Easter Ross, the owner of *Alness* in Berbice. Details of other cases, and of sexual relationships with 'free coloured' women, can be found in my article 'A Forgotten Diaspora'.[41]

A number of female domestic slaves, like Susannah, gained or regained their freedom and some detail of their lives can be gleaned from correspondence and other records, but it is almost impossible to recover anything of the lives of the vast majority of enslaved Africans who became field, rather than domestic, slaves. One man, renamed Inverness in slavery, is mentioned often enough to provide a sketch of someone determined to resist the fate imposed on him.[42] He probably came from the Gold Coast, was sold in Stabroek on 18 July 1803 by William Mackenzie & Co., acting as agents for the slave trader George Baillie, and was bought by Peter Fairbairn, the manager of Seaforth's estates, who purchased him as part of a lot of twenty 'prime negroes'. The ten men in the purchase were renamed Brahan, Britain, Kintail, Lewis,

Gordon, Crawfurd, Ross, Sutherland, Dingwall and Inverness. They were taken to plantation Brahan on the west sea-coast of Berbice, where, by back-breaking work, virgin land was being drained and brought into cultivation for cotton. Towards the end of the year Fairbairn reported that 'desertion was furious' and Inverness and Dingwall were among those who had escaped. An armed expedition in January found about fifty maroons in an encampment a day's journey away, 'with plantains, rice, tobacco, cassava etc in abundance'. Inverness was captured but Dingwall remained free.

Both shortage of food on the plantations, as a result of the failure of the plantain crop, and dry seasons, which made travel over the savannah easier, increased the number of escapes and Inverness once again disappeared into the bush. In subsequent years another of Seaforth's slaves, Favourite, was punished a number of times for the practice of African rites known as Obeah, which planters believed encouraged resistance. He was also suspected of 'having communication with Runaways and having formed a plan to carry off a number of the women to the Woods'. Favourite escaped for a second time in May 1809 but was caught at Brahan 'in the act of carrying off one of the negroes'. He had been assisted by Inverness, who was described as 'long absent but who it seems knows the way back and holds correspondence with the coast'.

This was a group of well-organised and determined people seeking to remain free, and to free others. Fairbairn reckoned that the maroon camp had grown to number about a hundred and he feared 'very serious consequences'. The response was the expedition mounted from Demerara in January 1810, led by Charles Edmonstone and described above. It is not known if Favourite and Inverness either escaped, or were seized, or were killed. To summarise, Inverness was enslaved in Africa, transported across the Atlantic, sold, renamed, forced to labour in creating a plantation from the mud of the Berbice coast, repeatedly escaped but was recaptured, and, perhaps, at the end was hunted down, killed and his right hand severed – all by Scots, or under the supervision of Scots, most of them from the Highlands.

It is unsurprising that resistance sometimes went beyond escape. Two large slave uprisings in Guyana are well known and extensively documented, the rising in Berbice under Dutch rule in 1763–4, whose beginning is now celebrated as a national holiday in Guyana, and the major rebellion in Demerara in 1823, which involved thousands of slaves, about 250 of whom were executed following its brutal suppression.[43] Between these dates, under both Dutch and British control, there were many other, smaller, uprisings in resistance to the conditions endured by enslaved Africans. These are an indication of the continual challenge to the tiny white community.

In 1804 the overseers at plantation Novar, in Berbice, were given instructions that on Christmas Day they should 'watch very closely for fear of disturbance among the Negroes'.[44] Three years later a young Scottish overseer on the east sea-coast informed the governor of Berbice of a planned insurrection on Christmas Eve, while the white people were celebrating. Twenty slaves were arrested and nine subsequently executed.[45] And in April 1813 Hugh Munro Robertson witnessed what he called 'an awful but necessary example of punishment in the execution of six Negro ringleaders' of another planned rising in the colony, which it was claimed was intended to spread to Demerara. A document written in what was thought to be Arabic was found among the possessions of one of those executed, fuelling the speculation that 'their plot was laid with a degree of policy & subtlety'.[46]

On Spencer Mackay's plantations in 1818, escape turned to revolt. Mackay, in London, received reports that between fifty and one hundred enslaved people on his estates at Mahaica, in Demerara, had escaped into the bush, taking with them a supply of plantains and many cattle. During negotiations to agree their return, two overseers were 'decoyed by a party of the estates' negroes (who had not absented themselves) . . . and . . . murdered in the most savage manner, their bodies being mutilated and their heads and limbs carried in triumph round the camp'. Retribution, of course, followed.[47]

FROM COTTON TO SUGAR: THE DOMINANCE OF THE MERCHANT HOUSES

Those who developed coastal cotton plantations in Guyana had not reckoned with the unpredictability of the climate, which was subject to the effects of both El Niño and La Niña. There were years of misfortunes, including droughts and destruction of crops by insects (probably El Niño effects) in 1803 and 1804, which was 'lamentably dry – only the oldest settlers can remember anything like it, 30 years ago', and extended wet seasons (probably La Niña effects) in 1806 and 1809, with 'weather most unfortunate that can be conceived – of all the seasons this is the worst'.[48] By 1810 there was, more importantly, increasing competition from cotton produced in the plantations of the southern United States.[49] One of Seaforth's partners had already come to regard Berbice as a 'poison' and those who had succeeded as 'low cunning characters

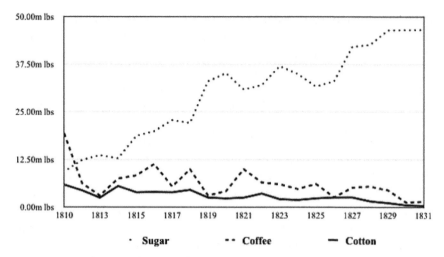

Figure 5.2 Production of principal crops in Demerara, 1810–31 (from data in Robert Montgomery Martin, *History of the British Colonies*, 5 vols (London: Cochrane & M'Crone, 1834), ii, p. 62)

versed in every subterfuge and ravelling'.[50] Guyana's allure had become tarnished and, although it still offered opportunities, the dramatic influx of young Scotsmen was at an end.

From about 1810 there was a transition to sugar production which, with a significant price rise in 1815, then saw more rapid growth in this sector than in any other colony. Unlike cotton or coffee estates, sugar plantations were not simply growers but also manufacturers, requiring greater capital investment and a larger labour force, forced to work under harsher conditions especially when sugar was harvested. The 'productivity' of slaves had been increased threefold by 1827, some of this being attributable to investment in machinery but also reflecting a strict regime.[51]

All the plantations established by Scots in Guyana had required effective relationships with merchant houses in Glasgow, Liverpool, London or Bristol, who bought their cotton and supplied them with essential goods. Many cotton planters had borrowed heavily and made plans based on overly optimistic expectations of production, and as a result there were many failures and a consolidation of ownership in the larger merchant houses, who had advanced funds on the security of mortgages over the estates and, as importantly, over their slaves. These larger concerns, with their access to investment capital, drove forward the transition to sugar.

Over time many of the coastal plantations, especially in Berbice, were simply abandoned and slaves transferred to more profitable sugar plantations, often in the neighbouring colony of Demerara, a move dreaded by the slaves who feared the harsher conditions.[52] Robert Bogle & Co. of Glasgow were responsible for an early attempt at 'asset stripping' when, in 1818, they bought a worn-out coffee plantation in Berbice with the aim of moving its 150 slaves to sugar plantations in Demerara. Such movement between colonies had become more difficult after the Slave Registration Act of 1817 and, under pressure from plantation owners who feared the rundown of the colony, the governor of Berbice refused permission. Nevertheless, between 1808 and 1825 some 4,000 enslaved people were legally transferred from Berbice to Demerara, and others may have been smuggled.[53]

Three Glasgow firms – John Campbell, senior, & Co., J., T. & A. Douglas & Co. and Robert Bogle & Co. – received large sums in compensation for slaves held in British Guiana. The first two partnerships had been involved in Guyana from 1800 and before, but Scots in Guyana did not necessarily work with Scottish-based merchants. There were close connections with Liverpool where the largest of its cotton importers, and the most successful in fostering trade with Guyana, was John Bolton & Co. They provided loans and acted as agent for Charles Lamont Robertson and John Noble, both from Inverness.[54] John Gladstone & Co. entered the Guyana cotton trade in 1804, contracting with Edward Fraser of Reelig and Seaforth's manager, Peter Fairbairn;[55] and William and Thomas Earle & Co., who were slave traders and major importers of cotton before they became involved in the sugar trade, had connections to John Ross, a carpenter's son from Golspie (Sutherland) who prospered in Berbice and later rose to become one of the founders of the Caledonian Bank in Inverness.

The most powerful Liverpool merchant house was, however, Sandbach, Tinné & Co. They were at first involved in the cotton trade, successfully competing with established Liverpool houses,[56] and then successfully made the transition to sugar production. At emancipation its partners received compensation of £150,242, the second-largest award to any mercantile firm in Britain and worth in today's values the equivalent of £12.9 million (comparative purchasing power). They were by far the largest plantation and slave owners in Guyana, where they had been 'looked up to as the Rothschilds of Demerara'.[57] Originally trading from both Glasgow and Liverpool, they made Liverpool their principal office from 1811, but had strong Scottish links (see Table 5.3).

Table 5.3 Early partners in Sandbach, Tinné & Co. (and its predecessor firms)

Name	Origins	History in firm	Other notes
James McInroy (1759–1825)	Son of a wadsetter in Moulin, near Pitlochry (Perthshire).	Demerara (1782); partnership formed 1792.	Bought estate of Lude (Perthshire).
George Robertson (1756–99)	Son of the parish minister of Kincardine (Ross-shire).	Grenada (late 1780s); partnership formed 1792.	Four nephews came to Guyana, including George Rainy (below); nieces married Parker and Sandbach.
Charles Stewart Parker (1771–1828)	Son of a Glasgow-born merchant in Norfolk, Virginia; educated in Edinburgh.	Apprentice to Robertson in Grenada, 1789; partnership formed 1792.	Married Margaret Rainy (Creich), niece of G. Robertson. Son married Sandbach's daughter.
Samuel Sandbach (1769–1851)	Son of a farmer and innkeeper in Tarporley, Cheshire.	Grenada from 1789; partnership formed 1792.	Married Elizabeth Robertson (Kiltearn), niece of G. Robertson. Daughter married Parker's son.
William McBean (d. 1822)	Son of minor landowner, Tomatin (Inverness-shire).	Partner in Demerara, 1803–c. 1808.	
Phillip Frederick Tinné (1772–1844)	Dutch merchant in Demerara.	Partner from 1813.	Married into family of Rose of Montcoffer (Banff-shire); son married daughter of Sandbach.
George Rainy (c. 1785–1864)	Son of parish minister of Creich (Sutherland).	Demerara from c. 1806; later partner.	Sister Margaret married Parker. Bought island of Raasay.

Sources: Friederich von Bouchenröder, *Kaart van de Colonie de Berbice* (Amsterdam, 1802); for details of individuals see the author's website *Slaves & Highlanders* available at http://www.spanglefish.com/slavesandhighlanders.

SUMMARY AND DIRECTIONS FOR FUTURE RESEARCH

Guyana underwent two periods of dramatic change after the colonies of Demerara, Essequibo and Berbice were surrendered to British forces in 1796. First, a scramble to acquire coastal land to develop cotton plantations, with an inrush of 'adventurers' seeking to make 'very rapid and splendid fortunes' and a corresponding explosion in the slave population; and then from about 1810, when this had largely failed, a ruthless transition to sugar production, driven by the merchant houses who had acquired many of the estates and slaves. The first stage, which had characteristics of a gold rush, was dominated by Scots, many of whom, particularly in Berbice, were from northern and Highland Scotland; the second was controlled more by large merchant houses, based in Glasgow, Liverpool, London and Bristol, in which a much smaller number of successful Scots still played an important role.

In 1810 there were about a thousand Scots in Guyana, the survivors of a larger number who had risked their lives, health, friendships, relationships and capital in pursuit of what had been, for most of them, the illusory prospect of becoming 'as rich as a Demerary man'. Judged by the number of adventurers, the scale of investment and the resulting deaths, this attempt to settle and exploit the tropical mainland of the Americas was something of a second Darien. Yet, unlike Darien, it brought wealth to a fortunate few.

The rapid development of cotton estates in Guyana pushed the system of plantation slavery to its limits and at least some of the details of this are apparent from correspondence of Scots isolated on the coastal plantations. But fully understanding the role of Scots in the slave plantations of Guyana, and the British Caribbean in general, must include further study of their role in the firms which were the largest recipients of compensation. Barkly & Davidsons of London and Sandbach, Tinné & Co. of Liverpool were pre-eminent and both had large holdings of slaves in Guyana (see Table 5.4). The records of Sandbach, Tinné & Co., the extensive Parker family papers, and over four hundred personal letters in the correspondence of the Robertson family at Kiltearn, together with other sources, constitute a particularly large and under-researched body of material which would illuminate the roles of the inter-related Robertson, Parker, Sandbach, Tinné and Rainy families.[58]

As elsewhere in the Caribbean, Scots put down few roots in Guyana and left little mark on the character of the colony. Their legacy, nevertheless, was profound. They helped to establish a colony with a small white population of European descent and a much larger population of African descent, with a vital, but later marginalised, population of 'free coloured' people. After emancipation, liberated slaves generally preferred to become smallholders rather than plantation workers, and it was in Guyana that the system of indentured Indian labour was pioneered, to provide a new workforce for the sugar plantations. This subsequently led to the movement of more than a million Indians to the Caribbean, Mauritius and Fiji, and to the creation of the largest ethnic group in Guyana.[59] Scots were heavily involved in this aftermath to slavery and Guyana, although optimistically branded as 'The Land of Six Peoples', has remained one of the most fractured and poorest societies in the world.[60]

CODA

Scotland's historical relationship with Guyana abounds in unexpected connections and ironies. The abandoned settlement of Hallaig in Raasay has become, through Sorley Maclean's poem *Hallaig*, an icon of the Highland clearances. Yet few note that its people were removed, not by an aristocratic landowner, but by George Rainy, who rose from childhood in a manse in Sutherland to become a partner in Sandbach, Tinné & Co., and bought the island with the fortune he had made from the sugar plantations of Demerara.

Rainy had followed his older brother George to Guyana where, with their cousin Gilbert Robertson, they had established plantation Kiltearn on the Courentyne coast of Berbice. The leading Caribbean writer and political thinker, Jan Carew, whose mother was a Robertson and who died in 2012 at the age of 92, was a descendant of both slaves and slave owners at Kiltearn. His great-grandmother had said:

> There are ghosts in our blood and we're lucky because the lowliest, the ones who suffer most in the world of the living, are always top dogs in the spirit world . . . We're blessed with the blood of the most persecuted folks on earth – Africans, Caribs, Portuguese Jews, French convicts from Devil's Island, Highland Scots and the Lord alone knows what else.[61]

This was a generous comment on the Highland Scots who, like the Robertsons and their cousins the Rainys, had come to Guyana to exploit others. Her magnanimity had a profound influence on Carew who used her words, in his conversations with Malcolm X, to summarise his own political creed:

So whenever we cut ourselves, we can see ghosts of those others peeping out from the African and Amerindian blood. The ghosts are always there talking their conflicting talk until there's a Tower of Babel inside your head. So you've got to listen well and search out the kindest, the strongest, the most human of these voices and make them your own.

Table 5.4 Firms receiving compensation for slave ownership in Guyana with their Scottish links (ranked by total received for all slaves in the West Indies)

Firm	City	Scottish links	Notes
Davidson, Barkly	London	Both families had origins in Cromarty (Ross-shire). Davidsons owned Tulloch estate (Dingwall, Ross-shire).	Involvement in Guyana after transition from cotton to sugar.
Sandbach, Tinné & Co.	Liverpool	See Table 5.3.	See Table 5.3.
T Daniel & Co.	London/Bristol	None known.	
Chauncy, Lang	London	Firm grew out of George Baillie & Co. Eric Mackay (Lord Reay) partner to 1805.	
John Gladstone	Liverpool	Scottish origin. Married to Elizabeth Robertson (Dingwall, Ross-shire) through whom he was known or related to a number of plantation owners.	Non-resident. Original partner John Wilson, resident in Berbice. Agent from 1804 for Fraser (Reelig, Inverness-shire) and Lord Seaforth.
Hall, M'Garel	London	None known.	
H. D. & J. E. Baillie	Bristol	Dochfour (Inverness-shire). Related to many Scots who were in Guyana from 1790s.	Involvement in Demerara from c. 1790 and Berbice from later 1790s.
J. Campbell senior	Glasgow		Active in Guyana from early 1790s. Partners in Demerara and Berbice until 1811: Angus and Evan Fraser (Fort William, Inverness-shire).
R. Bogle/ Bogle, King	Glasgow		Involvement in Guyana after transition to sugar.

Table 5.4 (*Continued*)

Firm	City	Scottish links	Notes
C., W. & F. Shand	Liverpool	Not clear – may be connected to John Shand of Arnhall (Fettercairn).	
J., T. & A. Douglas	Glasgow	Three brothers of whom the oldest, John, was resident in Guyana.	Sister Cecilcia m. Gilbert Douglas (Balcony, Ross-shire) who had interests in Demerara.
T. & W. King	London	None known.	
J. & H. Moss	Liverpool	None known.	
T. & H. Murray	Liverpool	None known.	

List and ranking from Nicholas Draper, *The Price of Emancipation* (Cambridge: Cambridge University Press, 2010), p. 236. For details of individuals see *Legacies of British Slave-ownership database* available at http://www.ucl.ac.uk/lbs/ and the author's website *Slaves & Highlanders* available at http://www.spanglefish.com/slavesandhighlanders.

NOTES

Details of all individuals named in this chapter can be found on the author's website, *Slaves & Highlanders*, available at http://www.spanglefish.com/slavesandhighlanders.

1. Henry Gibbs Dalton, *A History of British Guiana*, 2 vols (London: Longmans, 1855), i, p. 306.
2. Calculators available online at http://www.measuringworth.com/ukcompare (accessed 1 September 2014).
3. Nicholas Draper, *The Price of Emancipation* (Cambridge: Cambridge University Press, 2010), pp. 138–9.
4. Stephen Mullen, 'A Glasgow-West India Merchant House and the Imperial Dividend, 1779–1867', *Journal of Scottish Historical Studies*, November 2013, p. 223.
5. Donald Wood, 'Berbice and the Unification of British Guiana', in Michael Twaddle (ed.), *Imperialism and the State in the Third World* (London: British Academic Press, 1992), p. 70; *The Trans-Atlantic Slave Trade Database* available online at www.slavevoyages.org (accessed 9 October 2014).
6. T. M. Devine, *To the Ends of the Earth* (London: Penguin, 2012), p. 42; Barry W. Higman, *Slave Populations of the British Caribbean 1807–1834* (Kingston: University of the West Indies Press, 1995), p. 77.
7. Alvin O. Thompson, *Unprofitable Servants: Crown Slaves in Berbice,*

Guyana 1803–1831 (Kingston: University of the West Indies Press, 2001), pp. 25–7.

8. Kit Candlin, *The Last Colonial Frontier* (Basingstoke: Palgrave Macmillan, 2012).

9. Johannes Postma, *The Dutch in the Atlantic Slave Trade, 1600–1815* (Cambridge: Cambridge University Press, 1990), p. 216; *Naamlyst der bestierders, officieren en bediendens &c. op de Colonie der Berbice, 1794*, transcribed by Paul Koulen, available at http://www.rootsweb.ancestry.com/~nyggbs/Transcriptions.htm (accessed 9 August 2014).

10. Wood, 'Berbice', p. 67.

11. P. M. Netscher, *History of the Colonies of Essequebo, Demerary, and Berbice* (The Hague: Provincial Society of Utrecht, 1888), translated by W. E. Roth (Georgetown, British Guiana: Daily Chronicle, 1931), Chapter X, p. 7.

12. Bryan Edwards, *History of the British Colonies in the West Indies*, 3 vols (London: John Stockdale, 1793), ii, p. 268.

13. Higman, *Slave Populations,* p. 63.

14. Wood, 'Berbice', p. 68.

15. Henry Bolinbroke, *A Voyage to the Demerary* (London: Richard Phillips, 1807), p. 176; National Archives of Scotland [NAS] Seaforth Muniments GD/46/17/14 f337, Draft memorandum from Lord Seaforth to the Duke of Portland.

16. Dalton, *British Guiana,* i, pp. 307–8.

17. Douglas Hamilton, *Scotland, the Caribbean and the Atlantic World, 1750–1820* (Manchester: Manchester University Press, 2005), p. 50.

18. Gravestone in Dallas parish church, Moray.

19. *Essequibo & Demerary Royal Gazette* [E&DRG], 18 April 1812; Lloyd Kandasammy, 'St Andrew's Kirk: A concise history of a national heritage site', in *Stabroek News,* 25 November 2005.

20. Highland Council Archive [HCA], D238/D/1/17/6 Thomas Fraser, St Vincent, to Simon Fraser, baker, Inverness, 4 January 1790.

21. NAS GD46/17; Finlay McKichan, 'Lord Seaforth: Highland Proprietor, Caribbean Governor and Slave Owner', *Scottish Historical Review*, Vol. 90, Issue 2 (Edinburgh: Edinburgh University Press, 2011), pp. 204–35.

22. Thompson, *Unprofitable Servants*, pp. 25–7; Robert Montgomery Martin, *History of the British Colonies*, 5 vols (London: Cochrane & M'Crone, 1834), ii, p. 32; Higman, *Slave Populations*, p. 77.

23. David Alston, 'A Forgotten Diaspora: The Children of Enslaved and "Free Coloured" Women and Highland Scots in Guyana before Emancipation', *Northern Scotland*, 6 (Edinburgh: Edinburgh University Press, 2015).

24. *Guyana Colonial Newspapers* available at http://www.vc.id.au/edg (accessed 8 August 2014).

25. Bolinbroke, *Voyage to the Demerary*, p. 186; NAS GD46/17/14 Draft memorandum to the Duke of Portland.
26. *London Chronicle*, 30 October 1798; *Royal charter, list of subscribers, state of funds, &c., &c. of the Tain Academy* (London, 1810); Aberdeen University Library [AUL] KC Ms874 f234; *Edinburgh Advertiser*, 22 November 1822.
27. For analysis, see 'Families of Ministers' available at http://www.spanglefish. com/slavesandhighlanders/index.asp?pageid=577455 (accessed 14 August 2014).
28. HCA D456/A/10/49, Donald Mackintosh to Colonel Baillie of Dunain, 24 May 1796.
29. *Aberdeen Journal*, 12 January 1801.
30. HCA D122/2 /3, Donald McRae, Demerary, to Simon Fraser, shoemaker, Church Street, Inverness, 24 July 1801.
31. NAS GD46/17/23/290, Fairbairn to Lord Seaforth, 18 January 1804.
32. NAS GD23/6/391, Letters of Donald Mackay to James Grant.
33. NCA D122/2/3, Duncan Matheson to Alexander Fraser, Inverness, 21 October 1813.
34. Devine, *To the Ends of the Earth*, pp. 35–7.
35. Hamilton, *Scotland, the Caribbean and the Atlantic World*, pp. 88–92.
36. *Guyana Colonial Newspapers* available at http://www.vc.id.au/edg (accessed 8 August 2014).
37. Mary Turner, 'The 11 O'clock Flog: Women, Work and Labour Law in the British Caribbean', in Sylvia R. Frey and Betty Wood (eds), *From Slavery to Emancipation in the Atlantic World* (New York: Frank Cass, 1999), pp. 38–58.
38. Wood, *Berbice*, p. 77.
39. Sylvia van Kirk, *Many Tender Ties: Women in Fur-trade Society, 1670–1870* (Oklahoma: University of Oklahoma, 1983); Martin Daunton and Rick Halpern (eds), *Empire and Others: British encounters with indigenous peoples, 1600–1850* (Philadelphia: University of Pennsylvania Press, 1999).
40. *E&DRG*, 11 September 1817.
41. Alston, 'A Forgotten Diaspora'.
42. For details, see 'Inverness' available at http://www.spanglefish.com/slavesandhighlanders/index.asp?pageid=172832 (accessed 14 August 2014).
43. Emilia Viotti da Costa, *Crowns of Glory, Tears of Blood* (Oxford: Oxford University Press, 1994).
44. National Register of the Archives of Scotland [NRAS] 2696, Fraser family of Reelig: family and estate papers, Edward Fraser to his mother, 15 January 1804.
45. Thomas Staunton St Clair, *A Residence in the West Indies*, 2 vols (London: Richard Bentley, 1834), ii, p. 142.
46. National Library of Scotland [NLS], Papers of Thomas Stewart Traill,

MS 19332 f102, Hugh Munro Robertson to Dr Traill, 17 April 1813.
47. *Sydney Gazette and New South Wales Advertiser*, 10 October 1818.
48. NAS GD46/17/23, Peter Fairbairn to Lord Seaforth, 22 February 1804; GD46/17/24, Fairbairn to Seaforth, 15 February 1806; GD46/17/35/51, Fairbairn to Seaforth, 20 April 1809; Thompson, *Unprofitable Servants*, pp. 20–1.
49. Wood, 'Berbice', p. 71.
50. NAS GD46/17/35/332, Edward Satchwell Fraser snr to Lord Seaforth, 30 November 1810.
51. Higman, *Slave Populations*, p. 63.
52. Higman, *Slave Populations*, p. 63.
53. Wood, 'Berbice', p. 71.
54. Alexey Krichtal, Master's Thesis: 'Liverpool and the Raw Cotton Trade: A Study of the Port and its Merchant Community, 1770–1815' (University of Wellington, 2013), p. 46.
55. Krichtal, 'Liverpool and the Raw Cotton Trade', p. 43; NAS GD46/17/26, Peter Fairbairn to Lord Seaforth, 8 December 1804.
56. Krichtal, 'Liverpool and the Raw Cotton Trade', p. 47.
57. University of London, SOAS Library, 'Journal of J. C. Cheveley', ii, p. 124.
58. Senate House Library, University of London, MS 667, papers of Sandbach, Tinné & Co., Liverpool; Liverpool Record Office, PRO PAR, Parker family papers; NLS GB233, papers of Thomas Stewart Traill, MSS 19329–19334.
59. David Hollett, *Passage from India to El Dorado* (London: Fairleigh Dickinson, 1999), p. 65; Gaiutra Bahadur, *Coolie Woman: The Odyssey of Indenture* (London: Hurst & Co., 2013), p. xx.
60. The groups referred to are Amerindian, East Indian, African, Portuguese, Chinese and British.
61. Jan Carew, *Potaro Dreams: My Youth in Guyana* (Hertford: Hansib Publications, 2014), p. 12; Jan Carew, *Ghosts in Our Blood: with Malcolm X in Africa, England, and the Caribbean* (Chicago: Lawrence Hill Books, 1994), pp. 49–50, 62, 138–46.

6

The Great Glasgow West India House of John Campbell, senior, & Co.

Stephen Mullen

WHEN THE HISTORIAN John Guthrie Smith majestically surveyed the landed estates of the West of Scotland in *The Old Country Houses of the Old Glasgow Gentry* in 1878, he cited one family in particular that epitomised Glasgow's elite 'sugar aristocracy':

> The Campbells of Possil, or rather of John Campbell sen. & Co., deserve more than a passing notice. They were a representative family of those West India magnates, who came after the Virginia Dons, and came in for much of their social and commercial supremacy . . . [The sugar trade] probably was never entitled to the consideration it got. Being in few hands, it yielded fortunes that bulked in the public eye, and less showy trades may have been of more real importance . . . It left behind it no single fortune equal to the largest fortunes left by the tobacco trade.[1]

In his landmark study *The Price of Emancipation*, Nicholas Draper underlined the exceptional standing of the great merchant house of John Campbell, senior, & Co. On the abolition of plantation slavery in 1834, partners in the firm received over £73,000 compensation, which ranked the merchant house as the eighth-largest 'mercantile beneficiary' in Great Britain and the highest in Scotland.[2] Given their prominence and the availability of business records, it is surprising the firm has not attracted serious attention by historians.[3] This case study will address this lacuna, thus adding to a developing historiography on Scottish–West India merchants, planters and firms in the colonial period.[4]

The rise of the firm in Glasgow, including capital stock and partnership structure, can be traced in some detail from surviving business records. This will be placed in a transatlantic context. The colonial activities of the firm will be illustrated through dealings with correspondents in Scotland and the Caribbean. Early commercial ventures in Grenada and

Carriacou provided the foundation for the firm's later expansion into the frontier colony of Demerara, which was joined with Berbice and Essequibo to become British Guiana in 1831. Colonial operations will be outlined through deeds and mercantile correspondence. Finally, the firm's compensation claims and the financial interests of co-partners will be traced through parliamentary sources, and wills and confirmation inventories generated on the death of individuals concerned.

The founder, John Campbell senior (c. 1735–1807), was the third son of Alexander Campbell of Kinloch, captain in the Black Watch. This branch was descended from a gentry family led by Sir John Campbell of Lawers of the house of Campbell of Glenurchy. John Campbell senior (so called to differentiate him from other merchants of the same name in Glasgow) initially owned shares in one of the largest tobacco firms, John Glassford & Co., which was headed by the prominent 'tobacco lord' John Glassford.[5] It is possible that Campbell's marriage to the daughter of John Murdoch, another 'tobacco lord', assisted in his mercantile career. He registered as Burgess and Guild Brethren in April 1780 as married to the daughter of a Burgess.[6] He subscribed to the Merchant's House the next year and became a member of the Town Council merchant rank.[7] After the American War of Independence, Campbell worked out of a counting house in Argyle Street with his cousin, Alexander Campbell of Hallyards.[8] The family soon reached the upper echelons of the colonial elite in Glasgow by establishing what became a major West India firm.

The rise of the merchant house of John Campbell, senior, & Co. was similar to that of contemporaries Leitch & Smith.[9] Both firms were established by younger sons from cadet branches of minor landed families resident outside Glasgow. Although Campbell had a more distinguished lineage, neither individual hailed from 'gentry capitalist' families.[10] However, both John Campbell and Archibald Smith improved their respective wealth and status through the Virginia trades before shifting commercial focus to sugar and the Caribbean after Glasgow's tobacco monopoly ended in 1783. Each firm was therefore led by mercantile patriarchs who groomed younger male relatives to take control across successive generations, thus creating an extensive family fortune.

The partnership structure of John Campbell, senior, & Co. was based on kinship networks which provided the firm with capital, skills and colonial connections. In the firm's co-partnership contracts between 1790 and 1848, fifteen separate individuals have been traced. The initial five co-partners were John Campbell, his brother Colin Campbell of Park and their cousin, Alexander Campbell of Hallyards, also known as Business Sandy due to his work ethic. The other co-partners were based in

Table 6.1 Capital Stock and co-partners of John Campbell, senior, & Co., 1790–1848

Year	Partners	Capital Stock
1790	Five	£40,000
1801	Five	£54,000
1806	Five	£80,000
1812	Six	£140,000
1817	Six	£152,000
1821	Six	£180,000
1828	Seven	£180,000
1841	Five	£50,000
1848	Four	£20,000

Source: GCA, TD1696, 'Contracts of co-partnership', 1790–1848.

the West Indies. In 1790 John's brother Thomas was described as a merchant resident in Grenada alongside their nephew Alexander Campbell of Haylodge and Marran.[11] Thus, like Leitch & Smith, the co-partners and associates of the firm focused on the new British colony of Grenada from the outset. Although not a partner in the firm, John's other brother Mungo Campbell of Hundleshope owned Marran, a sugar estate in the parish of St John. His son Alexander Campbell of Haylodge, who was a partner in the firm, inherited the plantation on his death and took the nickname 'Marran' from the colonial property.

As individuals died or retired, they were replaced with younger family members, and the number of co-partners remained almost constant throughout the firm's life cycle. There were five between 1790 and 1812, six up to 1828 and seven up to 1841. The sharp increase in levels of capital stock underwrote the dramatic rise of the firm: a total of £40,000 was invested in 1790, peaking at £180,000 in 1828 (see Table 6.1). Five of John Campbell's sons became co-partners: John Murdoch Campbell, Colin (later of Colgrain), Alexander (later of Possil), Thomas, James, as well as a grandson, Colin, 2nd of Colgrain. Marran recruited his son 'Black' Mungo Campbell, while the son of Hallyards, 'White' Mungo Campbell, also joined. Another nephew, Mungo Nutter Campbell, also had a prominent role over many years.

The protection offered to mercantile concerns under Scots law could be viewed as a contributory factor to their remarkable success. Under Scots law, merchant firms were legally defined as separate entities, meaning they could transact on their own terms. This offered more protection than equivalent English legislation as the personal wealth of individual co-partners was protected in the event of a firm's bankruptcy. This has been cited by T. M. Devine as a reason why Scottish firms usually had more co-partners than similar concerns in England.[12] Consequently, firms could rely on diverse capital reserves and the risk was spread across many individuals. Senior partners in Glasgow must have been confident promoting the next generation into a prestigious occupation which safeguarded personal wealth. In this case, there was a direct transfer of colonial capital as younger male relatives were primed for commercial careers, firstly through education.

Although the arts curriculum at Old College – the predecessor of the University of Glasgow – attracted strong criticism in this period from merchants, four of John Campbell's five sons attended between 1792 and 1804.[13] It is likely the young men subsequently served an apprenticeship in the family counting house. The mercantile passage of rites was also dependent on peer monitoring. As a nineteen-year-old in 1801, the second-eldest son was warned that any promotion to co-partner in the firm was conditional on his father being 'of opinion that the said Colin Campbell's conduct continues to deserve such transfer being made in his favour'.[14] He evidently behaved himself and inherited four shares worth £4,000 on 27 January 1803, three weeks after reaching twenty-one. Some of this capital had previously been advanced to his elder brother John Murdoch Campbell, who died in 1802. Thus, through patrimony, John Campbell promoted his sons and developed the family firm. It is also possible he was consulted for marriage advice.

Recent work by Katie Barclay has noted that economic resources were an important consideration in the selection of potential spouses in this period.[15] Certainly, the younger Campbells were matched with daughters of several notables. Alexander married Harriet, daughter of Donald McLachlan, Advocate of Argyllshire, also a co-partner in the firm before 1808. Other sons established connections with elite merchant houses. Colin married Janet Millar, the daughter of Provost John Hamilton of North Park. James married Elizabeth Bogle, the youngest daughter of Robert Bogle of Gilmorehill, of Robert Bogle, junior, & Co. Thomas Campbell's first wife was Agnes Finlay, daughter of Kirkman Finlay. Mungo Nutter Campbell perhaps exemplifies the almost incestuous relationships among the sugar aristocracy. He was son of Alexander Campbell of Dallingburn, Collector of Customs at Port Glasgow, a cousin of John Campbell and brother in law as he was married to his sister Elizabeth. Mungo Nutter Campbell married John's daughter, Helen. From 1806 Mungo Nutter was therefore at once John Campbell's co-partner, his nephew, his son-in-law and his cousin's son.[16]

The marriages of other co-partners further increased the firm's influence. Alexander Campbell of Marran married Catherine, daughter of John Robertson, a partner in Robert Mackay & Co. Their son, 'Black' Mungo, married Isabella Craigie Alston, the daughter of John Gordon, senior partner in the firm of Stirling Gordon & Co. Alexander Campbell of Hallyards married Barbara Campbell, daughter of Archibald Campbell of Jura, in 1800. They had six sons, including 'White' Mungo Campbell. The Campbells of Jura were related through marriage to the Dennistouns and all were involved with the West India firm of Campbell, Rivers & Co. Thus, both 'Black' Mungo and 'White' Mungo were sugar princes descended from elite colonial families on both paternal and maternal sides. The inter-related marriages established close kinship ties which underpinned commercial links between five prominent Glasgow–West India firms.

Several co-partners in the firm were members of social clubs and formal lobbying bodies which confirmed their elite personal standing. With their Highland origins, the Campbells naturally took a leading role in the Gaelic Club of Glasgow. Indeed, Hallyards added a taste of the Caribbean to the powerful fraternity when he presented a 'splendid turtle' at the first meeting on 11 July 1798 in the Black Bull Inn.[17] John Campbell also attended the West India Club that met in Glasgow between 1787 and 1791.[18] This club was essentially the predecessor of the Glasgow West India Association, a ruthlessly effective lobbying group formed in 1807, described at more length elsewhere in this book. Like Leitch & Smith, John Campbell, senior, & Co. was ranked among the initial top seven company subscribers to the Association, placing it among the elite firms. At least four co-partners were founder members; Hallyards, Mungo Nutter Campbell, John Campbell and his son Colin.[19] Another two sons, Thomas and James, later became members with the younger Mungo Campbell in the 1820s and 1830s. John Campbell was a founder member of the Chamber of Commerce in Glasgow in 1783. The most prominent local officeholder in the firm, however, was Mungo Nutter Campbell, who was elected Dean of Guild of the Merchant House (1822–3) and Lord Provost of Glasgow (1824–5). Thus, members of the merchant house connected regional politics and transatlantic commerce. This chapter will now consider the true source of the wealth: the exploitative operations located in the Caribbean.

FIRST-PHASE OPERATIONS IN THE WEST INDIES

The rise of the firm and co-partners in Glasgow was initially based on wealth generated in Grenada and Carriacou, although their colonial operations there remain obscure. H. Gordon Slade's study of plantations Craigston and Meldrum in Carriacou, a cotton island off Grenada, provides context. These estates were owned by the Urquharts, a gentry family of Meldrum near Aberdeen in the North-east of Scotland. While Slade noted the Urquharts imported much of their cotton to Glasgow, the relationship with their preferred merchants John Campbell, senior, & Co. was not explored.[20] The privately held Urquhart papers therefore allow a glimpse into activities of the merchant house and associates in the south-eastern Caribbean.[21]

Thomas Campbell, brother of John, had the experience and contacts required for the early expansion of the merchant house in the West Indies. Prior to the firm's formal establishment in 1791, he was an 'imperial careerist' with interests in Grenada, Bristol, London, Liverpool and across Scotland.[22] Although Campbell eventually viewed the West Indies as his home, he maintained a transient lifestyle which allowed him to cultivate transatlantic networks:

> I must postpone my Northern jaunt till next summer . . . I promise myself, much pleasure in . . . a long summer among my friends in the west and north of Scotland, before I return to what I call my own country between the tropics which after long use I find agrees best with me, and where also I find more employment than in this country.[23]

In this way, Thomas Campbell promoted transatlantic commerce between suppliers and markets in Scotland and the Caribbean. In the summer of 1786 he visited William Urquhart at Meldrum, with discussions evidently focused on the import of cotton. Thomas recommended his brother John and cousin Alexander in Glasgow, which was by then an important trade hub supplying local manufacturing industry. In order to make a formal connection, Thomas Campbell organised a letter of introduction for Urquhart, who agreed 'to establish a correspondence and to be connected with you for my Concerns in the West Indies . . . I believe your prices . . . were rather higher'.[24]

This letter established a long-term relationship between cotton plantations in Carriacou, the merchant firm in Glasgow and the estate owner in northern Scotland. John Campbell immediately initiated a discussion regarding credit with the absentee planter: 'any accommodation in money matters that you may happen occasionally to want, will be at your service'.[25] The first account current between William Urquhart and the firm also outlined trade connections between the Clyde and the Caribbean. Campbell exported stores including Scottish herring to feed the resident slaves on the Urquhart plantations.[26] The firm charged

Table 6.2 John Campbell, senior, & Co., advertised shipping voyages from the Clyde, 1806–34

	1806–10	1811–20	1821–30	1831–4	Total
Demerara	2	25	27	11	65
Grenada	4	19	18	5	46
New Providence	1	0	0	0	1
St Vincent	3	21	19	6	49
Tobago	2	15	8	0	25
	12	80	72	22	186

Source: *Glasgow Herald, 1806–34.*

Urquhart for foodstuffs and other goods that were shipped on large sea-going vessels from Port Glasgow to Carriacou via Grenada. In return, the insured cotton was shipped to the Clyde at six-monthly intervals. At point of sale, the firm charged 2.5 per cent commission.

John Campbell, senior, & Co. had access to a fleet of ships which facilitated regular trade between the Clyde and Grenada (see Table 6.2). From the late eighteenth century the firm also transported sojourners to the West Indies, sometimes advertising positions in newspapers. In one such advertisement they required 'TWO OR THREE YOUNG MEN brought up in the country' to be employed as overseers in Grenada.[27] Before he died in 1795, Thomas Campbell acted as mentor to arrivals such as William Arbuthnot, a nephew of the Urquhart family who travelled on the *Tivoli* which landed in Grenada in early 1787.[28] Campbell was particularly adept at cultivating close relationships with Scots at home and abroad.

Thomas Campbell assumed full co-partnership status in John Campbell, senior, & Co. around 1790 and immediately requested the Urquhart trading account be officially transferred to his brother's firm.[29] Thus, John Campbell's informal arrangement with kinsmen was ratified in a legal partnership. On 30 April 1791, William Urquhart was sent a printed letter stating the firm would hereafter be known as 'John Campbell, senior, and Co.' The letter further informed him the firm's partnership structure had altered and included signatures of each partner, which offered an early form of authentication on future correspondence.[30]

After 1791, the co-partners of John Campbell, senior, & Co. embarked on an ambitious strategy across the West Indies which almost ended in bankruptcy. Much of their business at this point was based on financing plantations or individuals, and a series of letters from William Arbuthnot offers a detailed account of how credit was obtained. In this period, he received 'every assurance of support, they [John Campbell, senior, & Co.] are well pleased with speculation'.[31] One example illustrates how this worked on a practical level. In early 1790 Arbuthnot pondered over the purchase of a cotton estate in Carriacou from Messrs Robertson of Glasgow. He wrote to his uncle William Urquhart to request a loan, although he first consulted their preferred merchant whose firm were also prepared to finance the deal:

> I would go down to Grenada & consult Mr Thomas Campbell whose knowledge in business & Experience in the World, as well as personal friendships I have upon all occasions found to be very great, & with which you are indeed well acquainted . . . Should it be inconvenient for you to advance any money, Mr Campbell is so good . . . that he will interest his brother Mr John Campbell in the business, who he is confident will give me any assistance I may wish . . . I should think it proper to give him full powers to make the bargain.[32]

On the same day, Thomas Campbell wrote to William Urquhart outlining a detailed plan of the location of the plantation as well as the character of Arbuthnot's co-partner, Dr John Bell. Thomas Campbell also wrote to his brother John to inform him of the Bell–Arbuthnot partnership and instructed him to initiate negotiations with Robertson. Although they were ultimately unsuccessful in the purchase, as Campbell expected, the correspondence illustrates how a transatlantic credit relationship between a Glasgow–West India merchant house and correspondents was established through existing networks which could lead to the financing of Caribbean plantations.

In the same period, the firm's main colonial representative established a foothold in the developing frontier colony of Demerara which was, at that stage, still under Dutch control. In 1792 Thomas Campbell compiled a dossier of commercial information on Cellsborough cotton plantation situated on the windward sea-coast of Demerara.[33] This information was sent to William Urquhart, although Campbell eventually acquired the plantation himself. The main co-partners of John Campbell, senior, & Co. therefore not only financed correspondents in the colonies but also diversified into the direct purchase of plantations.

A series of events that struck the firm in this period demonstrated the risky nature of transatlantic commerce and life in the tropics. In June 1793 John Campbell, senior, & Co. stopped payments to creditors, which was most likely due to over-speculation. While the merchant house avoided collapse, their colonial representative was not so lucky. By 1795 Thomas Campbell was part of the colonial council in Grenada who took control of Government at the outbreak of the Fedon Rebellion on 2 March that year. Thomas quickly fled and died in Demerara on

14 May 1795.[34] By this point he was a large-scale plantation owner, having acquired shares in three estates in both Grenada and Demerara, including Cellsborough and Taymouth Park. A deed lodged in Grenada Register Office in 1793 ensured his real and personal estate passed to his brothers, who subsequently appointed attorneys 'in our names to manage the foresaid plantations . . . to the best advantage' in 1796.[35]

The events of the mid-1790s initiated a shift in mercantile strategy for John Campbell, senior, & Co. Firstly, the firm's co-partners relocated their Caribbean operations from Grenada to Demerara. Secondly, they financed plantation owners and purchased estates directly. Thirdly, instead of sending representatives from the direct family matrix to the colonies, they depended on colonial sojourners already in Demerara to undertake their business. Thus, associates were recruited from kith networks – notably based on a shared Highland heritage – which replaced the traditional kinship ties.

SECOND-PHASE EXPANSION

After 1795 the co-partners of John Campbell, senior, & Co. expanded into Demerara in South America. The focus on the southern Caribbean offered lucrative commercial opportunities, although the contested region was marked by warfare among the European powers as well as rebellions by the rapidly increasing enslaved population. The pioneering work of David Alston has outlined the wealth-generating activities of Highlanders in Berbice.[36] This section traces the operations of John Campbell, senior, & Co. and their Highland associates in Demerara.

The shift in location in the Caribbean was matched by a transfer of power in Glasgow. After the death of senior partners John Campbell in 1807 and Alexander Campbell of Hallyards in 1817, Mungo Nutter adopted a management role alongside Colin, James and Thomas. The two sugar princes 'Black' Mungo and 'White' Mungo both assumed formal partnership status in 1828. It is evident this younger generation managed a diverse transatlantic business that had evolved since the establishment of the merchant house in 1791. Indeed, shipping advertisements of the firm's voyages from the Clyde suggest that Demerara had replaced Grenada as the firm's principal Caribbean trade destination by the 1810s (see Table 6.2).

The activities of the firm in Demerara after 1827 can be gleaned from a surviving letter-book and minute-book which provide a rare glimpse into the operations leading up to and beyond emancipation.[37] Like their mercantile contemporaries, Leitch & Smith, the firm of John Campbell, senior, & Co. operated a commission business, although the latter firm operated on a larger scale. While the Smiths traded mainly in Grenada and Jamaica, the Campbells had a diversity of interests in Demerara, Trinidad, Grenada and St Vincent which they retained after emancipation.

The establishment of a sister firm in London – Alexander and James Campbell & Co. – expanded operations into the commercial heart of empire. A five-year co-partnership agreement of 1827 outlined the capital stock was split among the firm John Campbell, senior, & Co. and two associates, Colin Macrae and Alexander George Milne, junior.[38] The firm's correspondence suggested the London establishment was intended to be a stand-alone business designed to allow the firm to take advantage of both markets, although it was wound up in April 1831.[39]

The London venture also demonstrates the firm's continuing dependence on transatlantic professionals. However, while Thomas Campbell was a direct blood relation, the connection with Colin Macrae – their attorney in the 1820s – was reinforced by shared Highland origins. Colin was the son of Farquhar Macrae of Inverinate in the Kyle of Lochalsh. The young Highlander took up a commercial career in Demerara as merchant and planter and assumed a position of some importance as a Colonel Commandant of the Colonial Militia. He later acted as a negotiator when Demerara was transferred to British rule.[40] This chapter will illuminate his little-known role as an attorney in Demerara.

The earliest reference to this colony in the surviving records of John Campbell, senior, & Co. was in May 1823, when the partners were especially concerned about 'the great and rapide increase in many of the Demerary outstandings'.[41] Evidently, capital or supplies had been advanced to resident merchants and planters before this point. The co-partners had further expanded into plantation ownership by acquiring Endeavour and Enterprise, located on Leguan Island in the delta of the Essequibo river. Both estates were purchased before 1823.[42] The firm's colonial operations were rapidly expanding in this period, although the co-partners preferred their business to be managed by one individual as outlined in correspondence to Macrae:

> Besides it is very desirable & indeed necessary for us, to put all our business into the hands of one attorney, in order to insure its being better done, & with less trouble to ourselves, as well as to make it always an object worth the acceptance of a person of respectability and experience as a planter.[43]

This was clearly a prestigious commission and Colin Macrae held a senior position for several years. He 'took charge of House matters' in

July 1826, although he had left for London a month previously.[44] Thus, the day-to-day management of the estates was delegated to kinsmen Alexander Macrae and Archibald MacQueen while Colin ran the firm's operations in London.

While in the capital in November 1827, Colin Macrae appeared before the Privy Council hearing set up to examine the proposed Compulsory Manumission of Slaves in Demerara and Berbice. This followed a petition in November 1826 from planters in Glasgow – including James, Mungo and Colin Campbell – who appealed to the King to avert the introduction of compulsory manumission. Several resident planters, including Colin Macrae, also signed a similar petition, which suggests transatlantic collusion.[45] At the Privy Council, the Inverinate sojourner spoke with some authority, having spent almost twenty-five years on Demerara as an attorney and plantation owner. In 1827 he was part-proprietor of two estates, and although they were not named at the hearing they were Enterprise and Endeavour on Leguan Island, which he owned in partnership with John Campbell, senior, & Co. Macrae was therefore cited at a parliamentary inquiry as a supposed expert and questioned at length on the moral character and work habits of the enslaved population. The testimony not only provides an insight into the *mentalité* of a Scottish sojourner in Demerara but also illustrates conditions on a Campbell-owned plantation.

In his evidence, Macrae described how his 230-strong 'gang of slaves' lived and worked on a sugar estate (either Endeavour or Enterprise) on Leguan Island. Macrae suggested the treatment of slaves had improved 'a very great deal' since 1807, particularly through educational provision. He further elaborated on working conditions. About half of the gang on his plantation were children, domestics and nurses not required for heavy labour. However, the other 115 slaves – the 'effective gang' – were made up of skilled and manual labourers. The majority of this gang were 'field slaves' split into two groups under the direction of two drivers. Up to sixty of the strongest slaves made up the 'man's gang of ablest men' and were employed in the most arduous work such as digging holes, while the other group comprised women and weaker men who undertook less intensive labour such as weeding. A skilled section of the gang – known as 'mechanics' – consisted of carpenters, masons, boilers and coopers who undertook complex tasks required for sugar production.[46]

Thus, an estate was a 'small community' where, Macrae alleged, 'good and bad [slaves] intermixed'. He warned compulsory manumission would lead to a complete breakdown in social order and that the rapid disintegration of the colonial economy would ensue.[47] In the aftermath of the Demerara slave rebellion in 1823, the testimony from a former Colonel of the Militia must have struck fear into members of the Privy Council. Perhaps the most invidious objection to manumission related to the emancipation of children. Macrae argued enslaved peoples would naturally want to buy their children's freedom, which would have been 'a most serious injury' to the planters of Demerara and Berbice, indeed, 'the greatest which can befall them'. The plantation economy, stated Macrae, was perpetuated 'only by a succession of children'.[48] Given these staunch views on compulsory manumission, it is unsurprising the firm's co-partners and their associates were opposed to full emancipation and they implemented a practical strategy which aimed to protect their joint interests in the colonies.

Alexander Macrae, Colin's nephew, was tasked by the co-partners of John Campbell, senior, & Co. to implement the firm's strategy for emancipation in Demerara. Alexander was employed by the firm before 1823, perhaps after a recommendation from his uncle. Alexander was further assisted in the Campbell business by his cousin Archibald MacQueen. The firm therefore had a close kinship network of Highlanders to rely upon for support. By 1830 Alexander Macrae replaced his uncle as the main attorney. His tasks included the management of estates and foreclosing mortgages of indebted correspondents. In this period the firm also embarked on a policy of purchasing estates brought to sale at auction after previous owners died or fell into debt.

The co-partners in Glasgow attempted to speculate on Demerara estates in order to accumulate compensation money from the British Government. In mid-1833 the firm sought to purchase Ridge plantation, situated on Wakenaam, an island in the delta of the Essequibo river. Macrae was sent instructions to bid £20,000 and granted a Power of Attorney which provided legal authority to make the purchase. However, the firm requested certain conditions must be met before any purchase was concluded:

> The property will have the sole, and undoubted register to the Compensation to be received from Government, and this is a matter which you must take care to ascertain clearly before bidding. Indeed, we should suppose that it will be stated in the Articles of Sale, but if not, you must ask the question, and have it fairly understood.[49]

The partners of John Campbell, senior, & Co. therefore made the decision to purchase Ridge in the knowledge that a compensation award was imminent, although they were ultimately unsuccessful in this venture. In any case, the co-partners had a clear strategy to deal with their existing interests and the Macraes provided support in London and Demerara.

While in London in 1830, Colin Macrae authored an economic tract which was submitted to the Tory Prime Minister, the Duke of Wellington. In this text Macrae acknowledged the abolition of plantation slavery was a *fait accompli* and the debate had become 'one of mere purchase and sale'.[50] As joint-owner of estates in Demerara, Macrae offered an astonishing solution. He suggested the British Government should take over the plantation economy of the British West Indies – via a commercial company – for a sum of £140 million with respective values set at £56 million each for the slaves and land and a further £28 million for machinery and stock. 'The West India Stock' would therefore recompense planters for the loss of their property while the institution of slavery would have been gradually abolished after a system of voluntary labour for former slaves. In reality, the terms of the emancipation were lower yet still staggering. The British Government set the level of compensation to slave owners at £20 million and the Apprenticeship scheme kept the slaves thirled to the plantations for a set period. While Macrae's suggestions were impractical and unrealistic in financial terms, the pared-down Abolition Act of 1833 still presented an unprecedented challenge for the British Government. In order to compensate slave owners for the loss of their property, each colony was assigned a proportionate share of the compensation, while individual slaves were classified according to individual socio-economic characteristics.

The Compensation Commission was established in London, with the main administrative responsibility undertaken by a central board consisting of lawyers and colonial administrators. Auxiliary committees were set up in each colony, although there was a conflict of interest as almost all of the working members were owners or managers of estates. The first issue – the proportion each colony should receive – was resolved by the Compensation Commission taking an 'ad valorem' award system into consideration. The compensation was awarded on the basis of the average value of slave prices from 1822 to 1830. British Guiana came fully under British control after the abolition of the slave trade in 1807 and slave prices were inflated in the 1820s due to limited stocks and the high costs induced by the inter-colony slave trade.[51] As the average price of slaves was the second-highest of all British West India colonies in this period, the rate of compensation was also second-highest.[52] The second issue – how to classify individual slaves – was resolved by establishing three major categories that ex-slaves would assume under the apprenticeship scheme; praedial attached, praedial unattached and non-praedial. Praedial categories referred to field slaves; those considered 'attached' worked on the land of their owner while 'unattached' slaves worked on land owned by someone else. All other slaves, such as domestics, fell into the third category. After emancipation, the former slaves categorised as praedial were intended to have an apprenticeship period of six years, while non-praedial were intended to have a four-year period. There were further sub-classifications within each category that decided rate of compensation and the colonial commissioners employed evaluators to decide.[53] Thus, the rates of compensation for slaves were set in the colonies based on a classification system that left much room for deception by vested interests. Perhaps unsurprisingly, the Campbells and Alexander Macrae collaborated to squeeze as much compensation and labour from the Government and apprenticed labourers as possible.

In February 1834 James Campbell wrote to Macrae after he had 'some time to consider . . . the change so soon to be made in the conditions of the Negro population, & to prepare for carrying it into effect'.[54] By this point the evaluators in British Guiana had not yet decided on individual compensation awards (at least not for the Macrae–Campbell slaves), although the British Government had set the categories attached to compensation. This delay provided the opportunity for 'deliberate misrepresentation' of non-praedial slaves as praedial.[55] Consistent with this view, senior partner James Campbell instructed Macrae on how to approach the evaluation of slaves:

> You are of course preparing for the classification of the Negroes as required by the emancipation act, and we presume it will be your endeavour to bring as much of that under your charge as possible under the class of 'Praedial Attached'.[56]

Thus the firm were keen to classify the majority of their slaves in Demerara as agricultural workers – instead of non-praedial – which should have meant an extra two years' labour from the ex-slaves under the apprenticeship scheme (although the duration was cut short for all apprentices after four years in 1838). As well as the extra labour, praedial apprentices attracted higher rates of compensation per individual. The highest and lowest rate in British Guiana for praedial slaves was £87 for 'head people' and £36 for 'inferior field labourers' respectively. The highest award for non-praedial was for 'head tradesmen' (£68) and the lowest was for 'inferior domestics' (£35). Compensation for children was set at £19, while 'aged, diseased and non-effective' slaves attracted awards of just £11.[57]

The co-partners also recommended a post-emancipation strategy designed to increase productivity under the apprenticeship scheme. After emancipation, apprentices on the estates were to be used for jobbing work in order to 'procure the greatest quantity of labor, at the least expense & trouble'. Echoing Adam Smith's views on labour and rational self-interest in *Wealth of Nations*, Alexander Macrae was advised to allow the formerly enslaved peoples a 'certain interest' in the produce of new sugar cane from 1 August 1834.[58] Thus the political and commercial strategy ensured the merchant house was well prepared for the landmark event.

THE FINANCIAL LEGACY OF THE MERCHANT HOUSE

Although the partners of John Campbell, senior, & Co. were opposed in principle to emancipation, they collected vast sums after 1 August 1834. The ongoing *Legacies of British Slave-ownership* project at University College London assists in the untangling the Gordian knot of mercantile compensation claims in Glasgow. The six remaining partners of the firm – Colin, Thomas and James as well as Mungo Nutter and 'Black' and 'White' Mungo – claimed compensation for enslaved peoples across at least twelve estates in British Guiana, St Vincent, Trinidad and Grenada.[59]

Some of these claims were made as mercantile beneficiaries, as trustees or split with the owners of slaves. However, partners of the firm collected full awards for the resident slaves on their own estates Endeavour and Enterprise. The level of compensation collected reduced outstanding debts owed to the firm:

> That the West India outstandings, consisting of debts and property in Estates, being greatly diminished in amount by Government Compensation money and other causes, the same extent of capital [£180,000] as formerly is not required to hold the property and carry on the business of the concern and the capital shall be accordingly reduced.[60]

Thus it seems the compensation allowed individual co-partners to pare back their own personal investment by up to one-third.

The strategy implemented by the partners meant the firm survived after emancipation, although it was eventually wound up on 30 May 1858. The five remaining co-partners were John Campbell's two sons, James and Thomas, as well as his grandson, Colin Campbell junior, who had learned his trade in the family firm after assuming partnership status in 1841. 'Black' and 'White' Mungo Campbell remained partners until the firm's commercial demise. That ended its almost seventy-year relationship between Scotland and the Caribbean. The legacy of the firm can be measured by tracing the financial interests of partners.

The use of confirmation inventories as indicators of personal wealth – analogous to English probate inventories – is problematic as they sometimes underestimate actual holdings or do not represent an individual's peak wealth. Nevertheless, William Rubinstein's study of nineteenth-century British wealth-holders utilised large samples of inventories which provide a comparative framework. This analysis defined individuals who died owning at least £100,000 of personal property as 'rich'.[61] Rubinstein's study therefore allows comparison of the fortunes made by the Campbell family to be placed in a national context.

It has been possible to trace wills and inventories of nine of the fifteen individuals who registered as co-partners in John Campbell, senior, & Co. during the period 1790 and 1848 (see Table 6.3). The personal wealth totalled over £1 million sterling. First-phase fortunes, such as that made by John Campbell senior, were on a par with average holdings of elite West India merchants in Glasgow in the same period.[62] On his death in 1807, much of his fortune was held in stock and shares in the merchant house. As well as bequeathing heritable property, he left explicit instructions that his three sons were to be the major financial beneficiaries of £10,000 each, some of which had been administered before he died.[63]

The family investments in landed estates, urban property, banks, manufactories, insurance companies and British railways were typical of the Glasgow–West India mercantile elite.[64] Partners of the firm

Table 6.3 Landed estates and personal wealth of nine co-partners of John Campbell, senior, & Co., 1790–1848

First name	Surname	Year of death	Landed estate	Wealth on death
John	Campbell senior	1807	Morriston	£53,548
Alexander	Campbell	1817	Hallyards	£34,432
Alexander	Campbell	1835	Haylodge	£17,574
'Black' Mungo	Campbell	1859		£6,830
Mungo Nutter	Campbell	1862	Ballimore	£23,274
Colin	Campbell	1863	Colgrain	£169,350
'White' Mungo	Campbell	1866		£14,901
Thomas	Campbell	1866	Hailes House	£31,494
Colin	Campbell II	1886	Colgrain	£680,890
			Total	**£1,032,293**

Source: National Records of Scotland; Will and Confirmation Inventories from Commissary Courts of Edinburgh and Glasgow and Sheriff Courts of Dunoon, Dumbarton, Edinburgh and Glasgow.

inherited or purchased several landed estates in Glasgow, Peeblesshire and Argyll. John Campbell senior was elevated to the landed class when he purchased Possil. After the award of compensation in 1836, his son Colin acquired Colgrain estate near Cardross – formerly owned by the Dennistouns – which passed onto his son. Many of the partners' inventories on death listed townhouses in Glasgow and Edinburgh, such as Mungo Nutter Campbell who seems to have owned two properties in the capital.[65]

Three of the initial co-partners – John Campbell, Hallyards and Haylodge – died while still active in the firm, explaining why the majority of their wealth was held in capital stock and account current. Much of their fortune was subsequently passed to their sons. The inventories of the partners who died after the dissolution of the firm in 1858 outline a partial investment shift from the West Indies to Great Britain. These partners held extensive holdings in insurance firms, banking institutions and railways. With a personal fortune of over £160,000, Colin Campbell seems to have acquired the most wealth of the original partners. His notable investments include over £54,000 in the Union Bank. Similarly, his younger brother Thomas held almost £20,000 in balance and stock in the same institution. At least three partners retained mortgages on properties in the West Indies beyond 1834.

The direct male line of John Campbell senior continued the family's involvement in the sugar trade. In the late nineteenth century, his grandson Colin Campbell junior resided permanently at Colgrain, although he spent much of his time in South Kensington Place in London where he died in 1886. He held large-scale investments in English firms such as Finlay, Campbell & Co., which had interests in the East Indies, particularly Ceylon. He also made domestic investments in Scottish and English railways. However, he retained an international focus with investments in the New Zealand and Australian Land Company, and even loaned capital to the Chilean Government.[66] The family fortune established by John Campbell senior in Virginia and the West Indies was remitted to Glasgow and was subsequently invested across the globe.

Rubinstein has noted that comparisons of intergenerational wealth and associated social mobility allow the historian to chart the source and rise of great fortunes. In this case, the sugar and cotton trade and related investments propelled the Campbell family into the ranks of the super-wealthy in Great Britain. Based on successive infusions of West India capital across two generations, Colin Campbell junior left a personal fortune of over £680,000. By means of comparison, there were just twenty-eight half-millionaires in Scotland during the period 1880 to 1939.[67] Thus the inheritor of the family fortune seems to have been one of the wealthiest merchants in Scotland during the colonial period.

This chapter has traced the rise of the Campbells of Possil, many of whom were associated with the great Glasgow merchant house John Campbell, senior, & Co. The firm was established by John Campbell who recruited close family members as co-partners. Several of these partners became notable figures in Glasgow during the city's 'golden age' of sugar. The increase in capital stock provides quantitative evidence of the dramatic rise, and this chapter has revealed the exploitative activities in Grenada, Carriacou and subsequently Demerara. The firm depended on family members to undertake their business in the former and employed Highland sojourners in the latter. The merchant house operated a commission system based on the exportation of goods from Scotland, the importation of produce from the Caribbean and the provision of credit to plantation owners in Grenada and Carriacou. The partners eventually inherited and purchased estates in Demerara. The extent of this involvement can be gauged by the large compensation awards made to the partners on emancipation in 1834, as well as the fabulous wealth noted in confirmation inventories. Indeed, this case study suggests that John Guthrie Smith was premature if not myopic when he asserted in *The Old Country Houses of the Old Glasgow Gentry* in 1878 that the sugar trade did not create a large-scale fortune in Glasgow.

NOTES

1. John Guthrie Smith, John Oswald Mitchell, 'Possil', *The Old Country Houses of the old Glasgow Gentry* (Glasgow: James Maclehose & Sons, 1878).
2. Nicholas Draper, *The Price of Emancipation: Slave ownership, Compensation and British Society at the End of Slavery* (Cambridge: Cambridge University Press, 2010), p. 236.
3. Glasgow City Archives (hereafter GCA) TD1696 'Campbell of Hallyards papers'.
4. For example: T. M. Devine, 'An Eighteenth-Century Business Elite: Glasgow-West India Merchants, 1750–1815', *Scottish Historical Review*, 57/163 (1978), pp. 53–67; Allan I. Macinnes, 'Scottish Gaeldom from Clanship to Commercial Landlordism, c. 1600–1850', in A. I. Macinnes, S. M. Foster and R. K. MacInnes (eds), *Scottish Power Centres from the Early Middle Ages to the Twentieth Century* (Glasgow: Cruithne Press, 1998), pp. 162–90; Allan Karras, *Sojourners in the Sun* (USA: Cornell Press, 1992); Douglas Hamilton, 'Scottish Trading in the Caribbean: The Rise and Fall of Houston & Co.', in Ned C. Landsman (ed.), *Nation and*

Province in the First British Empire: Scotland and the Americas, 1600–1800 (Lewisburg: Bucknell University Press, 2001), pp. 94–126; Douglas Hamilton, *Scotland, the Caribbean and the Atlantic World, 1750–1820* (Manchester: Manchester University Press, 2005); Anthony Cooke, 'An Elite Revisited: Glasgow West India Merchants, 1783–1877', *Journal of Scottish Historical Studies*, 32/2 (November 2012), pp. 127–65; Stephen Mullen, 'A Glasgow-West India Merchant House and the Imperial Dividend, 1779–1867', *Journal of Scottish Historical Studies*, 33/2 (November 2013), pp. 196–233.

5. T. M. Devine, *The Tobacco Lords* (Edinburgh: John Donald, 1975), p. 178.
6. James Anderson, *The Burgesses and Guild Brethren of Glasgow, 1751–1846* (Edinburgh: J. Skinner & Co., 1935), p. 118.
7. GCA C1/1/36 'Town Council Minutes', 5 October 1781, p. 531.
8. Nathaniel Jones, *Reprint of Jones's Directory for the Year 1787* (Glasgow: William Love, 1868), p. 34.
9. For a comparative case study, see Mullen, 'A Glasgow-West India Merchant House'.
10. S. D. Smith, *Slavery, Family and Gentry Capitalism in the British Atlantic: The World of the Lascelles, 1648–1834* (Cambridge: Cambridge University Press, 2006), p. 9.
11. GCA TD1696 'Contract of co-partnership', 1790, p. 1.
12. T. M. Devine, 'Sources of Capital for the Glasgow Tobacco Trade, c. 1740–1780', *Business History,* 16/2 (1974), p. 122; Hamilton, 'Scottish Trading in the Caribbean', p. 120.
13. W. Innes Addison, *The Matriculation Albums of the University of Glasgow* (Glasgow: James Maclehose & Sons, 1913), pp. 169, 175, 211, 212.
14. GCA TD1696 'Contract of co-partnership', 1801, pp. 4–5.
15. Katie Barclay, *Love, Intimacy and Power: Marriage and Patriarchy in Scotland, 1650–1850* (Manchester: Manchester University Press, 2011), p. 80.
16. Guthrie Smith, Oswald Mitchell, 'Possil', *Old Country Houses*.
17. John Strang, *Glasgow and its Clubs* (London: Richard Griffin & Co., 1857), p. 113.
18. Henry Hamilton, *An Economic History of Scotland in the Eighteenth Century* (Oxford: Clarendon Press, 1963), p. 273.
19. GCA TD1683/1/1, 'Minutes of the Glasgow West India Association', pp. 6–8.
20. H. Gordon Slade, 'Craigston and Meldrum Estates, Carriacou, 1769–1841', *Proceedings of the Society Antiquaries of Scotland,* 114 (1984), pp. 481–537.
21. National Register of Archives for Scotland (hereafter NRAS), 2570, 'Plantation records of the Urquharts of Craigston and Meldrum'. With thanks to William Pratesi Urquart for access to these papers.
22. D. Lambert and A. Lester (eds), *Colonial Lives across the British Empire:*

Imperial Careering in the Long Nineteenth Century (Cambridge: Cambridge University Press, 2006).

23. NRAS 2570/131, 18 September 1790.
24. NRAS 2570/120, 7 July 1786.
25. NRAS 2570/120, 17 July 1786.
26. NRAS 2570/120, 'Account Current', August 1786.
27. 'For Grenada', *Glasgow Herald,* 30 September 1808, p. 4.
28. NRAS 2570/131, 18 February 1787.
29. NRAS 2570/131, 17 February 1791.
30. NRAS 2570/122, 30 April 1791.
31. NRAS 2570/130, 14 November 1792.
32. NRAS 2570/118, 3 March 1790.
33. NRAS 2570/120, 15 July 1792.
34. *The Edinburgh Magazine,* Vol. VI (London: James Symington, August 1795), p. 160.
35. Supreme Court Registry, St George's, Grenada, Vol. F2, 9 May 1796, pp. 178–80.
36. David Alston, 'Very rapid and splendid fortunes'? Highland Scots in Berbice (Guyana) in the early nineteenth century', *Transactions of the Gaelic Society of Inverness,* LXIII (2002–4), pp. 208–36 (Inverness, 2006).
37. GCA TD1696, 'Private Letter book, J. C. Senr. & Co., 1827–1847'; 'Minute book, 1803–1842'.
38. GCA TD1696, 'Co-partnership agreement', 1827.
39. GCA TD1696, 'Letter book', p. 74.
40. Rev. Alexander Macrae, *The History of the Clan Macrae* (Dingwall: George Souter, 1910), pp. 97–104, 116.
41. GCA, TD1696, 'Minute book', p. 13.
42. Alexander Macrae, *A Manual of Plantership in British Guiana* (London: Smith, Elder & Co., 1856), p. 34.
43. GCA TD1696, 'Letter book', p.83.
44. Ibid., p. 41.
45. *Proceedings before the Privy Council against Compulsory Manumission in the Colonies of Demerara and Berbice* (London: J. Moyes, 1827), pp. 2, 77, 124.
46. PP 1828 (261) Slaves: Berbice and Demerara, November 1827, pp. 26–39.
47. Ibid., p. 28.
48. Ibid., pp. 36–9.
49. GCA TD1696, 'Letter book', pp. 104–5.
50. Colin Macrae, *Suggestions of a Plan for the Effectual Abolition of Slavery in all the British West India Colonies* (London: H. I. McLary, 1830), p. 4.
51. K. M. Butler, *The Economics of Emancipation* (London: University of North Carolina Press, 1995), pp. 27–9.
52. P 1837–38 (64) Slavery Abolition Act.
53. Butler, *Economics of Emancipation*, pp. 30–1.

54. GCA TD1696, 'Letter book', p. 110.
55. Butler, *Economics of Emancipation*, p. 32.
56. GCA TD1696, 'Letter book', p. 110.
57. PP 1837–38 (215) Accounts of slave compensation claims, p. 352.
58. GCA TD1696, 'Letter book', pp. 111–12.
59. 'Legacies of British Slave-ownership website' available at http://www.ucl.ac.uk/lbs (accessed 12 August 2014).
60. GCA TD1696, 'Minute book', 12 July 1836.
61. William D. Rubinstein, *Who Were the Rich? A Biographical Directory of British Wealth-holders, vol. I, 1809–1839* (London: Social Affairs Unit, 2009), p. 13.
62. Cooke, 'An Elite Revisited', p. 143.
63. NRS, SC36/48/3, 'Inventory of John Campbell senior', 3 October 1808, pp. 57–63.
64. Cooke, 'An Elite Revisited'.
65. NRS SC51/32/12, 'Inventory of Mungo Nutter Campbell', 1863, pp. 270–81.
66. NRS SC65/34/29, 'Inventory of Colin Campbell junior', 1886, pp. 391–416; NRS SC65/34/30, 'Additional Inventory of Colin Campbell junior', 1887, pp. 383–5.
67. William D. Rubinstein, *Men of Property* (London: Social Affairs Unit, 2006), pp. 131, 146–7.

7

Scottish Surgeons in the Liverpool Slave Trade in the Late Eighteenth and Early Nineteenth Centuries[1]

Suzanne Schwarz

I

ON 6 APRIL 1792 James Irving junior, a Scottish slave ship surgeon, met James Currie, an abolitionist and Edinburgh-trained doctor, at Liverpool Infirmary. The occasion for their meeting was a formal examination by Currie and two other practitioners to establish whether Irving had sufficient medical knowledge to qualify for certification under the terms of the Dolben Act of 1788.[2] Irving and Currie were both from Dumfriesshire, and their places of birth in Langholm and Kirkpatrick Fleming were located only fourteen miles apart. In other respects they had little in common. Currie studied medicine in Edinburgh and graduated MD from Glasgow University, whereas Irving was a barber-surgeon whose more limited medical knowledge was built up through his apprenticeship to his older cousin and namesake as a surgeon's mate on slave ships.[3] Their views on the trade in enslaved Africans were dia-metrically opposed; Currie had already written various condemnations of the trade, whereas Irving had displayed some eagerness in calculating the bonus he would receive depending on how many Africans died in the course of the Middle Passage on the *Ellen* in 1791.[4]

Other Scottish surgeons, who either felt no moral qualms about the dehumanisation of Africans as cargo or who had become inured to the brutality of the trade, undertook a series of slaving voyages from Liverpool. James Irving senior (later Captain Irving) from Langholm in Dumfriesshire undertook his first slaving voyage on the *Vulture* in 1783 and five years later persuaded his younger cousin (James Irving junior) to join him as surgeon's mate on his fifth voyage as a surgeon.[5] The Edinburgh-trained surgeon Archibald Dalzel became involved in slave trading following his discharge from the Royal Navy at the end of the

Seven Years War. He accepted a position as surgeon at Anomabu fort in the employ of the Company of Merchants Trading to Africa in 1763, and was subsequently appointed as governor of the fort at Whydah in 1767. Born in Kirkliston, West Lothian, Dalzel also captained a number of slave-trading voyages during his career, including one from Liverpool.[6] In a letter to Dr Percival in 1788, Currie referred to Dalzel as 'a person who was first a surgeon, and afterwards a master of a Guinea-ship: after this, a governor on the coast; a planter on the Mississippi; & finally, from the misfortunes he sustained in the Revolution of America, reduced to the station of a slave-captain again'.[7] Dalzel initially had some moral reservations about participating in the slave trade, but overcame these fairly quickly and commented in May 1764 on how 'I have at last come a little into the spirit of the slave trade and must own (perhaps it ought to be to my shame) that I can now traffick in that way without remorse'.[8]

Thomas Trotter, in contrast, was unable to reconcile his employment as a surgeon in the slave trade with his conscience. In common with his English counterpart Alexander Falconbridge, he was appalled by the conditions that he witnessed during a period as a surgeon in the slave trade and subsequently gave evidence to parliament in support of the abolitionist cause.[9] Trotter, born in Melrose in Roxburghshire and educated in Edinburgh, testified that he had accepted the position as surgeon on the *Brooks* in 1783 as a result of limited career opportunities in the Royal Navy following the cessation of the American War of Independence.[10] As the *Brooks* sailed up the Mersey on its return to Liverpool in August 1784 Trotter, aged twenty-four, disembarked from the vessel at his earliest opportunity and undertook no further slaving voyages during his career.[11]

The medical skills of these surgeons were highly valued as a means of maximising profits through the control of shipboard mortality, and merchants in London, Bristol and Liverpool frequently employed surgeons before it was made compulsory by the Dolben Act. Stephen D. Behrendt argues that experienced surgeons could reduce mortality rates, and that 'merchants hired competent captains and qualified surgeons who could screen and inoculate slaves on the Coast, maintain some degree of hygiene and sanitation on board ship, and treat slaves with stimulative and supportive medicines'.[12]

The rapid expansion of slave ship clearances from Liverpool in the late eighteenth century provided new career openings for surgeons, as well as prospects for swift promotion and high financial rewards if they were able to survive the many perils of the Africa trade.[13] In contrast, the trade from Scottish ports had petered out by the 1760s and the last recorded slaving voyages of the *Juba* and the *Coats* cleared from Clyde ports in 1766, more than forty years before the British abolition of the trade in 1807.[14] Scottish slave ship clearances accounted for the forced migration of an estimated 4,830 Africans, of whom 4,029 were disembarked in the Americas.[15]

The small number of recorded voyages from Scotland gives the misleading impression that Scots had limited involvement in the Atlantic slave trade. Advances which have taken place in scholarship in recent years point to extensive Scottish participation in the trade from the principal English ports.[16] As T. M. Devine has noted and the chapters of this book confirm, it is clear that 'Victorian assumptions about Scotland's peripheral role in slave trafficking were largely unfounded'.[17] Thomas Trotter, Archibald Dalzel and Captain James Irving and his younger cousin (James Irving junior) were part of a much larger commercial diaspora of Scottish men involved in the Atlantic slave trade in England.[18] Scots can be identified in all ranks of the trade, ranging from slave merchants to rank-and-file seamen, but they formed a large and disproportionate number among ship captains and officers. This Scottish presence among the most responsible and skilled groups is significant, as the selection of suitably qualified men to manage the complex business of slave trading was an important 'risk management strategy' deployed by merchants in a trade that was highly volatile and precarious.[19] Scottish men made a distinctive contribution to the expansion of the slave trade in Liverpool through the transfer of their specialist labour skills to the port in the eighteenth and early nineteenth centuries.

This chapter traces the career profiles of a number of Scottish surgeons who were active in Liverpool during a period of increasingly fractious debate on the morality of the transatlantic slave trade in the closing decades of the eighteenth century. These cases bring into sharp relief the clash of abolitionist and anti-abolitionist values characteristic of national debate, although the strength of vested interests in Liverpool added considerable vehemence to arguments in defence of the trade.[20] The views of James Currie and Thomas Trotter contrast directly with those of Archibald Dalzel and James Irving and his younger cousin. Scottish surgeons were prominent among those who spoke out against the trade in Liverpool, which reflected the numerical importance of this group of skilled men in the port. However, in a town where open opposition to the trade could provoke violent responses, Currie's support for the abolitionist cause was expressed anonymously in print.[21] His covert opposition was also pragmatic as his role in certifying surgeons involved regular encounters with men whose livelihoods depended on the trade.

Currie's outlook reflects the ideas of Scottish Enlightenment thinkers who by the late eighteenth century had condemned the slave trade as immoral and inhumane.[22] In contrast, Dalzel was an ardent defender of the trade in Liverpool and used his first-hand experience of governance at slave forts in West Africa to bolster his pro-slavery arguments.[23] Captain Irving and his cousin also reflect entrenched attitudes typical of an 'older mentality of toleration' of the slave trade, which were out of step with changing national opinion.[24] Even after a period of captivity in North Africa forced them to confront their own attitudes to slavery, they both returned quickly and apparently without any moral unease to the business of transporting Africans to the Americas.[25]

II

Scottish migrants contributed substantially to the 'reservoir of slave-trading expertise' which gave Liverpool such a marked competitive advantage over its rival slaving ports of London and Bristol. Behrendt's analysis of muster rolls indicates that 7 per cent of the crew of Liverpool vessels between 1798 and 1807, and 6 per cent of crewmen in Bristol between 1789 and 1794, originated from Scotland. Disaggregating the results by rank indicates that a disproportionate number of officers on Liverpool vessels were Scottish. In this more restricted sample, 14.3 per cent originated from Scotland, compared with 8.7 per cent from Ireland and 2.5 per cent from Wales.[26] This Scottish influence is still greater if the sample is restricted to captains, as 20 per cent of those active in Liverpool between 1785 and 1807 were Scottish, with a similar Manx proportion.[27]

Limited career openings at home and the lure of profits in the slave trade influenced the outward migration of Scottish surgeons to England, with the result that almost two-fifths of surgeons in the trade in the late eighteenth century originated from Scotland.[28] Between 1750 and 1800, over 85 per cent of medical graduates in Britain were trained in Scottish universities. There were simply not enough openings in the homeland for more than a fraction of them. Thus, the expatriate Scottish physician became a familiar figure throughout the Empire and beyond.[29] Behrendt has identified surgeons on 1,660 Liverpool slaving voyages between 1753 and 1807. Of the 369 men identified with birth-counties, 142 came from Scotland (38 per cent). As part of this professional diaspora, surgeons in Liverpool originated from a wide range of areas including Argyll and Bute, Aberdeenshire, Ayrshire, Midlothian, Moray, Borders, Fifeshire, Perthshire, Renfrewshire, Lanarkshire and Roxburghshire.[30]

Intelligence about employment opportunities would have been conveyed to Scotland in personal correspondence and by mariners and returning migrants. James Irving senior, baptised in Langholm in December 1759, could well have gleaned intelligence of career openings in Liverpool during his apprenticeship as a surgeon. There were certainly strong connections with the Liverpool slave trade in Dumfriesshire which predated Irving's maritime career. Thomas Brown, a slave merchant from Dumfriesshire, organised up to eighteen slaving ventures from Liverpool between 1763 and 1775, and James Carruthers organised an estimated forty-three slaving ventures between 1753 and 1786.[31]

Behrendt identifies twenty-four surgeons from Dumfriesshire who were active in Liverpool between 1771 and 1807. Roger Aikin and John Wright undertook their first slaving voyages in the 1770s, and Christopher Robson, James Robertson and David Hannay first sailed as surgeons in 1785, 1787 and 1791 respectively. John Laidley and Alexander Armstrong from Langholm were entered on board Liverpool ships as surgeons in 1784 and 1786. The supply of surgeons from Dumfriesshire continued right up until abolition, as William Geddies [Geddes] and John Campbell both undertook their first voyages in 1807.[32] Campbell was entered on board the *Kitty's Amelia* in command of Captain Hugh Crow, but his career was short-lived.[33] Crow recorded that during the voyage 'we lost no fewer than thirty whites and fifty blacks: amongst the former were our two doctors, who died immediately after our arrival at Kingston'.[34] In common with James Irving junior, a number of these Dumfriesshire-born surgeons seeking employment in the Liverpool slave trade were examined at Liverpool Infirmary by James Currie. David Hannay was assessed by Dr Currie, Dr Gerard and Mr Park on 1 April 1791, and his successful examination was reflected in his payment of a fee of £3 3s. 0d. Alexander Wilson was examined by Dr Currie and Dr Lyon on 2 August 1798, and his payment of a fee of £5 5s. 0d. indicates that his examination took place at a special meeting outside the usual time scheduled for 'examining Affrican [sic] Surgeons' on the first Tuesday of every month at 4 pm. John Campbell, examined by Dr McCartney and Dr Lyon on 25 April 1807, was the last surgeon listed in the 'Register of Certificates granted by the Medical Faculty of the L[iver]pool Infirmary to the Surgeons for the African Trade'.[35]

The importance of family connections in shaping patterns of outward migration from Scotland is reflected in how James Irving's younger cousin and namesake followed him into the slave trade at the age of fifteen or sixteen in 1787.[36] Three years earlier, James Irving junior would have seen how his older cousin had earned sufficient money on his first slaving venture on the *Vulture* in 1784 to purchase buildings in Langholm. Irving earned approximately £140 from his monthly wages, the value of two privilege slaves and 'head money' of one shilling for each of the 592 enslaved Africans who survived the Middle Passage.[37] Within a month of returning to Liverpool from this voyage to Africa and Jamaica, Irving entered into a contract of feu to purchase houses and a yard which were bounded on the north-western side by the 'dwelling house' of his uncle Janetus Irving.[38] James Irving later explained that he was the cause of his younger cousin taking up a career at sea.[39]

Irving's contacts built up through four previous voyages as a surgeon enabled him to secure a good position for his cousin as a surgeon's mate on the *Princess Royal* in April 1788. Through this apprenticeship, James Irving junior had the opportunity to learn his trade on one of the largest ships engaged in the trade. Furthermore, he would have benefited from the expertise of William Sherwood, one of the leading Liverpool captains who had developed specialist knowledge of trade in the Bight of Biafra. As the ship was bound there to secure its cargo, Irving junior began his training in an area that was characterised by face-to-face trading with African suppliers. This 'ship trade', conducted in areas without European forts, was more complex than the 'fort trade' and relied on the skills of officers in building up trust with African merchants. The surgeon's mate would have gone on shore with his more experienced cousin and observed how trade was conducted with African merchants based at Bonny or New Calabar in the Niger Delta.[40] It is not clear which port acted as the principal source of supply for the 771 Africans embarked on the *Princess Royal* in 1788.[41] Bonny had been the principal source of supply for 798 Africans embarked by Sherwood a year earlier, and if this pattern was repeated in 1788 the younger Irving would have observed trading in an area noted for its efficiency, rapid loading rates and the effective protection of credit through powerful centralised African authority.[42] It was also advantageous that his training commenced in an area that formed the 'cornerstone of Liverpool's slaving activities' and which could command salaries double the rate of those paid in the fort trade.[43] Four of the previous voyages undertaken by his older cousin had traded in the Bight of Biafra, and this practical schooling of younger men reflected how Liverpool had built up a dominant position in the region through 'commercial knowledge developed through iterative exchange across generations of traders on both sides of the trading nexus'.[44]

Scottish networks in Liverpool appear not to have had a discernible impact on the career of James Irving senior, as he was employed by

English merchants and worked mainly with officers from England and the Isle of Man. Although a number of leading Scottish merchants, including William Begg, Robert Sellar, Charles Shand and Samuel McDowal, were active in Liverpool in the 1780s and 1790s, Irving took up employment with William Boats and John Dawson.[45] His decision to work with English merchants may have been informed primarily by the size of their operations and the prospects for promotion, as large slaving firms had the capacity to employ captains for repeat voyages over a number of years.[46] Boats organised up to 156 slaving ventures between 1752 and 1795, and Dawson probably invested in 129 voyages between 1772 and 1795. The number of voyages organised by Scottish merchants was low in comparison with totals of up to 102 voyages for Begg (1799–1807), 36 for Sellar (1787–1807) and 34 for Shand (1796–1805).[47] Irving may not have been typical in this respect, as clear networks can be traced among other Scottish captains and investors. When Thomas Mullion, born near Perth in 1777, sailed in command of the *Kingsmill* in 1798 and 1800, all the investors were Scottish.[48]

In the case of James Irving junior, family ties not only influenced his entry into the trade but also shaped his rapid advancement. The promotion of his older cousin to his first captaincy provided an opportunity for him to attain the position of surgeon on the *Anna* at the age of sixteen or seventeen. This was exceptionally young, as surgeons normally entered the slave trade in their mid-twenties.[49] The captain (James Irving senior) had also been promoted a year earlier than the average age at first command. His promotion from surgeon to captain was not typical of most Liverpool captains, although this became more common practice after the outbreak of war in 1793 as the number of available officers was restricted by recruitment to the Royal Navy.[50] Other Scottish surgeons appointed to command can be identified, however, including James Swanson from Hawick who attained the status of captain after completing three voyages as a surgeon. Following a voyage in command of the Liverpool ship *Prudence*, he returned home and died in September 1803 aged twenty-three.[51] He was accompanied home by the son of an African trader at Cape Mount, and the boy later named Thomas Jenkins developed a significant role as a teacher and a missionary.[52]

Among the twenty-four Dumfriesshire surgeons active in Liverpool between 1774 and 1807, Christopher Robson also progressed to captain. In a letter from Liverpool dated 22 September 1790, Robson wrote to Dr William Graham, a physician in Gibraltar, and informed him that 'the Merchants has given me the Ship and I shall sail again in the course of three weeks or a month – as <u>Captain</u>'. The letter indicates that

Robson, Graham and Irving all originated from south-west Scotland, as Robson referred to how:

> About the time we was taking the fresh air last Summer in the Boarders [sic] and sporting Among the rose buds on the banks of the Esk Jimmy Irving got the Command of a Schooner to go to the coast of Africa.[53]

Robson sailed for Africa and Barbados in command of the *Porcupine* in April 1792, and this voyage of the 183-ton brig was financed predominantly by Lancashire-born men.[54]

On 3 May 1789, James Irving senior set sail as captain of the *Anna*, a brand-new schooner of 50 tons burthen capable of carrying approximately eighty Africans. Although it was more usual for experienced captains to be given the command of newly constructed vessels,[55] the instructions Irving received to trade at forts on the Gold Coast may have been an attempt by the merchants to test out his skills in command in a less complex area of slave supply. Even so, the selection of trusted officers by the captain was vital. In addition to appointing his cousin as surgeon, Captain Irving recruited a number of English mariners with whom he had previously sailed on the *Jane* and *Princess Royal*. John Clegg, appointed as first mate, was a Manxman who had served as fourth mate on the voyage of the *Jane* to New Calabar in May 1786.[56]

Trade conducted at forts and in other areas where Europeans acted as intermediaries could still present considerable risks and difficulties. When Dalzel commanded the *Tartar* from Liverpool in 1785, the ship was subject to lengthy delays in West Africa and took 540 days to complete the journey. Even though Dalzel had specialist knowledge of trading at the Bight of Benin built up during a period as governor of the fort at Whydah, he was unable to expedite the efficient loading and departure of the vessel.[57] Neither could his experience as a surgeon's mate in the Royal Navy and as a surgeon at the Gold Coast fort of Anomabu prevent high losses among the Africans and crew. The mortality level among Africans was extremely high, accounting for 120 of 360 embarked (33.3 per cent), and crew mortality accounted for 15 of the 37 crew embarked (40.5 per cent) at the outset of the voyage.[58]

During Trotter's period on the *Brooks* in 1784, mortality levels were substantially lower than the *Tartar*, accounting for 23 of 619 (5.3 per cent) of the Africans embarked at Anomabu. In evidence given in May 1790, Trotter described how the Africans experienced 'extreme anguish' during the voyage, which was expressed through a 'howling melancholy kind of noise'. He was clearly at odds with the captain, Clement Noble, whom he accused of excessive cruelty towards the enslaved Africans

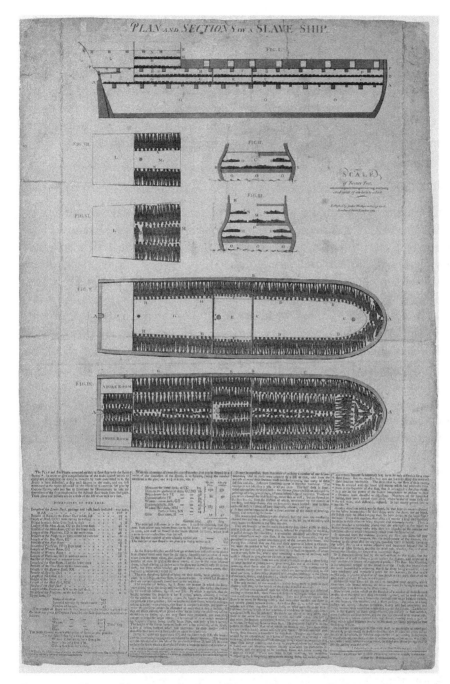

Figure 7.1 'Plan and Sections of a Slave Ship', 1789. Source: ZBA2745 © National Maritime Museum, Greenwich, London, Michael Graham-Stewart Collection

and crew.[59] Scottish involvement in this voyage was also reflected in the profile of investors, as James Carruthers was listed as one of six owners. Carruthers's career as a captain on eight slaving voyages and as an investor in up to forty-three ventures suggests that he was unlikely to have had any sympathy for Trotter's humanitarian concerns.[60] Three years after Carruthers's death in 1786, the publication of the image of the *Brooks* (Figure 7.1) captured the public imagination as a symbol of the horrors experienced by Africans in the Middle Passage.[61]

III

Currie did not have any first-hand experience of a voyage in the Middle Passage but, in common with other abolitionists, used the Atlantic crossing as a site of imagination to explore the reactions of Africans to their violent separation from home and family. After a night spent among friends from the Roscoe Circle in Liverpool in 1788, Currie explained how he imagined 'a negro in the hold of a ship, in chains, his companions sleeping around him, awake in the middle of the night, & bursting into a soliloquy on his wretched condition . . .'[62] Published as 'The African', this sentimental poem co-authored with Roscoe focused on the plight of Maraton, who had been torn away from 'the groves of Angola'. The poem, originally named 'The Negroes Complaint', lamented the 'wild anguish' of Africans 'from country and liberty torn'. Although Currie considered that he was 'intitled to one half of the merit' for the poem, he was anxious to remain anonymous due to the hostility it might engender in Liverpool, where he had practised as a physician at Liverpool Infirmary since 1786.[63] He explained to his friend Lieutenant Graham Moore that if it was known that he had written the poem 'our polite negro-dealers' would consider it 'an unpardonable offence'.[64] In order to retain his anonymity, Currie asked Moore to arrange for the poem's publication in 'the Morning Herald, Post, or the World, as you judge best'. Moore was to submit it in his 'own hand' as a way of disguising Currie's authorship.[65] Currie was also the anonymous author of the preface to Roscoe's poem on *The Wrongs of Africa*, in which he condemned 'this traffic in the human species, which is so direct and daring an infringement of every principle of liberty and justice . . .' In a letter to his uncle, Rev. George Duncan of Dumfries, Currie asked him to re-read the preface to the poem as 'I wrote it'. He cautioned his uncle that his authorship 'must not be known, for it would play the duce with me here'.[66]

Currie was aware that Dalzel had written in defence of the trade using the pen name 'Vindex' in the Liverpool press, but he considered

Figure 7.2 James Currie, MD FRS, aged thirty-five. 'Taken from an Original Picture by Williamson in 1791 in the Possession of William Roscoe, Esq.', October 1830. Source: PAD3092 © National Maritime Museum, Greenwich, London

that Dalzel's manuscript had been altered by 'several slave-Merchants here'.[67] In an article published in *Williamson's Liverpool Advertiser* on 14 January 1788, Dalzel defended the trade from what he regarded as false assertions in articles published in the name of 'Africanus' and 'Philo-Africanus'. Presenting arguments that would become standard elements in the defence of the trade in parliamentary debate later the same year, Dalzel argued that slave ships incorporated 'well adapted contrivances for the commodious reception of the negroes'. He emphasised how observers would 'be pleased to see with what attention and tenderness the slaves are treated, and how conveniently they are lodged'. In his defence of surgeons, Dalzel argued that 'I know no description of men more attentive to their duty, which is very fatiguing during the middle passage'.[68]

Currie considered that the arguments Dalzel presented were 'more fatal to the cause it proposes to support than almost any thing that has appeared'.[69] Even so, the local attention generated by these letters may have influenced Dalzel's selection by Liverpool Corporation as a witness in defence of the trade, particularly as he had first-hand knowledge of trading on the African coast.[70] As one of the 'Liverpool delegates' sent to London to represent the town's interests in 1788, Dalzel reiterated a number of the arguments in his 'Vindex' articles. According to Thomas Clarkson, Dalzel's testimony was completely undermined when he was challenged on the record of mortality among crew and slaves on the *Tartar*:

> this champion of the merchants, this advocate for the health and happiness of the slaves in the middle passage, lost nearly a hundred and sixty of the unhappy persons committed to his superior care, in a single voyage![71]

Dalzel's interest in defending the trade was also reflected in his *History of Dahomy*, published in 1793, in which he argued that Africans transported in the slave trade were saved from a worse fate of savagery in Africa.[72] The list of subscribers indicates that the book was supported by the upper ranks of Liverpool's slave merchants, including Moses Benson, John Bolton, John Dawson, William and Thomas Earle, Thomas Leyland and John Tarleton. Of the leading 201 slave merchants in Liverpool in the period 1750–1807, thirty subscribed to Dalzel's book.[73] John and Alexander Anderson, London merchants who inherited the slave fort at Bance Island in the Sierra Leone estuary from their uncle Richard Oswald, were also listed.[74] Not all subscribers were defenders of the slave trade. Currie's support for the book reflected his wider interests in Africa, as well as his personal contacts with Dalzel.[75]

In correspondence with Dr Percival he had noted how Dalzel was a 'gentle moderate man & of a good understanding'.[76]

Currie's antipathy towards the slave trade predated his appointment as an examiner for slave trade surgeons at Liverpool Infirmary and, together with the financial remuneration offered, may have influenced his decision to accept this regulatory role. From 18 August 1789, the date of his first examination, Currie was brought into regular contact with Scottish surgeons applying for certification.[77] By the time James Irving junior presented himself for examination, Currie had three years' experience in this role. Discharged two months earlier from the *Ellen* on 14 February 1792, Irving had served as surgeon on the vessel.[78] However, he did not have his own surgeon's certificate but relied instead on the fact that his older cousin sailing as captain carried evidence of his qualification from the Company of Surgeons.[79] This may have been technically permissible, as the legislation stipulated that slave ships should have 'one Surgeon at least engaged' who could produce evidence of having passed the relevant examination.[80] As the captain had died during the voyage of the *Ellen* on 24 December 1791, the younger Irving could not sail again as surgeon without first obtaining his own qualification.

By this stage, Irving junior had served as surgeon's mate on board the *Princess Royal* and as surgeon on two vessels commanded by his older cousin. Although his track record was not impressive, he must have demonstrated sufficient knowledge of tropical diseases and their treatment to convince the board that he was competent.[81] The experience gained in his first venture as surgeon's mate on the *Princess Royal* in 1788 may have been sufficient to convince the panel, as he had experience of dealing with over seven hundred Africans during the voyage. His performance on the *Ellen* in 1791 was less impressive, as 47 of 253 Africans embarked did not survive the Middle Passage (19 per cent). During the voyage of the *Anna* he had no opportunity to gain any medical experience as the vessel was wrecked on the Atlantic coast of Morocco on 27 May 1789. The eleven-man crew, which included the nephew of John Dawson, was held captive at various locations before a ransom for their release was agreed by consular officials at Tangier and Essaouira.

On his return to England in November 1790, James Irving junior wrote a 'very short account' of his experiences in captivity which was added at the end of a longer journal written by his older cousin. His account indicates that he was purchased by Mawlay Abd. Al-Rahman, the exiled son of the Sultan, and held in the remote southern Saharan

provinces of Morocco. In common with his older cousin, he characterised his captors as 'barbarians' and stated defiantly that he preferred
death to slavery 'amongst unfeeling moors who would spit in my face,
and call me an infidel or unbeliever when I spoke'.[82]

The temporary loss of his own freedom certainly did not lead the
younger Irving to change his outlook on the slave trade. Within two
months of returning to Liverpool he embarked on the *Ellen* in January
1791 and calculated the profits that could accrue from the sale of
Africans. He informed his 'Honoured Parents' in Langholm that 'if we
only bury 6 slaves my Couzin will receive £100 and I £50 Bounty. If
we bury not more than 9 slaves my Couzen will receive £50 and I £25
bounty.'[83] He was well aware of the terms of the Dolben Act, which
introduced bonuses for the captain and surgeon if mortality levels were
kept below 3 per cent. This may well have been the type of attitude that
Currie had in mind when he referred to how the slave trade led men
to sacrifice 'the principles of justice and the feelings of humanity to the
acquirement of wealth'.[84]

IV

The attitudes of these five Scottish surgeons were split across different sides of the debate on the morality of the Atlantic slave trade and
reflected wider fissures in national opinion. The pro-slavery views of
Archibald Dalzel, Captain Irving and James Irving junior mirrored the
general outlook in late eighteenth-century Liverpool. The extent to
which the views of the wider Scottish migrant population in Liverpool
were aligned with the economic interests of the port or reflected new
Enlightenment attitudes from north of the Border is difficult to assess.[85]
This would have been influenced in significant measure by the extent
to which individuals' business interests were intertwined with the
slave trade either directly through investment in voyages, or indirectly
through the supply of trade goods. A number of Scottish merchants in
Liverpool, including Edgar Corrie, had no direct involvement in the
slave trade.[86]

Differences in outlook on the slave trade in Liverpool were expressed
in pamphlet literature, poetry, newspaper articles and in parliamentary
debate. Conversations between people with opposing views on the trade
may well have taken place after service at Benn's Garden Presbyterian
Chapel and other places of worship attended by Scots.[87] In a letter to
Moore on 23 March 1788, Currie described how 'the general discussion of the slavery of the negroes has produced much unhappiness in

Liverpool – Men are awaking to their situation, & the struggle between interest and humanity, has made great havock in the happiness of many families . . .'[88]

Thomas Trotter, in common with John Newton and Alexander Falconbridge, was regarded as a valuable source of propaganda by abolitionists as he had first-hand knowledge of the trade which could be used to counter the evidence presented by Dalzel and other Liverpool delegates.[89] Trotter's public renunciation of the trade was not typical of other Scottish slave traders in Liverpool; a more typical mindset is reflected in the private correspondence of James Irving senior. Although he wrote to his wife from Tobago in December 1786 complaining that he was 'nearly Wearied of this Unnatural Accursed trade', this phrase did not reflect any incipient abolitionist sentiment as it was followed swiftly by a bitter complaint that 'our Black Cattle are intolerably Noisy and I'm almost Melted in the Midst of five or six Hundred of them'. An earlier reference in the same letter to how they had 'not yet disposed of any of our very disagreeable Cargo' also confirms Irving's dehumanisation of the enslaved Africans.[90]

The opposing views of Currie and Dalzel were incorporated within the 'literary memorial' of abolition published by Thomas Clarkson in 1808.[91] In view of the hostile and highly charged atmosphere in Liverpool, Clarkson considered that Currie was one of three individuals who merited recognition for their 'early' work 'as labourers' in advancing the abolitionist cause.[92] Clarkson also included Currie's name on his schematic map of abolition; he was not the only Scot listed on this imaginary map of rivers and streams, but his opposition to the trade in such close proximity to slave traders was a factor that impressed Clarkson.[93] Dalzel, in contrast, was used by Clarkson as a means of laying bare the feeble arguments presented in defence of the trade by the Liverpool delegates. It is clear that migrant Scots not only formed a sizeable portion of the skilled labour force in the slave trade in Liverpool, but some individuals also emerged as influential protagonists in the debate on the rights and wrongs of slavery in the 'pre-eminent slaving port of the North Atlantic world'.[94]

NOTES

1. An earlier version of this paper was presented as a keynote address at the conference 'Africa in Scotland, Scotland in Africa', University of Edinburgh, 30 April 2009. I would like to thank Stephen Behrendt, Robin Law, David Pope and David Richardson for their helpful comments and advice. I would

also like to thank Stephen Behrendt for his generosity in providing information from his database on surgeons in the slave trade.

2. Liverpool Record Office [hereafter LivRO], 614 INF 9/1, List of African Surgeons 1789–1807. Accounts & Minutes of the Medical Board of the Liverpool Royal Infirmary 1807–1826, p. 5. The Dolben Act placed restrictions on the number of enslaved Africans who could be carried in relation to the tonnage of ships. The legislation also stipulated that slave ships had to carry a surgeon who had passed an examination at Surgeons' Hall in London. The right to conduct these examinations was extended in 1789 to the Royal College of Surgeons of Edinburgh, as well as to a number of county and public hospitals including Liverpool Infirmary. Stephen D. Behrendt, 'The British Slave Trade, 1785–1807: Volume, Profitability, and Mortality', PhD, University of Wisconsin-Madison, 1993, pp. 175–8; Richard B. Sheridan, *Doctors and Slaves. A Medical and Demographic History of Slavery in the British West Indies, 1680–1834* (Cambridge: Cambridge University Press, 1985), pp. 120–1.

3. Margaret DeLacy, 'Currie, James (1756–1805)', *Oxford Dictionary of National Biography*, Oxford University Press, 2004, http://www. oxforddnb.com/view/article/6954 (accessed 19 August 2014).

4. See below, p. 158.

5. The older cousin and later slave ship captain was born on 15 December 1759. Dumfries Archive Centre [hereafter DAC], MF 67, Langholm Parish Registers, 1668–1854. James Irving junior was born in the early 1770s. A gravestone in Langholm old churchyard dedicated to the 'memory of Janetus Irving, Baker, who died on 8th April 1815, aged 74' and 'Helen Little his spouse who died 17th August 1797 aged 60' refers to 'James their son, surgeon, who died at Lagus in Africa 22nd June 1793, aged 21'.

6. I. A. Akinjogbin, 'Archibald Dalzel: Slave Trader and Historian of Dahomey', *The Journal of African History*, 7, 1 (1966), pp. 67–70, 73–8; James A. Rawley, 'Dalzel, Archibald (1740–1818)', *Oxford Dictionary of National Biography,* Oxford University Press, 2004, online edition, January 2009, http://www.oxforddnb.com/view/article/47570 (accessed 19 August 2014); James A. Rawley, 'Further Light on Archibald Dalzel', *International Journal of African Historical Studies,* 17, 2 (1984), pp. 317–18, 320–1. Dalzel is listed as the captain of five slave ships between 1775 and 1789; David Eltis et al., *Voyages: The Transatlantic Slave Trade Database*, www. slavevoyages.org, *Hannah,* voyage 75602, *Europa,* voyage 81323, *Gosport & Havre Packet*, voyage 81632, *Saint Ann,* voyage 83454, *Tartar,* voyage 83725. Archibald Dalzel was also an investor in three slaving vessels which sailed from Liverpool between April and November 1804: *Dart,* voyage 80964, *Hope,* voyage 81866, *President Ince,* voyage 83172.

7. LivRO, 920 CUR 111, Dr James Currie to Dr Thomas Percival, 16 January 1788.

8. Cited in Akinjogbin, 'Archibald Dalzel', p. 69.

9. Christopher Fyfe (ed.), *Anna Maria Falconbridge: Narrative of Two Voyages to the River Sierra Leone During the Years 1791–1792–1793 with Alexander Falconbridge An Account of the Slave Trade on the Coast of Africa* (Liverpool: Liverpool University Press, 2000), p. 193; Sheridan, *Doctors and Slaves*, pp. 111–13.

10. J. Wallace, 'Thomas Trotter (bap. 1760, d. 1832)', *Oxford Dictionary of National Biography*, Oxford University Press, 2004, http://www.oxforddnb.com/view/article/27763 (accessed 19 August 2014).

11. Sheila Lambert (ed.), *House of Commons Sessional Papers of the Eighteenth Century* (Wilmington, DE: Scholarly Resources, 1975), vol. 73, pp. 86–97, 109–10, 118.

12. Behrendt, 'British Slave Trade', pp. 186–8.

13. Stephen D. Behrendt, 'The Captains in the British Slave Trade from 1785 to 1807', *Transactions of the Historic Society of Lancashire and Cheshire*, 140 (1991), pp. 94, 111–15.

14. Eltis et al., *Transatlantic Slave Trade Database*, *Tiger*, voyage 26303, *Juba*, voyage 26097, *Coats*, voyage 26098.

15. Mark Duffill, 'The Africa Trade from the Ports of Scotland, 1706–66', *Slavery and Abolition*, 25, 3 (December 2004), pp. 102–8; T. M. Devine, 'Did Slavery make Scotia great?', *Britain and the World*, 4, 1 (2011), pp. 42–5.

16. George A. Shepperson, 'Introduction', *Scotland and Africa* (Hawick: HMSO, 1982).

17. Devine, 'Did Slavery make Scotia great?', pp. 44–5; Eric Graham, 'Abolitionists and Apologists: Scotland's Slave Trade Stories', *NLS*, 6 (2007), pp. 20–2.

18. Duffill, 'Africa Trade', pp. 104, 107; Devine, 'Did Slavery make Scotia great?', pp. 44–5; David Hancock, 'Scots in the Slave Trade', in Ned C. Landsman (ed.), *Nation and Province in the First British Empire: Scotland and the Americas, 1600–1800* (Lewisburg: Bucknell University Press, 2001), pp. 62–3; Mark Duffill and Eric Graham, 'Scots in the Liverpool Slave Trade, 1789–1805. Robert Hume of Jedburgh Surgeon and Master', *History Scotland*, 8, 2 (March/April 2008), pp. 30, 33.

19. David Richardson, Keynote Address, 'Transatlantic Triangles: Retracing Connections between Europe, Africa, and the Americas in the Age of the Slave Trade', Conference on 'History and Public Memorialization of Slavery and the Slave Trade: Liverpool–Nantes', National Museums Liverpool, 2 July 2014.

20. Seymour Drescher, 'The Slaving Capital of the World: Liverpool and National Opinion in the Age of Abolition', *Slavery and Abolition*, 9, 2 (1988), pp. 128–43; F. E. Sanderson, 'The Liverpool Delegates and Sir William Dolben's Bill', *Transactions of the Historic Society of Lancashire and Cheshire*, 124, 1972, p. 58.

21. DeLacy, 'Currie, James'.

22. Devine, 'Did Slavery make Scotia great?', pp. 63–4; Iain Whyte, *Scotland and the Abolition of Black Slavery, 1756–1838* (Edinburgh: Edinburgh University Press, 2006), pp. 5–6; Hancock, 'Scots in the Slave Trade', pp. 61–3.
23. Rawley, 'Dalzel, Archibald'; Sanderson, 'Liverpool Delegates', pp. 64, 67.
24. Drescher, 'Slaving Capital', pp. 128–9.
25. Suzanne Schwarz (ed.), *Slave Captain. The Career of James Irving in the Liverpool Slave Trade,* 2nd edn (Liverpool: Liverpool University Press, 2008), pp. 38–69.
26. Stephen D. Behrendt, 'Human Capital in the British Slave Trade', in David Richardson, Suzanne Schwarz and Anthony Tibbles (eds), *Liverpool and Transatlantic Slavery* (Liverpool: Liverpool University Press, 2007), pp. 75–82, 88.
27. Behrendt, 'Captains', pp. 87, 89, 129.
28. Behrendt, 'British Slave Trade', p. 177.
29. I am grateful to T. M. Devine for this information. T. M. Devine, *Scotland's Empire, 1600–1815* (London: Penguin, Allen Lane 2003), pp. 234–5; Cairns Craig, 'Empire of Intellect: The Scottish Enlightenment and Scotland's Intellectual Migrants', in John M. Mackenzie and T. M. Devine (eds), *Scotland and the British Empire* (Oxford: Oxford University Press, 2011), pp. 86, 96–7.
30. Stephen D. Behrendt, Database of surgeons in the slave trade in the late eighteenth and early nineteenth centuries. Biographical information on Liverpool slaving surgeons will appear in www.liverpoolmaritime. org.
31. David Pope, 'The Wealth and Social Aspirations of Liverpool's Slave Merchants of the Second Half of the Eighteenth Century', in Richardson et al., *Liverpool and Transatlantic Slavery*, Appendix 1, pp. 194–207.
32. Other examples include William Clark of Dumfries who was entered on board the *Alexander* on 23 October 1798, and William Dunlop of Dumfries who was entered on the *Eliza* on 22 July 1790. William Hutson [Hotson] of Dumfries was entered on the *Vulture* on 10 September 1791. William Kirk of Dumfries was entered on the *Elizabeth* on 19 April 1807 and Alexander Wilson of Dumfries was entered on the *Bridget* on 20 August 1798. John Alexander from Closeburn was entered on the *Henry* on 18 June 1803 and John Dickson of Dumfries was entered on the *Sally* on 15 September 1804. John Duff of Keir, Dumfries was entered on board the *Earl of Liverpool* on 15 August 1803 and died on 28 February 1804. Thomas Kirkpatrick was entered on board the *Bolton* on 12 November 1798, and another individual of the same name served as surgeon on the *Polly* of Liverpool from 6 July 1804. Adam Murphy was entered as surgeon on the *Princess Royal* in January 1805 and died in September 1805. James Wallace of Dumfries was entered on the *Admiral Nelson* on 23 January 1805. He died six months later on the homeward passage. Robert Wallace from Dumfries

and Galloway was entered on board the *King George* in May 1802 and died in January 1803. This information is based on Stephen D. Behrendt, Database of surgeons.

33. Behrendt, Database of surgeons.

34. Eltis et al., *Transatlantic Slave Trade Database,* voyage 82203; Hugh Crow, *Memoirs of the Late Captain Hugh Crow of Liverpool* (London: Frank Cass, 1970 [1830]), pp. 149, 157.

35. LivRO, 614 INF 9/1, List of African Surgeons 1789–1807, pp. 1, 3, 14, 18, 24, 33.

36. Paul E. Lovejoy and David Richardson, 'African Agency and the Liverpool Slave Trade', in Richardson et al., *Liverpool and Transatlantic Slavery,* pp. 42–3.

37. Eltis et al., *Transatlantic Slave Trade Database,* voyage 83976.

38. DAC, RS 22/5, Register of Sasines, 1781–1820, number 2551, Contract of Feu, 1784.

39. The National Archives [hereafter TNA], FO 52/9, Morocco Series, Various, 1772–1792, Captain James Irving at 'Telling' to John Hutchison, Vice-Consul at Mogador [Essaouira] in Morocco, 24 June 1789, ff. 115–16. Transcript in Schwarz, *Slave Captain,* pp. 92–3.

40. Behrendt, 'Human Capital', pp. 68–70, 74, 85.

41. Lancashire Record Office [hereafter LRO], DDX 1126/1/34, James Irving on board the *Princess Royal* to Mary Irving in Liverpool, transcript in Schwarz, *Slave Captain,* p. 90; Eltis et al., *Transatlantic Slave Trade Database,* voyage 83240.

42. Eltis et al., *Transatlantic Slave Trade Database,* voyage 83239; Lovejoy and Richardson, 'African Agency', Table 2.4, p. 58.

43. Behrendt, 'Human Capital', pp. 68–9.

44. Lovejoy and Richardson, 'African Agency', pp. 49, 60–1.

45. Duffill and Graham, 'Scots in the Liverpool Slave Trade', p. 34. Samuel McDowal invested in thirty-seven slaving voyages between 1795 and 1807. Information supplied in email correspondence by David Pope, January 2015.

46. Behrendt, 'Captains', pp. 104–5.

47. This information on the number of voyages has been supplied by David Pope in email correspondence, January 2015. Pope, 'Wealth and Social Aspirations', Appendix I, pp. 194–207.

48. Eltis et al., *Transatlantic Slave Trade Database,* voyages 82167 and 82168.

49. Behrendt, 'British Slave Trade', p. 177.

50. Behrendt, 'Captains', pp. 97–8.

51. Behrendt, 'Captains', pp. 97–100, 111, 128.

52. Eric J. Graham and Mark Duffill, '"An Intelligent Negro". Thomas Jenkins: Scotland's First Black Educator and Foreign Missionary', *History Scotland,* 7, 4 (2007), pp. 36–9; Graham and Duffill, 'Scots in the Liverpool Slave Trade', p. 32.

53. LRO, DDX 1126/1/29. Christopher Robson to Dr William Graham, 22 September 1790. Transcript in Schwarz, *Slave Captain*, pp. 115–16.
54. Eltis et al., *Transatlantic Slave Trade Database*, voyage 83151; Pope, 'Wealth and Social Aspirations', Appendix 1, pp. 194–207.
55. Behrendt, 'Captains', p. 101.
56. TNA, BT 98/47, Muster Roll of the *Jane*, 27 February 1787.
57. Rawley, 'Further Light', pp. 317–18; Sanderson, 'Liverpool Delegates', p. 65.
58. The *Tartar* sailed from Liverpool on 8 September 1785 and returned on 29 June 1787. Eltis et al., *Transatlantic Slave Trade Database,* voyage 83725; Rawley, 'Further Light', p. 321.
59. Lambert, *House of Commons Sessional Papers*, vol. 73, pp. 86–101.
60. The other investors were Clement Noble, Thomas Staniforth, Joseph Brooks junior, Francis Ingram and William Denison. Eltis et al., *Transatlantic Slave Trade Database*, voyages 80664, 90402, 90403, 90503, 90651, 90693, 90704, 90705, 91114; Pope, 'Wealth and Social Aspirations', Appendix I, pp. 194–207.
61. Marcus Wood, *Blind Memory. Visual Representations of Slavery in England and America 1780–1865* (Manchester: Manchester University Press, 2000), pp. 14–19.
62. LivRO, 920 CUR 108, Dr James Currie to Lieutenant Graham Moore, 23 March 1788.
63. DeLacy, 'Currie, James'. The issue of anonymity in the Roscoe Circle is discussed by Florence Baggett, 'The Slaving Capital in the Era of Abolition: Liverpool's Silent Rejection of the Slave Trade, 1787–1807', MA dissertation, Victoria University of Wellington, 2013, pp. 48–52.
64. LivRO, 920 CUR 108, Currie to Moore, 23 March 1788.
65. LivRO, 920 CUR 106, Dr James Currie to Lieutenant Graham Moore, 16 March 1788.
66. LivRO, 920 CUR 110, James Currie to Rev. George Duncan, 5 July 1788.
67. LivRO, 920 CUR 111, Dr James Currie to Dr Thomas Percival, 16 January 1788.
68. *Williamson's Liverpool Advertiser*, 14 January 1788.
69. LivRO, 920 CUR 111, Currie to Percival, 16 January 1788.
70. Sanderson, 'Liverpool Delegates', p. 63; Rawley, 'Further Light', pp. 317–23.
71. Thomas Clarkson, *The History of the Rise, Progress, and Accomplishment of the Abolition of the African Slave-Trade by the British Parliament,* vol. I (London: Longman, Hurst, Rees & Orme, 1808), pp. 542–3, 546; Sanderson, 'Liverpool Delegates', p. 71.
72. Rawley, 'Dalzel, Archibald'; Philip D. Curtin, *The Image of Africa. British Ideas and Action, 1780–1850* (London: Macmillan, 1965), p. 24.
73. Pope, 'Wealth and Social Aspirations', Appendix I, pp. 194–207.
74. Christopher Fyfe, *A History of Sierra Leone* (London: Oxford University Press, 1962), p. 7; Behrendt, 'Human Capital', p. 85.

75. Archibald Dalzel, *The History of Dahomy, An Inland Kingdom of Africa; Compiled from Authentic Memoirs* (London: Printed by T. Spilsbury, sold by J. Evans, 1793), pp. xxvii–xxxi.
76. LivRO, 920 CUR 111, Currie to Percival, 16 January 1788.
77. LivRO, 614 INF 9/1, List of African Surgeons 1789–1807, p. 1.
78. TNA, BT 98/52, Muster Roll of the *Ellen*, 31 July 1792.
79. Five months before taking command of the *Ellen*, Captain Irving explained his concern about the 'loss of my Certificate as a Surgeon, which it will be necessary (let whatever may happen) to get renewed'. LRO, DDX 1126/1/28, James Irving at Mogador to Mary Irving, 9 August 1790, transcript in Schwarz, *Slave Captain*, pp. 114–15.
80. LivRO, 614 INF 9/1, List of African Surgeons 1789–1807, unnumbered page.
81. LivRO, 614 INF 9/1, List of African Surgeons 1789–1807; Behrendt, 'British Slave Trade', p. 178.
82. Beinecke Rare Book and Manuscript Library, Yale University, Osborn Shelves c. 399, 'A Narrative of the Shipwreck of the *Ann,* Captain Irving'. Transcript in Schwarz, *Slave Captain*, p. 151.
83. James Irving junior to his parents in Langholm, 2 January 1791. Letter in private ownership. Transcript in Schwarz, *Slave Captain,* pp. 119–20.
84. William Roscoe, *The Wrongs of Africa, Part the First* (London: R. Faulder, 1787), http://www.brycchancarey.com/slavery/roscoe1.htm (accessed 27 April 2009).
85. Devine, 'Did Slavery make Scotia great?', pp. 63–4.
86. F. E. Sanderson, 'The Liverpool Abolitionists', in Roger Anstey and P. E. H. Hair (eds), *Liverpool, the African Slave Trade, and Abolition* (Liverpool: Historic Society of Lancashire and Cheshire Occasional Series, vol. 2, 1989), pp. 215–16.
87. Richard Brooke, *Liverpool as it Was* (Liverpool: Liverpool Libraries and Information Services, 2003 [1853]), p. 405.
88. LivRO, 920 CUR 108, Currie to Moore, 23 March 1788.
89. Sanderson, 'Liverpool Delegates', pp. 66–9.
90. LRO, DDX 1126/1/6, James Irving to Mary Irving, 2 December 1786. Transcript in Schwarz, *Slave Captain*, pp. 85–7.
91. J. R. Oldfield, *'Chords of Freedom'. Commemoration, Ritual and British Transatlantic Slavery* (Manchester: Manchester University Press, 2007), pp. 32–55.
92. Clarkson, *History*, pp. 542–3. Contemporary commentators showed an awareness of who was included on the map, as William Rathbone III referred to the exclusion of Hugh Mulligan. Baggett, 'The Slaving Capital in the Era of Abolition', p. 16.
93. Wood, *Blind Memory*, pp. 1–6.
94. Drescher, 'Slaving Capital', p. 129.

8

Scotland and Colonial Slave Ownership: The Evidence of the Slave Compensation Records

Nicholas Draper

THIS VOLUME AS A whole and many of the individual chapters within it explore the importance of slavery to Scotland. This chapter, by contrast, primarily addresses the importance of Scotland to slavery. It is based on work undertaken by the *Legacies of British Slave-ownership* (LBS) project at University College London which allows us, for the first time, to locate Scotland within the totality of slave ownership in the United Kingdom and hence to gauge the relative importance of Scotland within overall British and Irish colonial slave ownership *at the end of slavery*.[1] This last is an important qualification that readers need to bear in mind in assessing the evidence presented here, which reflects the end-position of slave ownership in the early decades of the nineteenth century and does not include analysis of the ownership patterns in the preceding two centuries of British colonial slavery.[2] Nevertheless, the work of LBS to date both provides an overall context in which to place consideration of Scotland's role in colonial slavery and establishes an empirical framework for a synchronic comparative 'four-nations' approach to British and Irish colonial slave ownership.[3]

The title of our project, *Legacies of **British** Slave-ownership*, was consciously chosen. The team comprised historians of England, steeped in English economic, social, cultural and political history and not equipped to do the same type of work in analysing national and local elites in Scotland (or Ireland or Wales) as we have done for England. But the single metropolitan archive at The National Archives in Kew which was the foundation of our work captured the universe of slave owners across all four nations (and indeed across the Caribbean), and we adopted the same practices of recording, classification and digitisation for the records of all slave owners resident in Britain and Ireland. As a result, we have accumulated, organised and published data from the four nations which we believe is of considerable value to those who can use it better than we can ourselves. We fully recognise that the connections between Scotland and slavery have been and continue to be the subject of active work based on archives in Scotland and the Caribbean.[4] This volume is testimony to the vibrancy of that work. Our own research represents a resource that can potentially contribute to the wider project of reassessing Scotland and empire, and in turn we will benefit from the knowledge and material of scholars versed in Scotland's wider history. Scotland's history in relation to slavery is its own subject, but placing it in the context of the equivalent histories of England, Ireland and Wales illuminates both it and them. Together we can contribute to an improved understanding of the importance of slave ownership to the historic United Kingdom as a whole.

For, among other things, the *Legacies of British Slave-ownership* project provides one lens for looking at the importance or otherwise of wealth from slavery to Britain's commercial and industrial transformation of the eighteenth and nineteenth centuries.[5] We understand that slave **ownership** is only one of the ways that slavery contributed to the United Kingdom's wealth. We do not claim that our work addresses the systemic effects of increased demand for manufactures, of lower raw material costs, or of institutional innovation in credit and commerce. We believe instead that in two ways it supplements the work of others. First, by identifying the slave owners it allows scrutiny of the ways in which individually and collectively they operated as transmitters of slavery into the metropole through their redeployment of slave-derived wealth (and the concomitant status) at the imperial centre(s). Secondly, while much of the work on slavery's impact on Britain has treated the nineteenth century as an addendum to a story fundamentally over by the close of the eighteenth century, we are challenging that periodisation by drawing attention to flows of wealth, reinvestment in Britain and the role of slave owners and former slave owners in institutional change for up to a half-century after the end of slavery itself.[6]

THE SLAVE COMPENSATION RECORDS

The 'slave compensation' which is the basis of our work was part of the wider package negotiated between the British Government, representatives of the slave owners and parliamentary leaders of the abolitionist movement in the spring and early summer of 1833 and then enshrined in the 1833 Abolition Act.[7] The Act provided for £20 million in monetary compensation to the slave owners, interest on that compensation from 1

August 1834 (the effective date of the Act), and a period of 'apprentice-ship', four to six years of further enforced labour of 45 hours per week by the formerly enslaved for their former owners. The emancipated people themselves received nothing. New social relations of production were forged in the Caribbean in a very short period of time, with the former agrarian workforce of enslaved people withdrawing from the estates into subsistence agriculture where it was possible for them to secure access to land, and otherwise remoulding into a waged labour force.

For the slave owners, £20 million represented just over 40 per cent of the deemed value of the 800,000 people in a condition of chattel slavery in the British colonies to which the Act applied. The enslaved people themselves paid another part of the bill through the labour extracted in the Apprenticeship period, valued at between a further one-third and one-half of their value in slavery.[8] In total, therefore, the slave owners received somewhere between three-quarters and just over 90 per cent of the value of their 'property', and hence contributed the least to the bill for compensation among the parties who paid (the British taxpayer, largely through consumption taxes to service the debt of the British state; the enslaved people; and the slave owners). For slave owners in Jamaica, abolition gave the chance to take money off the table; but for slave owners in frontier territories like British Guiana, emancipation disrupted a very profitable system. The differential allocation of compensation, £25 on average per enslaved person in Jamaica versus £50 in British Guiana, was intended to reflect these structural differences in profitability.

The compensation was spread among more than 45,000 individual awards, not just to owners, but to mortgagees, legatees and annuitants, all those with a claim secured either on enslaved people directly or more commonly on an estate and the enslaved population upon it as a unit. The distribution of compensation was an extraordinary bureau-cratic achievement by the fledgling pre-Victorian state. A central body in London, the Commissioners of Slave Compensation, with a small staff, arbitrated almost all the awards in fewer than four years, at a time when a letter took six weeks to reach Jamaica and the reply another six weeks to reach London, and when suits in Chancery could last fifty years.

Initially, even the distribution of basic information beyond London was problematic. The agent in the Gazette Office in Edinburgh wrote in April 1834 on publication of the Commission's Rules to point out that he had been subject to repeated applications for information concerning compensation, 'and as that is to be found in the *London Gazette* alone, one copy of which is filed at this office and not more than five in Scotland besides', he had on his own initiative 'in order to the better dissemination of a matter so important to the community of Scotland', printed it in the *Edinburgh Gazette*, for which he sought payment equivalent to the *London Gazette*, 'our charges being similar'. The Commissioners (who refused to pay the agent of the *Edinburgh Gazette*) eventually drew on designated merchant firms in Glasgow, Bristol, Dublin and Liverpool to republish notices in the local newspapers for the benefit of the communities of interested parties in and around each city.[9]

The process of administering the compensation spanned colony and metropole: claimants had to file in colonies but arbitration and payment of awards was in London. All claims had to be made by individuals, not by legal bodies. Successful claimants were obliged to collect their awards from the National Debt Office either in person or by appointed attorney. The filing of claims in the colonies posed comparable problems for Scots, Welsh, Irish and English claimants (especially the smaller-scale claimants), who required agents to act on their behalf in the Caribbean, while the London-centric mechanisms of payment represented a separate challenge for those living in Scotland, the English provinces, Wales, Ireland and the colonies themselves: again, the successful claimants were obliged to provide powers of attorney to intermediaries to collect the compensation (in the form of a Treasury warrant or for some colonies as Government stock) from the National Debt Office. So centralised a process imposed costs on the claimants, but benefited the historian in that the Commissioners left behind a meticulously compiled single set of records. The importance of these records lies not only in the compensation money itself – although that might individually and cumulatively be material – but also in their function as a screen to identify and define connections between individuals and the slave economy which certainly require more work to elaborate their significance but which in aggregate represent the totality of such connections at the end of slavery. Our start-point had been tracing the compensation money but our scope in following the slave owners beyond compensation became progressively wider.

We sought to make a distinction between 'rentier' and 'mercantile' claimants, the latter defined as those with a recognisable affiliation with a commercial firm or partnership, although we recognise that over a lifetime individuals passed from one of these categories to the other. The claimants and awardees of compensation included many people acting as executors and trustees, as well as owners and mortgagees, because 'slave-property', in common with other forms of property of the period, was gendered, and was often transmitted like landed property through the devices of entail and settlement as generations of men contested control of property (and control of women's access to property). Despite the legal and social subordination of female beneficiaries to males who were awarded the compensation on their behalf (especially in Britain and Ireland – the greater agency of women in the urban centres of the Caribbean is in marked contrast), women nevertheless represent some 40 per cent of the named awardees overall, a notably high proportion relative to other forms of property of the era.[10]

We have placed particular emphasis in identifying and researching the absentee slave owners as transmitters of slavery into British and Irish life, although we recognise the potential fluidity of 'absentee' as a category. Our allocation of British/Irish absentees among England, Scotland, Wales and Ireland has been determined by attributed addresses in the slave compensation records where such exist, supplemented by material drawn from the *London Gazette* and the *Edinburgh Gazette*, trade directories and secondary material. It has necessarily been a mechanical process of classification: did the individual have what appears to be a primary address in Scotland (or England, Wales or Ireland) in the mid-1830s?[11] Our methodology of course throws up a number of issues, and not just for the Scottish slave owners. We are freezing what were often patterns of sustained mobility in order to provide a snapshot as of the mid-1830s, the period of slave compensation. Even within the few years of the mid-decade, people moved, between colony and metropole, between Scotland and England, and between Scotland and other parts of the Empire. Edward Clouston, for example, who had been an attorney in Jamaica and a small-scale slave owner in his own right, returned to Scotland c. 1834 with his natural children, and married in Edinburgh in 1838 'late of Jamaica': we classify him as a British/Irish absentee with a primary address in Scotland. Moreover, we are simplifying not only such patterns of mobility but also still more complex problems of identity and allegiance. For example, the brothers William Maxwell Alexander and Boyd Alexander, the sons of Claud Alexander of Southbar (an East India Company servant), were in the 1830s living in London as partners in the West India merchant firm of the Hon. William Fraser, Alexander and Neilson, and in that capacity shared in the compensation for hundreds of enslaved people in St Vincent and Grenada: but the brothers were reabsorbed into Scotland in the 1840s. Boyd Alexander's grandson, Sir Claud Alexander 2nd Bt (d. 1947), again 'moved South' around 1900 according to his grandson in turn, Sir Claud Hagart Alexander (1927–2006), who once more reclaimed the family's Scottish identity as a campaigner for the Burns House Museum. Our categorisation treats the brothers in the 1830s as mercantile British/Irish absentees with a primary London address.

Above all, our focus on absentees introduces a 'survivor bias' into the picture of slave owners as a whole. First-generation absentees (those returning to the United Kingdom from the colonies) were by definition those who had physically survived and often (not invariably) those who had economically thrived; later generations of absentees typically held larger estates and larger numbers of enslaved people than did resident slave owners in the colonies; and there is some evidence from St Vincent that absentee slave owners were less indebted than resident slave owners.[12] Our analysis of the impact of slave ownership on metropolitan Britain is not affected by this bias, but it is clear that the absentees cannot stand as representative of the experience of slave owners as a whole, for many of whom life in the colonies was brutish, short and financially disastrous (although not as brutish and short as the lives of the enslaved Africans).

It is possible today to construct a mass prosopography of people in pre-Victorian Britain in a way which would not have been possible even twenty years ago.[13] Among the slave owners identified within the compensation records as resident in Britain, there are very few about whom we have been able to find nothing whatsoever. Critically, we have been able to identify the estate in almost every major award, despite struggles with variant spellings and transcriptions familiar to all historians of the period. Hence in general we can link compensation, estate and owner, and have made some sense of the 'path to ownership': how a specific absentee individual came to hold enslaved people at the time of compensation.

We have found the compensation money in the awards was paid to (1) around 42,000 residents in colonies and (2) some 3,500 absentees in metropolitan Britain. Absentees tended to own more of the larger units, estates with lots of enslaved people, so in total about half the enslaved people were owned by absentees. What our work shows is that between 5 and 10 per cent of British elites were close enough to the slave economy to appear in the compensation records, as owners, mortgagees, legatees, trustees or executors, the latter two categories often linked to the underlying beneficiaries by family ties. This 5 to 10 per cent figure is valid across a whole range of definitions of national elites: MPs, nobility and peers, baronets, county sheriffs.[14] In particular locations the 5 to 10 per cent national average goes up: slave owners were concentrated in a number of regions (the South-west of England, Liverpool and its hinterland, parts of London, the southern and south-eastern counties of England, and Scotland as a whole, which has been our unit of analysis for Scotland up to now) and thinly spread though present elsewhere

(Ireland, the North-east, the new industrial towns of the West Midlands, and the East Midlands).

Having identified the universe of absentee slave owners, we have sought to trace forward their legacies in Britain (and particularly in England) over the ensuing decades. By 'legacies', we mean the totality of the ways in which these slave owners transmitted slavery into metropolitan life. The legacies in which we have been interested are not simply the financial ones – the commercial legacies, the reinvestment of wealth from slavery in new opportunities such as railway shares – although those are important, but also the physical legacies (their building of country houses and their participation in urban development), their philanthropic activities, their cultural accumulation, their political legacies, their imperial legacies (through service or investment or settlement in other parts of the Empire) and their historical legacies, by which we mean how they shaped the memory of slavery through writing – whether poetry, fiction or non-fiction.

We have thus been focused primarily on **absentee** owners living in Britain. The published database includes **all** slave owners, whether resident or absentee, at the end of slavery by name and by details of their compensation awards: but we are developing detailed legacies only for the absentees. For Scotland, we have documented what we know for these absentee slave owners, but for the reasons given above we have not sought to speak to their legacies in the same way as for England. Our knowledge of Scotland's social and economic context is too limited. Nevertheless, the data we have made available should be of value to historians of Scotland.

We cannot conceivably exhaust ourselves of the possibilities of the material. We have made the raw data available in a structured form, as an online database, a perverse version perhaps of the *Oxford Dictionary of National Biography*, although freely accessible and intended to continue to grow through crowd-sourcing: there is an enormous volume of knowledge among local and family historians on specific families and individuals that we have already tapped and plan to tap further.

As noted above, we understand that our material cannot pretend to be a complete account of linkages to slavery. In particular, to reiterate, we are looking at slave **ownership**, not at the slave trade, nor at the systemic effects in the metropole of raw material production in the colonies, nor at dealing in tropical produce like sugar, cotton, indigo or mahogany, nor at the development of credit networks, nor at the supply of provisions to slave estates, linkages and multipliers highlighted for Scotland by Devine and others.[15] There are often overlaps of individuals between the metropolitan mercantile and financial sectors on the one hand and slave ownership in the colonies on the other; but the impacts of slave ownership and of the wider slave economy are different categories.

The second limitation, also already highlighted, is that we have to date been looking at the **end** of the slave system, in the 1830s. There are long continuities of ownership by absentee families, often spanning more than two centuries, and therefore our work on the slave owners of the 1830s tends to pick up many of the families who were owners in the eighteenth century and even earlier. But we do not capture people who were slave owners in the eighteenth century but who exited the slavery business well before Emancipation. The Fairholme family of Edinburgh, for example, who sought to rebuild their fortunes after the collapse of their eponymous Edinburgh bank by developing slave estates in Tobago, alongside many fellow-countrymen, left no traces in the slave compensation records: the estates and enslaved people must have been sold off after the death on Tobago of Thomas Fairholme in 1786 and of his widow in 1797.[16] Finally, and especially significantly in addressing the importance of slavery to Scotland given the commercial role of tobacco in Glasgow's history, we do not capture the slave economies of the American colonies for the period prior to 1783.

SCOTLAND IN THE SLAVE COMPENSATION RECORDS

It has recently become clearer that Scottish people were active players in the formation and maintenance of the slave economy in many colonies.[17] Our new material offers the opportunity to gauge the relative importance of absentee slave owners in Scotland, because it provides both a full census of such slave owners in Scotland at the end of slavery, and the context of comprehensive details of overall British and Irish slave owning at that time. However, because the database contains all slave owners who were awarded compensation for enslaved people held in the British colonies, it can therefore potentially illuminate all three concentric rings of 'Scottish' slave owners: not only (a) the slave owners resident in Scotland itself; but also (b) slave owners of the Scottish diaspora in Britain and Ireland; and (c) slave owners among the Scottish diaspora in the colonies themselves. In these latter two cases, the data is not systematically searchable in the way that the database can be mined for Scottish absentee slave owners, but relevant material is nevertheless embedded in the database and can be explored there. Our work also offers the possibility, however, for other approaches to gauging Scotland's weight within the colonial slave economy: for example, our recording of the names of more than four thousand estates across the Caribbean would allow systematic analysis of the naming practices of the estates, where Scottish place names proliferate.[18]

Slave owners in Scotland

Slave owners in Scotland ranged from owners of a single enslaved person, such as the minor Anna Archibald of Round Toll, Black Quarry, Glasgow, whose grandmother and guardian Eliza T. Thomas (herself the widow of a planter in Dominica) was awarded the compensation for Anna Archibald's single enslaved person in Trinidad,[19] to large-scale slave owners and mortgagees such as the partners in John Campbell senior or in J. T. & A. Douglas & Co., merchant powers of Glasgow, owning hundreds of enslaved people and receiving tens of thousands of pounds in compensation.[20] This diversity of slave owning, between small-scale owners and large-scale proprietors of estates, and the presence among the former of women, often widowed and dependent on the income from their slave property in the Caribbean, is consistent with the patterns we have found elsewhere in Britain and Ireland.

The extent, however, of absentee slave owning is markedly different for Scotland. Of 3,500 or so absentee slave owners identified in Britain and Ireland at the time of writing, we have identified addresses for two-thirds (2,400), of whom over 350 were individuals resident in Scotland in the compensation records, accounting for almost 1,000 awards out of 7,000 to absentees. Scotland thus had 15 per cent of the identified absentees, versus 10 per cent of the population (which was 26.8 million for the United Kingdom in 1841). By contrast, only some one hundred were individual Irish absentees, accounting for almost 170 awards out of the total of 7,000 awards associated with British and Irish absentees as a whole. Ireland was thus wildly under-represented among slave owners. This was a very different pattern from the one displayed by Scotland, whose population was one-third that of Ireland. On a per capita basis, therefore, there were proportionately many Scottish absentees and Scotland played a disproportionately large part in the story of British and Irish slave ownership.

This pattern could reflect four different dynamics, acting in isolation or in combination. It could reflect a higher proportional propensity for people to move from Scotland to the slave economy in the first place. It could reflect the higher propensity of Scottish people to move **back** to Scotland by the 1830s. It could reflect the higher propensity of slave owners in the colonies to bequeath slave property to legatees in Scotland.

And it could reflect the strength of a mercantile community in Scotland providing credit to the slave economy and becoming mortgagees, and/ or eventually owners, of enslaved people. We believe that of these four factors, the key drivers of the difference between Scotland and Ireland were most probably the first and the second.

A further step in the analysis is the distribution of absentee ownership by people in Scotland among the colonies of the Caribbean. Absentee ownership (whether English, Scottish, Irish or Welsh) per se was not evenly spread throughout the Caribbean. Overall, two-thirds of the awards over £500 were made to absentee owners, accounting for half the enslaved people (the other half were owned by a much more numerous class of resident slave owners, each of whom on average owned relatively few enslaved people). But the rate of absentee ownership ranged from 98 per cent of the larger awards in Tobago to 22 per cent in St Lucia.[21] For Jamaica, often seen as the *locus classicus* of absentee ownership, two in three of the larger awards went to absentees, while in Barbados the ratio was two in five, confirming Barbados's peculiar position as a largely resident, relatively well-articulated white settler society.

Absentees in Scotland owned slaves across the Caribbean.[22] Our data confirm this permeation of Scottish absentees, and also highlight patterns within the Caribbean that are relevant for considering not only the importance of Scotland to slave ownership in different colonial sites, but also the question dealt with elsewhere in this volume, the importance of slavery to Scotland. For among the absentee slave owners in Scotland, there is a particular concentration of absentees in Scotland associated with (1) the Ceded and Neutral Islands of Grenada, St Vincent and Tobago (although not Dominica), which collectively passed to Britain in 1763, and (2) the 'frontier' slave colony of British Guiana in which serious amounts of money were still being made from slavery right until Emancipation.[23] In Jamaica, the largest single site of British colonial slave ownership as a whole, absentees in Scotland are slightly underrepresented relative to the average for the Caribbean as a whole. It has long been understood that the land sales to new settlers in Grenada, St Vincent and Tobago went disproportionately to Scots. David Alston's work has also emphasised the component of Highland Scots in British Guiana.[24] The impact in Scotland of the presence of absentee slave owners there was therefore potentially amplified by disproportionate exposure on their part to the areas in which new men were making new fortunes in the slave economy of the early nineteenth century. By contrast, there was a markedly lower than average penetration of Scottish absentees in the older colonies of Barbados and the Leewards (Antigua,

Table 8.1 Awards identified with absentees in Scotland for selected colonies*

Colony	Total awards associated with absentees in the United Kingdom	Awards associated with absentees in Scotland
All Colonies	6042	644
Jamaica	2785	274
British Guiana	637	139
Trinidad	344	31
Antigua	344	13
Tobago	230	55
Barbados	447	9

*Key colonies only. These numbers differ from those in Draper, *Price of Emancipation*, p. 152, primarily because the latter included only awards above £500. It should also be noted that this analysis is by award, not by awardee: Scots have a lower penetration by proportion of awards than by proportion of awardees.

St Kitts, Nevis). Barbados was a major centre of the slave economy with 80,000 enslaved people (15 per cent of the total in the British Caribbean colonies), with proportionately a markedly more resident population than any other major colony. However, of the over two hundred absentees in Barbados, fewer than ten were living in Scotland at the time of Emancipation: the island's title as 'Little England' reflected a number of different characteristics of its population, one of which was their distinct national origin. Levels of Scottish absentee ownership were also negligible for St Kitts, Nevis and (for different reasons) St Lucia, which remained francophone with very little penetration by Britons as a whole after its permanent cession by the French in 1814. Only Jamaica stands out against the conclusion that Scots never caught up in the islands colonised before the Act of Union in 1707.

Slave owners in the Scottish diaspora in Britain

The second component part of 'Scottish' slave owning consisted of those absentee slave owners living elsewhere in Britain in the 1830s who were of Scottish descent and had (either themselves or through their immediate ancestors) (1) returned or relocated from the Caribbean to England (rarely Wales or Ireland) rather than Scotland, or (2) absented themselves from Scotland (either retaining no property there, or representing 'double absentees' as absentee owners of land in Scotland and of land and enslaved people in the Caribbean) by moving directly to England (again, rarely to Wales or Ireland) without passing through the Caribbean but nevertheless engaging, or continuing to engage in, the slave economy from a new English base.

The prominence of mercantile owners among these diasporic Scots in England is marked, and merchant firms in England of recognisable Scottish heritage reflect both types of diasporic slave owning. Three merchant firms in Scotland – John Campbell Senior, R. Bogle and J. T. & A. Douglas – appear among the top twenty-five mercantile recipients of slave compensation in Britain and Ireland, against twenty-one from port-cities in England (of which eleven were in London, six in Liverpool, three in Bristol and one in both London and Bristol), and one in Dublin.[25] But of the twenty-one merchant firms in England among the top twenty-five mercantile recipients of compensation, seven (all of which figured in the top fifteen) had identifiable roots in Scotland: Davidsons Barkly, Sandbach Tinné, John Gladstone, H. D. & J. E. Baillie, C., W. & F. Shand, Reid Irving, and Wm. Fraser Alexander. Hence, in total ten of the top fifteen mercantile recipients were either Glasgow firms or firms in England with founding partners of known Scottish origin. This is a noteworthy result. It reflects in part the propensity of Scottish-origin firms to address the opportunities in British Guiana: seven of these ten Scottish firms (against six of the fifteen non-'Scottish' firms) did business mainly or exclusively with British Guiana, rather than older colonies. The fortunes made by such merchants qualify the 'decline' of West India by highlighting the fact that individual slave owners were still becoming rich in the newer slave colonies until Emancipation.[26] Of these seven firms with Scottish origin, two were founded in the Caribbean (Sandbach Tinné in British Guiana and C., W. & F. Shand in Antigua), while the other five were founded by expatriate Scots in England.[27] Among these merchant Scots, the 'double absenteeism' of families such as the Baillies has been highlighted by Hamilton.[28] Although absenteeism was problematised for Scotland as for the Caribbean (and for Ireland), the structure of Scottish (and Irish) absentee landlordism and Caribbean absenteeism was very different: the lack of a system of tenant farming on West India slave estates is very striking, with owners remaining directly exposed to fluctuations in profitability, and accessing the fruits of exploitation through profit, not rent.

While diasporic mercantile Scots in England are important to British slave ownership as a whole, rentier owners also feature in the Scottish diaspora in England. John McArthur, for example, probably originally from Greenock (where his sister was living at the time he made his will) and the absentee owner of Plantation Arthurville in British Guiana, who died at Catherington in Hampshire in 1840, is one of dozens of such slave owners and merchants of Scottish origin in the database who together form a meaningful component of slave owners living in England at the time of Emancipation. McArthur is among the Scottish slave owners in England known to have contributed to the maintenance of diasporic Scottish identities: he had, according to his will, been involved in the publication of 'Ossian's Poems in three volumes' with Sir John Sinclair Bt under the sponsorship of the Highland Society of London, and had subscribed 50 guineas to the Caledonian Asylum which he had originally proposed in 1808, again under the auspices of the Highland Society, of which he was then one of the treasurers.[29]

Slave owners in the Scottish diaspora in the colonies

The database, containing as it does all awardees of slave compensation named in the records of the Commissioners of Slave Compensation, includes an unknown number of slave owners of Scottish ancestry who were resident in the colonies in the 1830s. We have not systematically researched these resident slave owners, either those of Scottish heritage or those of English, Irish and Welsh ancestry, but the database provides the raw material for such systematic work person-by-person, either as a whole or – more plausibly – by colony. As it stands, the database lends itself to some fairly crude searches that might be broadly suggestive in exploring Scottish slave ownership, and suggests that the relative distributions by colony of (1) Scottish absentee owners, and (2) resident owners of Scottish extraction are correlated. For example, British Guiana has around 120 slave owners whose names begin 'Mc' or 'Mac' not identified as absentee against a total of 2,200 claims not associated with absentees, a ratio of 1:18, while Jamaica has over 400 slave owners whose names begin 'Mc' or 'Mac' not identified as absentee against a total of some 11,500 awards not associated with absentees, a ratio of 1:27. Barbados, by contrast, has fewer than 100 slave owners whose names begin 'Mc' or 'Mac' not identified as absentee against a total of some 5,000 awards not associated with absentees, a ratio of 1:58. That higher levels of Scottish absentee ownership should be associated with higher levels (by one unsophisticated indicator) of Scottish *resident* ownership and vice versa is not perhaps a surprising overall suggestion: but the material exists in the LBS database for more granular work by colony on the relationship between the two.

IMPORTANCE OF SLAVE OWNERSHIP TO SCOTLAND

Although this chapter is primarily about the important role that Scotland played within the wider pattern of British and Irish slave ownership, some of our material could help illuminate the inverse question, the importance of slave ownership to Scotland, and this section briefly highlights a few of the directions we have taken in examining this question for England, and their potential transferability. It is probably necessary to reiterate that we understand that our prosopographical approach is only one way in to the relationship between Scotland (or England) and slavery. It privileges the individual as transmitter of slave wealth, appropriate in an era of small-scale firms and very limited corporate as opposed to personal ownership, with few intermediary institutions between savers and investors at the time either in Scotland or England, despite the greater receptivity of Scottish law to collective legal bodies. But we recognise the systemic effects of the slave economy on demand, on raw material supply and on the evolution of institutions are often only hinted at, rather than captured, in our material.

The national average for Britain as a whole is that 5 to 10 per cent of the elites, however defined, were involved in the slave compensation process: for Ireland as a whole the equivalent figure is less than half that, that is, no more than 2 to 3 per cent of the elites. It appears *prima facie*, that if absentee slave ownership in Scotland was disproportionately high (relative to population) as we have argued, and that Scotland was poorer than England on a per capita basis (as Devine has stressed), such involvement in the slave economy would be expected to leave a greater mark in Scotland than it did on Britain as a whole, unless dramatically different mechanisms for the transmission 'home' of slavery through slave ownership applied in Scotland. The figure for Scotland should thus be above that for Britain as a whole.

The national figures disguise regional and local concentrations, and although slave ownership pervaded the country, there were clusters of connections in specific communities. We have undertaken mapping work for districts of London that highlight dense concentrations of slave owners in Marylebone, Fitzrovia and Bloomsbury. In the case of Scotland, one-fifth of the absentees and the awards associated with them relate to Glasgow, which had less than 10 per cent of the nation's population: and within Glasgow there are likely to be districts of especially intense slave ownership. As with England, the impact of slavery might well be significantly greater at a local than national level. The intense local impact of individual slave owners in England, such as William

Hudson Heaven in the case of Lundy Island, is mirrored in Scotland by figures such as George Rainy, who returned a very rich man from British Guiana, bought the island of Raasay in 1846 and was subsequently highly instrumental in its clearance.

The slave compensation records also allow us to put some dimensions around slave-derived wealth as a stream within some forms of industrial and commercial investment. Whether or not capital from slavery was *necessary* to help fund industrial, commercial and infrastructure projects in Britain, it is clear from our work that capital from slavery *did* help fund a wide variety of such projects. This continued to be the case even beyond the end of slavery into the mid-nineteenth century, when capital generated in industrialisation itself is widely accepted to have become more than sufficient to finance continued domestic transformation and expansion. Wealth derived from slavery certainly flowed into conspicuous consumption in Britain as a whole, but it also flowed into the hands of a significant number of individuals, in Scotland as well as the rest of Britain, who were active as investors and sometimes as entrepreneurs in new industries.[30]

Slave compensation obviously coincided with the beginning of the railway boom, an event that galvanised capital and mobilised investors throughout Britain and Ireland. We have looked systematically at the part played by slave owners in the railway boom by comparing our database of compensation recipients with three sets of railway investors, those captured by the 1837, 1845 and 1846 parliamentary returns of subscribers to railway contracts.[31] The amounts of capital represented were huge, and dwarf the slave compensation.[32] By definition, slave compensation could only be a small fragment of the total. Again, there are tens of thousands of subscribers listed, and while several hundred slave owners permeate these lists, they are again by definition going to be thinly spread. But we have found that (1) slave owners were often among the most active investors and directors; (2) in some railway companies, but a distinct minority, slave owners subscribed a significant part of the total. For example, the Glasgow, Paisley, Kilmarnock and Ayr Railway Co. was one of the foci of investment by slave owners, who subscribed 10 per cent of the total of £452,900 raised in 1837; the Secretary of the company, John Fairfull Smith, was married to the daughter of a Jamaican slave owner; and in 1846 Thomas Dunlop Douglas subscribed an extraordinary £336,100 to eleven railway companies in Scotland, the bulk of it to extensions of the Glasgow, Paisley, Kilmarnock and Ayr.

Like many English banks, banks in Scotland had mortgage business with slave owners, but in most cases this appears to have been a small part of their overall activity: credit provision to slave owners remained the preserve of merchant firms rather than the evolving banking sector. For the Edinburgh banking firm of Sir William Forbes, James Hunter & Co., for example, we have found only a single case of mortgage lending, to a female slave owner called Helen Watt, 'a gentlewoman of Manchester' Jamaica. The Royal Bank of Scotland, of course, is an amalgam of hundreds of provincial banks whose cumulative exposure to slavery is more material. RBS published an account of its linkages to slavery in 2006 and revised it in 2008, in part to take account of some of our early findings: many of those connections came through English banks absorbed by NatWest, which RBS took over in 1999.[33]

Slavery and slave ownership permeated the whole of the City of London and the evidence suggests it also permeated Scottish commerce and finance. But it was not always material to the development of individual institutions: it was 'thin' in many cases (especially in Edinburgh), and 'thick' in others (notably in Glasgow). Hence, in order to validate Eric Williams's thesis, work has to be done institution by institution and firm by firm: the compensation records provide an empirical base for such explorations, at least of the early nineteenth century.

CONCLUSION

We conceive of the LBS project and its associated database as contributions to the process of reinscribing slavery into the history of Britain and Ireland as a whole. That process of attempted reinscription is also underway in France and the Netherlands, as well as in Britain and Ireland; the breadth and depth of recent academic work in this area for Scotland, including this volume, place Scottish history writing at least on a par with those parallel efforts elsewhere in Britain and continental Europe.

We hope our work will be a tool for everybody interested in national, regional, local and family histories of all four nations in nineteenth-century Britain and Ireland, as well as those who are engaged in the struggle to incorporate the history of the enslavement of Africans into the national narratives. The database lends itself to searching by individual or by town/city/county. While the absence of a person or place from the database does not mean that they were not associated with slavery, in many cases such searches will bring confirmation or new news about linkages with slavery, with enough ancillary detail to stimulate new lines of enquiry and new work. In turn, we hope that new work can feed the database.

The database can answer such questions as: were these specific people in Scotland close enough to the slave economy to appear in the slave compensation records? If they do appear, why are they there? What were the estates they were connected with? How many enslaved people did they own or control and how much compensation did they receive? But the database can also help provide context: how typical, how representative were particular families in their slave owning? What kinds of community or network of slave owners did they participate in? We are eager to engage: to provide information, but also to benefit from the knowledge that many local and family historians, as well as academic historians, have on individuals of interest to us. In providing such a tool and in establishing a forum for exchange, we hope not only to engage the public but also to accelerate the dissemination of academic research on slavery's role in the formation of modern Britain, and to begin to help reshape national narratives that have privileged the history of abolition and elided the history of slavery. We would be delighted to hear from users of the database with questions, corrections or information, at lbs@ucl.ac.uk.

NOTES

1. Catherine Hall, Nicholas Draper, Keith McClelland, Katie Donington and Rachel Lang, *Legacies of British Slave-ownership: Colonial Slavery and the Formation of Victorian Britain* (Cambridge: Cambridge University Press, 2014).
2. *The Legacies of British Slave-ownership* project (2009–12), funded by the ESRC, has been succeeded by a second project, *The Structure and Significance of British Caribbean Slave-ownership 1763–1833* (2013–15), funded by the ESRC and the AHRC, in which we are extending our analysis of the final state of slave ownership over the preceding seventy years: http://www.ucl.ac.uk/lbs.
3. Work on Ireland and Wales includes: Nicholas Draper, '"Dependent on precarious subsistences": Ireland's Slave-owners at the Time of Emancipation', *Britain and the World*, 6, 2 (2013), pp. 220–42; Nini Rodgers, *Ireland, slavery and anti-slavery 1612–1865* (Basingstoke: Palgrave Macmillan, 2007); Bertie Mandelblatt, 'A Transatlantic Commodity: Irish Salt Beef in the French Atlantic World', *History Workshop Journal*, 63, 1 (2007), pp. 18–47; Chris Evans, *Slave Wales: The Welsh and Atlantic Slavery 1660–1850* (Cardiff: University of Wales Press, 2010).
4. We have benefited in particular in our work from conversations and exchanges of material related to Scotland with David Alston, Eric Graham, Stephen Mullen and Karly Kehoe.

5. For Scotland, the point of departure is of course T. M. Devine, 'Did Slavery make Scotia Great?' *Britain and the World*, 4, 1 (2011), pp. 40–64. A revised version of this article appears as Chapter 11 of this volume. For Britain as a whole, the position set out in Eric Williams, *Capitalism and Slavery* (Chapel Hill: University of North Carolina, 1944) that slavery was a necessary but not sufficient precondition of the Industrial Revolution appears once more to be gaining traction among economic historians not aligned with either side in the past controversies, for example Pat Hudson, 'Slavery, the slave-trade and economic growth: a contribution to the debate', in C. Hall, N. Draper and K. McClelland (eds), *Emancipation, Slave-ownership and the Remaking of the British Imperial World* (Manchester: Manchester University Press, 2014), pp. 36–59.

6. Hall, Draper, McClelland et al., *Legacies of British Slave-ownership*, especially Chapters 2 and 3.

7. *An Act for the abolition of slavery throughout the British colonies, for promoting the industry of the manumitted slaves, and for compensating the persons formerly entitled to the services of such slaves* 28 August 1833 (3 and 4 William IV cap. 73). The Act explicitly excluded Ceylon and St Helena, and did not apply to forms of bondage in India, while slavery continued in some of Britain's West Africa possessions until the early twentieth century. The records generated by the Commissioners under the Act are stored at The National Archives at Kew in the T71 series.

8. R. W. Fogel and S. L. Engerman, 'Philanthropy at Bargain Prices: Notes on the Economics of Gradual Emancipation', *Journal of Legal Studies*, 3.2 (1974), pp. 377–401 gives 49 per cent for the value of cash compensation and 47 per cent for the value of apprenticeship. Both these numbers appear, for different reasons, to be too high: Draper, *Price of Emancipation*, p. 106.

9. Circular Request T71/1592, 8 September 1835. The Glasgow merchant firm acting as agent of Commissioners in Scotland was given as 'A. Milne', which has not been traced with confidence.Alexander George Milne the younger, closely tied to John Campbell senior, with whose partners he had traded under the firm of Alex. and James Campbell of Copthall Court until 1835, was London- based.

10. In the 1870s women comprised only 15 per cent of the owners of a national shareholding sample: Janette Rutterford, David R. Green, Josephine Maltby and Alastair Owens, 'Who Comprised the Nation of Shareholders? Gender and Investment in Great Britain, c. 1870–1935', *Economic History Review*, 64:1 (2011), pp. 157–87. As the authors discuss, however, in the eighteenth century women comprised one-third of the holders of East India Company stock and had been more prominent in lower-risk investments such as railways and banks than in securities as a whole in the earlier decades of the nineteenth century.

11. The slave compensation records themselves generally distinguished

between England, Scotland or 'North Britain' and Ireland (although not Wales) in their characterisation of claimants, although for some four hundred individuals the records showed simply 'Great Britain', almost invariably in isolation rather than as an additional descriptor for a town or city.

12. Simon D. Smith, 'Slavery's Heritage Footprint: Links between British Country Houses and St Vincent Plantations, 1814–1834', in Madge Dresser and Andrew Hann (eds), *Slavery and the British Country House* (Swindon: English Heritage, 2013), pp. 57–68.

13. For the enslaved people, there is limited data in the Slave Registers allowing some minimal recapture of age, given name in slavery, birthplace (African versus Creole), sometimes skills and distinguishing features. This data has not been captured in the *Legacies* project but in the successor project we are striving to incorporate material on the enslaved people.

14. Nicholas Draper, *The Price of Emancipation: Slave Ownership, Compensation and British Society at the End of Slavery* (Cambridge: Cambridge University Press, 2010), p. 273. A number of such categories are more applicable to local elites in England and Wales than to Scotland or Ireland, where we have not performed a similar analysis.

15. T. M. Devine, 'An Eighteenth-Century Business Elite: Glasgow West-India Merchants c. 1750–1815', *Scottish Historical Review*, 57:1 (1978), pp. 40–67; Anthony Cooke, 'An Elite Revisited: Glasgow West India Merchants 1783–1877', *Journal of Scottish Historical Studies*, 32:2 (2012), pp. 127–65; Stephen Mullen, 'A Glasgow-West India Merchant House and the Imperial Dividend, 1779–1867', *Journal of Scottish Historical Studies*, 33:2 (2013), pp. 196–233.

16. Thomas Fairholme's slave ownership in Tobago is part of the current new phase of the *LBS* project, the results of which will be online in late 2015/ early 2016.

17. Alan Karras, *Sojourners in the Sun: Scottish Migrants in Jamaica and the Chesapeake, 1740–1800* (Ithaca: Cornell University Press, 1992); Douglas Hamilton, *Scotland, the Caribbean and the Atlantic World 1750–1820* (Manchester: Manchester University Press, 2005).

18. Barry Higman and Brian Hudson, *Jamaican Place Names*, (Kingston: University of the West Indies Press, 2009); Smith, 'Slavery's heritage footprint', p. 63.

19. *LBS* Database, 'Anna Archibald', http://www.ucl.ac.uk/lbs/person/view/-1461964810 and ibid., 'Eliza T. Thomas', http://www.ucl.ac.uk/lbs/person/view/29851 (both accessed 2 September 2014).

20. *LBS* Database, 'Archibald Douglas', http://www.ucl.ac.uk/lbs/person/view/45319; ibid., 'John Douglas', http://www.ucl.ac.uk/lbs/person/view/8520; and ibid., 'Thomas Dunlop Douglas', http://www.ucl.ac.uk/lbs/person/view/41768 (all accessed 2 September 2014).

21. Draper, *Price of Emancipation*, p. 152.

22. To date, we have found no absentees in Scotland at all associated with Anguilla, Bahamas, Bermuda or Honduras (all of which had almost negligible levels of absentee ownership overall), nor in Montserrat (a heavily absentee-owned island) or the Virgin Islands.

23. Nicholas Draper, 'The Rise of a New Planter Class? Some Countercurrents from British Guiana and Trinidad 1807–1833', *Atlantic Studies*, 9, 1 (March 2012), pp. 65–83.

24. David Alston, http://www.spanglefish.com/slavesandhighlanders/ (accessed 2 September 2014).

25. Draper, *Price of Emancipation*, p. 236. Of the twenty-five leading merchant partnerships, one further firm, Hall M'Garel of London, which is discussed below, had roots in Ireland. By contrast, in addition to the three Glasgow firms, a further seven firms based in England had their origins in Scotland.

26. Draper, 'The Rise of a New Planter Class?', pp. 65–83.

27. Earlier members of the Baillie family had certainly been in the Caribbean.

28. Hamilton, *Scotland and the Caribbean*, pp. 178–9.

29. Will of John McArthur Doctor of Laws of Catherington in Hampshire proved 24/10/1840 PROB 11/1935/126; J. K. Laughton, 'McArthur, John (1755–1840)', rev. Nicholas Tracy, *Oxford Dictionary of National Biography* (Oxford University Press, 2004); online edn, January 2008, http://www.oxforddnb.com/view/article/17338 (accessed 18 January 2015), says his origins are unknown: the entry makes no reference to his slave ownership.

30. For examples among Glaswegian West India merchants, see Devine, 'An Eighteenth-century Business Elite' and Cooke, 'Elite Revisited'; for specific sectors throughout Britain, see Hall, Draper et al., *Legacies of British Slave-ownership*, pp. 78–126 passim.

31. Hall, Draper et al., *Legacies of British Slave-ownership*, pp. 91–3. We know there are issues with these lists. Not all of these railways were built, for example, and there was sometimes fraudulent use of names on such lists. Nor is it always clear that a given individual was investing on his or her own account. In the case of railway schemes in Scotland, there is also the complexity that much of the capital for Scottish schemes was subscribed in England, and conversely that Scots subscribed to schemes in England. For example, the British Guiana slave owner and native of Larne in Ireland Charles M'Garel subscribed £5,000 into the Edinburgh and Northern as well as putting money into a series of railways in England. But it is the most extensive set of records of railway investors extant and all entries have (sometimes sketchy) details of occupation and address.

32. The 1837 lists have total subscriptions of £31.7 million; the 1845 equivalents show £61.6 million in subscriptions over £2,000 and a further £21.4 million in smaller amounts; the 1846 lists totalled £121.2 million. Thus in combination the three show total subscriptions over £230 million.

33. *Historical Research Report: Predecessor Institutions Research Regarding Slavery and the Slave Trade First published May 25, 2006 Updated May 29, 2009*, http://www.citizensbank.com/pdf/historical_research/pdf (accessed 2 September 2014).

9

'The Upas Tree, beneath whose pestiferous shade all intellect languishes and all virtue dies': Scottish Public Perceptions of the Slave Trade and Slavery, 1756–1833

Iain Whyte

'ALTHOUGH, IN THE PLANTATIONS, they have laid hold of the poor blacks and made slaves of them, yet I do not think that *that* is agreeable to humanity, not to say to the Christian religion. Is a man a slave because he is black? No. He is our brother; and he is a man, though not our colour, he is in the land of liberty, with his wife and child, let him remain *there*.'[1] Alexander Boswell, Lord Auchinleck, addressed these words in January 1788 to his fellow judges in the Court of Session in Edinburgh. They found, by a majority of eight to four, that the state of slavery was not recognised by the laws of Scotland, and Joseph Knight, a slave from Jamaica, was freed from the service of Sir John Wedderburn of Ballindean in Perthshire.[2]

There are distinct threads that run through Scottish thinking on slavery in the late eighteenth and early nineteenth centuries, two of which found an echo in Auchinleck's statement. The Scottish intelligentsia, possibly feeling the loss of national identity in the wake of the Union, were concerned about a self-image that encapsulated civilisation and humanity. Scots may have had an unusually harsh reputation in the colonies for their treatment of slaves, but they were keen to hide that from their countrymen at home. Robert Burns's poignant *The Slave's Lament* touched a popular chord, as did other poems proclaiming human feeling for others, even though the author was within an ace of sailing for Jamaica to help run a slave plantation.[3]

Another obvious strand was commerce. The fact that the wealth of Glasgow and other parts of Scotland, based on tobacco, sugar and cotton, was dependent on slavery, is demonstrated in Chapter 11. Scottish mariners were extensively involved in the slave trade, and Scottish cheap linen clothed bondsmen and women in the plantations. In a bizarre twist, those caddying for ships' captains on a two-hole golf course on

Bance Island, the slave station on the Sierra Leone river, were dressed in tartan manufactured in Bannockburn.[4] Economic ties with the trade and plantation slavery were emphasised by those who opposed the moves for abolition. *The Glasgow Courier* carried continuous reminders of this, with castigation of any who argued against the slave trade.

It would be impossible to consider Scottish attitudes to slavery without giving full consideration to the place that religion and theology played in national life. The legacy of John Knox and other reformers, with their passion for religious education, meant that many Scots were familiar with their Bible and used to discussing theological issues. In the court cases regarding slavery in the eighteenth century, extensive biblical references were cited by lawyers on both sides, a phenomenon that would not be seen south of the Border.[5] In contrast to Presbyterians in the United States, who struggled daily with the moral aspects of the 'peculiar institution' in their midst, hardly any in the churches in Scotland attempted to defend it.[6] When in Scotland, Christian evangelical zeal combined with an aspiration to humane values and stubborn Presbyterian independence, a powerful weapon was forged against a system that seemed to deny the very basis of Christianity. Given the very small number of black enslaved people in Scotland in the eighteenth century,[7] it was surprising that the actions of three of them led to extensive legal debates that engendered wide public engagement. Their cases are the starting-point for this investigation. Spanning either side of them were the intellectual challenges and reservations that occupied some of the major figures of the Scottish Enlightenment and which filtered down from the universities to coffee houses and other gathering places, and into the newspapers of the time.

Notices of enslaved people in Scotland who had sought freedom and departed from their owners were a regular feature in newspapers throughout the mid-eighteenth century. The first case to come before Scotland's Court of Session was *Sheddan v A Negro* in 1756. In 1750 James Montgomery had been brought by Robert Sheddan from Virginia to Beith in Ayrshire, to be trained as a joiner. When he learnt that his master intended to send him back to the colony to be sold as a valuable tradesman, he sought baptism from the local minister, Rev. John Witherspoon. Sheddan opposed this, he said, because he feared that it might give Montgomery 'fancies of freedom', and he assured the judges that the minister had 'again and again' told the slave that it made no difference to his status.[8] Two things call this contention into question. Witherspoon's insistence on the public baptism of James, despite the master's opposition, indicates the strong Scottish precedence of a Christian sacrament over the wishes of a master. Furthermore, Witherspoon furnished Montgomery with a certificate of Christian conduct 'so that he may be received as a member of any Christian society where Providence shall order his lot'.[9]

This was hardly an appropriate document for someone destined for the slave market in America, and indicated that Witherspoon in some way connived in the slave's bid for freedom. In the event, Montgomery was caught and imprisoned in Edinburgh but died before his status could be determined. Witherspoon himself moved to America in 1768, was a signatory to the Declaration of Independence, owned slaves himself, and was ambivalent on the question of the rights and wrongs of slavery.[10]

Public, and in particular church, support for a slave, and the assumption that baptism conferred freedom, played a strong part in the case of *Dalrymple v Spens* in 1759. 'Black Tom' from Grenada sought baptism in Wemyss parish church, and took the name David Spens. Accompanied by a local farmer and Kirk elder, John Henderson, he told his master, Dr David Dalrymple, that he was now free. The declaration, in which Spens had the assistance of three lawyers, included the assumption that his former status as 'an heathen slave' justified his enslavement. 'Now,' it stated, 'I am by the Christian Religion Liberate and set at freedom from my old yoke, bondage, and slavery, and by the laws of this Christian land there is no vestige of slavery allowed.' A bold claim that had little precedent, but it was backed by local churches, who collected money in his support, as did the miners and salters of the district. In the event, Dalrymple died before the Court of Session could adjudicate, and Spens was freed.[11]

Baptism was not so central to the third case in 1778, but Sir John Wedderburn was quite clear that he had fulfilled his duty by permitting Joseph Knight to be baptised. As with other masters, he and his Counsel, James Ferguson, argued that reception into the Christian community in no way altered a slave's situation, citing English legal opinion that tended to confirm this.[12] He also argued that the Old Testament showed divine sanction for slavery, something, he maintained, that neither Jesus nor St Paul disputed. Alan McConnochie, acting for Knight, relied heavily on the leading churchman and historian William Robertson, claiming that slavery was 'inconsistent with the spirit and principles' of the Christian faith. He contended that equality of all men under God flew in the face of slavery, and that Scottish law was not subject to Roman, let alone English, or colonial, law.[13] Lord Auchinleck was not alone in concurring with this last point. This was probably the argument which persuaded

Robert McQueen, Lord Braxfield, a staunch persecutor of any who challenged the status quo, and a man not easily swayed by religious or humanitarian appeals, to vote for Knight.[14]

The Knight judgement was made against a background strongly influenced by the Enlightenment, with which, in theory at least, most jurists were in sympathy. It has been claimed that Scotland's intelligentsia were united in their condemnation of slavery, while their friends and fellow countrymen were busy taking commercial advantage of it in the plantations of the West Indies, and in the triangular trade between Africa, the Caribbean and the Americas and Britain.[15] It was more complex than that. David Hume's infamous footnote about no black person being capable of anything but menial tasks, was a gift to the justifiers of slavery.[16] Frances Hutcheson, at the conclusion of his strong strictures against slavery, qualified that with the reservation 'where no public interest require it'. However, his successor in the Chair of Moral Philosophy at Glasgow, John Millar, was unambiguous in his opposition to slavery.[17] Although William Wilberforce told William Robertson, the Edinburgh historian and theologian, that his sermons had provided valuable material for the parliamentary campaign against the slave trade, Robertson stood aloof from supporting any petitions calling for the ending of the trade.[18] James Boswell was as supportive of slavery as his father was opposed to it, and Lord Monboddo, who loved to associate himself with enlightened thought, nonetheless voted against Joseph Knight's release. Scottish Enlightenment thinking on slavery held many different and contrasting colours.[19]

James Beattie was one of the few men of letters to take an active part in the campaign against the slave trade, which he did in Aberdeen. His anti-slavery lectures were renowned in Marischal College and had influenced a number of students, including, in the 1770s, James Stephen, who after legal service in the West Indies, became a prominent abolitionist, and drafted the bill to abolish the slave trade.[20] Beattie poured scorn on the coldness with which Scottish intellectuals treated the human issues, which, in his view, they simply mulled over in detached debate in coffee houses and learned societies.[21]

Keeping as quiet as possible about the slave trade and plantation slavery was seen as a wise precaution, lest too many questions were asked, and Scottish self-image suffer. The racial myth that slavery was acceptable to those who endured it, was of course extremely comforting to those who benefited from it both in Scotland and the colonies. When the tourist Janet Schaw from Edinburgh arrived at St Kitts, she was initially shocked at seeing the marks of the whip on the backs of slaves of both genders. She consoled herself, however, by concluding that when someone became better acquainted with 'the nature of the negroes', they would realise that there was no mental pain attached to such punishment, as with Europeans. At a slave sale she also interpreted the traumatic silence of parents being separated from their children as 'the most perfect indifference'.[22] This convenient myopia could not of course survive for long, but becoming detached from the human horror became the survival mechanism for many young Scots who found themselves involved in slavery in the colonies. The sixteen-year-old Zachary Macaulay, who was later to become a key figure in the abolitionist movement, wrote from Jamaica in 1785 to a friend in Glasgow that if he could see him in a cane field with a hundred slaves crying, as the whip resounded on their shoulders, 'it would make you imagine that some unlucky accident had carried me to the doleful shades'.[23] Later on he admitted, in a confession to his fiancée, Selina Mills, that he had become 'callous and indifferent', overcoming squeamishness that was 'inconvenient' for his position. 'I began', he said, 'to speak of the sufferings of the slaves with a levity which, as you will understand, marked my depravity.'[24]

A rather different picture emerged when James Ramsay, a former naval surgeon and Episcopal clergyman from Fraserburgh, and a contemporary and friend of Beattie, published his essay in 1784 on the treatment of West Indian slaves.[25] His biographer described the essay as 'lifting the veil from plantation slavery'. It was a mild document, and sought only to provide facts that he thought the public could bear. But its humanity indicated why he had been hounded out from St Kitts in 1781 after twenty years there. After his initial meeting with William Wilberforce in 1783, he bombarded the parliamentary campaigners with information from his first-hand experience of the slave trade and the plantations. The young Thomas Clarkson spent a week at his rectory in Teston, and left determined to devote his life to abolition. Ramsay's effectiveness was such a threat to the West Indians in parliament, that they were determined to drive him to an early grave in 1789 by their sustained attacks on his character.[26]

Less celebrated Scots were to make their views known by signing petitions sent to parliament in 1788 and 1792, and a few chose to submit letters to the newspapers. A three-month correspondence on the slave trade took place in the *Glasgow Courier* in 1792, the year that Scotland contributed one-third of the 561 British petitions to parliament against the slave trade.[27] A writer under the name of 'Hanway', who claimed extensive experience of the West Indies, warned of the threat to the colonies, commerce and civilisation. If the 'agitation' of the abolitionists should lead to rebellions in the British Caribbean, he said, that would match the 'dreadful calamities' and barbarous acts in San Domingue, the French island that had recently experienced a successful slave revolt. 'Hanway' staked a claim for the humanity of the trade, asserting that slaves in the West Indies enjoyed considerably more protection and freedom than in the 'barbaric' African countries from which they had been taken. He further warned that manufacturing and commercial interests would be so damaged by the abolition of the trade, that the wealth of Glasgow would be destroyed. Playing the patriotic card, in a year when the French Revolution was at its bloodiest, and fear of invasion from across the Channel was at fever pitch, 'Hanway' contended that the West African slaving voyages provided a training ground for sailors, who would be necessary for war at sea.[28]

This was too much for 'A Plain Citizen'. In his view, it was the barbarities of slavery in San Domingue that had caused the rebellion. 'It is just common sense', he contended, 'to see that if the slave trade was banned, the planters in the West Indies would have to treat their slaves better.' If that were so, he continued, 'it stands to reason that there would be less danger of rebellion from desperate people.' 'A Plain Citizen' scorned the claims made by 'Hanway' that slaves enjoyed more liberty in the West Indies than in Africa. 'If it is evident', he wrote, 'that taking the negroes to the coast in chains and imprisoning them in the hold of a slave ship, then selling them to planters, is all for the purpose of giving them more liberty, I suppose that the next step for Mr Hanway will be to claim that we should cut off their heads for the purpose of giving them more life.'[29]

'Columbus' supported 'Hanway', arguing that the British Government had encouraged the slave trade, and pointing out that the colonisation of America involved stealing land from the original inhabitants. The accusations of 'inhumanity' from the proponents of abolition, he thought, ignored the fact that those in Africa were 'cooped up' in 'barbarity, ignorance, and savagery'. Oladuah Equiano, who claimed to have experienced enslavement himself, responded to this, asserting that Europeans were responsible for the slave trade, and that governments in Europe were 'forced to connive at an evil which they were unable to prevent'. He assured the readers that as an African, he saw the abolition of the trade as a guarantor of more productive work on the plantations, securing the interests of all at home and abroad.[30]

A satirical touch was provided by one describing himself as 'A West Indian Planter'. He purported to agree with 'Hanway' and 'Columbus' that negroes were happy with their lot, and loved 'being ruled with a rod of iron'. Everyone, he considered, should be given free passages on slave ships to assist Africans to become Christian slaves. Five hundred million pounds should be paid to slavers, and British people should be forced by law to eat and drink a stated quantity of sugar and rum.[31]

Apart from letters from individuals such as these, there was no sustained public defence in Scotland of the slave trade, nor was it universally justified as a necessity of commerce. One of the first petitions to parliament on the issue came from the Edinburgh Chamber of Commerce in 1788. It declared their 'shame that this nation should enrich itself in a trade marked with cruelty and inhumanity'. Even if it was to be proved that commerce in this way was more profitable, the petitioners claimed that the Chamber would still be totally opposed to it.[32] Committees set up to abolish the trade had a number of businessmen on their committees, and David Dale, owner of New Lanark's cotton mills, chaired the Glasgow Society. At this point, abolition demands were strictly confined to the slave trade, and in many of the petitions it was argued that the limitation of supply would lead to better conditions and more efficient production on the plantations.[33]

Scottish petitions in 1788 were mainly instituted by the courts of the Church of Scotland. It was hardly surprising that most of them showed concern about the inhumanity of the slave trade, and the national shame accumulated by it. Many of them carried warnings of divine wrath and national punishment. This theme was taken up by some of the numerous petitions in 1792 from civic and trades bodies. The Incorporated Trades with Twenty-One other Societies declared that they shared the daily accumulation of guilt, and warned that if 'a timely stop' was not put to this, there was reason to conclude that such a system could not 'long escape the righteous judgment of God'.[34]

Despite the efforts of the abolitionists to distinguish between the trade and plantation slavery, many petitions by 1792 could not condemn the cruelty of the one without incorporating the other, now that conditions in the West Indies had been exposed. Some based their case on common humanity and equality in the eyes of the creator, others incorporated a doctrine of sin in arguing that an accident of birth and race condemned fellow humans to a life of 'undeserved punishment'.[35] Dr John Erskine of Greyfriars Church in Edinburgh had long argued that any missionary work in Africa would be severely hampered by the slave trade, and some of the petitions drew the obvious conclusion that Christian nations that stole people and kept them in chains were hardly likely to commend their religion to compatriots of the enslaved.[36]

Scotland's remarkable record of sending 181 petitions to parliament
in 1792 was largely attributable to the work of the Dumfries-born
William Dickson. Dickson, who had been secretary to the governor
of Barbados, offered his services to the London Committee for the
Abolition of the Slave Trade and Thomas Clarkson, whose 1791 visit
to Scotland had been none too successful, engaged Dickson to tour the
country in the early months of the next year. He did that with dogged
application, seeking the support of leading citizens from Kirkcudbright
to Inverness and carrying with him extracts of damning evidence on the
trade presented to parliament by the abolitionists. In the main he had
to make his own introductions, but James Beattie facilitated his time in
Aberdeen and the North-east.[37]

No Scottish petitions were sent to parliament opposing the abolition
of the slave trade. There were, however, voices raised in opposition to
action by the churches from within their ranks. When the Presbytery
of Glasgow petitioned in 1792, a lengthy dissent was recorded by Rev.
James Lapsley, minister of Campsie. Lapsley argued that the Presbytery
had stepped beyond its spiritual responsibility in dealing with a political matter, although as a spy in the pay of the Government he was
himself deeply involved in rather different politics.[38] He considered the
'abuses' in the West Indies of far less consequence than the moral lapses
at home, stated that it was dangerous to foment 'dissatisfaction' of the
present order, and affirmed that questioning Government policy would
risk interference in the privileged status of the Church of Scotland, and
threaten the livelihood of ministers.[39]

On the night of the Glasgow debate, the Presbytery of St Andrews
also faced an internal challenge to their decision to petition. Dr George
Hill and Dr Joseph MacCormick, Principals of two of the University's
colleges, opposed the motion on the grounds of insufficient evidence,
and claimed that such action might introduce 'amongst the people a
spirit of turbulence and a desire to dictate to the legislature'.[40] They were
voices against the stream, but William Dickson had been careful to warn
supporters of abolition to have nothing to do with revolutionary bodies,
or to express even the mildest support for any other cause at all.[41]

Before the main agitation on the slave trade had started, an extraordinary book appeared.[42] James Adair was a Fellow of the Royal College
of Surgeons in Edinburgh, who had practised as a surgeon and a judge
on the island of Antigua. Adair claimed that he was not attempting to
defend, or even palliate, 'the species of traffick which has been carried
on between Africa and America', but to absolve the planters from any
blame for it. He argued for better medical care for the slaves, in the

same way that Ramsay had done, but concluded that because the slaves 'often amuse themselves with singing and dancing', there was 'no reason to suppose that they regard bondage as a great evil'.[43]

If Adair's book was hardly a serious defence of the slave trade, one that appeared three years later certainly was. Archibald Dalzel, whose career in West Africa has been discussed in Chapter 7, was a rare combination of a merchant with experience of the African coast, and a man of letters. The Liverpool merchants employed him to write a justification of their trade, and when his *History of Dahomey – an Inland Kingdom of Africa* appeared, they rewarded him handsomely and gave him the Freedom of the Borough.[44]

Dalzel was not alone in arguing that the slave trade rescued Africans from a barbaric and brutish existence, and brought them into Western civilisation. He catalogued mass murders and grotesque forms of torture from his years of observation in the West African kingdom, claiming that cannibalism was endemic there. To the charges of Ramsay and others that Europeans fomented bloody conflict on the coast and inland, he responded that 'the haughty ferocity of a people born to war and rapine' was 'incompatible with the mild and steady spirit of commerce'.[45]

The abolition of the slave trade did not improve conditions on the plantations. In 1823 the national campaign for 'mitigation and eventual abolition of slavery' was launched throughout Britain, and once more Scotland saw many local committees formed to work for this end. They were well served by the constant flow of information from Zachary Macaulay. Macaulay's early experience in Jamaica had, in a very different way, been matched by a number of years in the governance of the settlement of Sierra Leone, under the Company set up by British abolitionists. After his return home in 1799, he undertook increasing amounts of research and dissemination of information on slavery. Macaulay was driven by the Calvinist work ethic, often at the cost of his health, and through pamphlets and the editorship of the monthly *Anti-Slavery Reporter*, became revered by Wilberforce and Stephen, and reviled by the advocates of slavery through the *Glasgow Courier* and the London-based *John Bull*.[46]

Anticipating this early pressure for full emancipation, two Scots published volumes that sought to demonstrate improvements in the slave colonies, and argued for a policy of non-interference. John Stewart, a former resident of Jamaica, made a survey of the island in 1823. He claimed that the abolition of the slave trade had led to more care for slaves on the plantations, and that the recent efforts of the abolitionists to secure registration of all slaves were counter-productive.

Stewart confessed that he wanted to steer a middle course between the contentions that the West Indian slaves were 'a happy and contented people', and that they were suffering 'under every species of revolting tyranny'.[47] He was a man caught between genuine feelings of humanity, and loyalty to the plantation system and his friends in the West Indies, whom he felt to be unfairly judged.

In 1826 Alexander Barclay, returning from Jamaica after twenty-one years' residence there, penned a response to James Stephen's delineation of West Indian slavery.[48] Barclay also identified with the bitterness of planters, who felt that they had been calumniated by the abolitionists. He countered Stephen's details of slave conditions and cruel practices in the West Indies by claiming, not that they had never existed, but that the facts provided by Stephen and Macaulay were outdated. Barclay was at pains to argue that old practices were limited to a few rogue individuals, and that the whip in the hands of the driver had 'become little more than a badge of his office'. Chains, he said, were virtually unknown, and compared with the situation of any unemployed British labourer, conditions for the fed, clothed and housed slave, who had access to medical care, were far better. One of his chapters was headed: 'Of the abundance of fish and crabs in Jamaica and the negro means of catching them', and another described 'plantation hospitals and nurseries'.[49]

The *Glasgow Courier*, although editorially opposed to the abolition of the slave trade in the late eighteenth century, had carried a variety of viewpoints within its columns and reported full accounts of meetings called to petition against the trade. That changed considerably under James McQueen's editorship, when the paper throughout most of the 1820s maintained a strong and sustained defence of the status quo in the slave colonies, and poured scorn on any attempts to alter this. McQueen had been manager of a plantation in Grenada. He interspersed editorial comment, especially on the problem-ridden 'free' colony of Sierra Leone, with pieces from Scottish planters, or those who had recently returned home. The Glasgow West India Association rewarded McQueen generously for his efforts on their behalf.[50]

In 1824 the *Courier* published extracts of three sermons from the minister of St Andrew's Scots Kirk in Demerara, Rev. Archibald Browne, entitled *On the Duties of Subjects to their Sovereign and Slaves to their Masters*. That same year McQueen reproduced his own publication, *Colonial Controversy*, which included an attack on the Sierra Leone Company.[51] In April 1826 Barclay's *A Practical View* was summarised in the *Courier*. In June three pages were devoted in successive issues to an anonymous, but 'prominent', Government figure, who offered *The*

West Indian Question Practically Considered.[52] Throughout the whole decade, and even beyond abolition, the *Courier* kept up a constant stream of vitriol against anyone challenging slavery.

The Glasgow West India Association was founded in 1808, the year after the abolition of the slave trade. It aimed to represent the interests of the planters and Caribbean commerce, and in its early years concerned itself with seeking lower tariffs on sugar, and a more efficient way to transport goods to the city. In the report of 1823 there was a reference to the injustice of other nations pursuing the trade to the detriment of the planters, and a report of a petition to the House of Commons from planters, merchants and shipowners of the city, seeking a review of customs duties for West Indian sugar.[53] Sugar became a disputed issue between defenders and opponents of West Indian slavery. In 1791 Thomas Clarkson had launched a campaign to boycott West Indian sugar, and several Edinburgh merchants then specifically advertised that they had sugar from 'free' sources. The Kirk Session of Largo, while declining to petition parliament on the slave trade, resolved to boycott West Indian goods, and Leslie's 'respectable inhabitants' published their determination to abstain from sugar and rum produced by slave labour. One spirited newspaper correspondent in Glasgow equated using West Indian sugar with whipping a slave.[54]

In 1823, when the campaign was launched to seek 'the mitigation and eventual abolition of slavery', the Glasgow West India Association sent a petition to the Earl of Liverpool at the Treasury. The Association presented itself as a benevolent organisation, stressing not only the importance of the sugar trade for the nation's economic health, but arguing 'that these benefits depend on the orderly and contented state of the negro, which your memorialists have ever been anxious to promote by attending to their comfort and happiness'. As if to prove this, the committee apportioned £100 towards religious instruction of slaves in the West Indies.[55]

Throughout the 1820s, Scottish abolitionist petitions to Westminster became progressively less cautious. More and more of them emphasised emancipation, rather than mitigation of conditions. The Glasgow West India Association, by the late 1820s, acknowledged the inevitability of abolition, but sought the support of King George IV in 1826 to ensure the 'safety' of the colonists, argued for a long period of preparation for the slaves, and above all pressed for considerable sums to be laid aside in order to compensate the slave owners.[56] These themes were reflected in a scattering of petitions to the parliament between 1824 and 1828. From Tain and Cromarty came appeals to calm the 'agitation', and give time for the slaves to be given Christian education and prepared for freedom. From planters and merchants in Glasgow and Greenock came complaints of victimisation towards those who ran the colonies that provided Britain's wealth. Planters living in Edinburgh and proprietors of West Indian estates in Aberdeen called for an impartial commission to be sent to the West Indies prior to any further action being taken.[57]

There is little doubt that had the colonists not shown such an ideological aversion to any ideas of amelioration suggested by the British Government, and brought in a gradual series of reforms, they would almost certainly have been able to drag out the institution beyond the end in 1838 of the 'apprenticeship' scheme, that replaced the false dawn of emancipation four years earlier. Macaulay's *Anti-Slavery Reporter* continued to provide well-researched and penetrating reports on the islands, showing, in most cases, little or no improvements in the conditions under which the enslaved lived.[58] This resulted in increasing public demands being made for speedy moves towards emancipation.

When Andrew Thomson, minister of St George's Church in Edinburgh, and one of Scotland's leading churchmen, rose to his feet in the Assembly Rooms on 8 October 1830, his words were described as 'the bursting of a bomb'. To the crowd of over two thousand gathered to press for abolition 'at the earliest possible opportunity', he declared loudly that he was opposed to this. In explanation, he said that it fell short of the necessity for immediate abolition. This marked the first call by a public figure in Scotland for such an uncompromising stand. The proposal by the meeting to have all the children of slaves freed on 1 January the following year seemed to be a radical one, but for Thomson it simply legitimised their parents' present enslavement.[59] 'Slavery', he declared at a meeting called eleven days later

> Is the very Upas tree of the moral world, beneath whose pestiferous shade all intellect languishes and all virtue dies. And if you would get rid of the evil, you must go more thoroughly and effectively to work than you can ever do by these palliatives, which are included under the term 'mitigation'. The foul sepulchre must be taken away. The cup of oppression must be dashed to the ground. The pestiferous tree must be cut down and eradicated; it must be, root and branch of it, cast into the consuming fire and its ashes scattered to the four winds of heaven. It is thus that you must deal with slavery. You must annihilate it, – annihilate it now, – and annihilate it for ever.[60]

In two speeches and in several sermons, Thomson spelt out the theological case for immediate abolition. He was careful not to be drawn into a tit-for-tat argument over the literal interpretation of the Bible, but echoed William Robertson in declaring that slavery was totally incompatible with 'the spirit of Jesus'.[61] Affirming the humanity of enslaved people 'for whom the Saviour died', he used traditional Calvinist doctrine to argue that fallen humanity could never be entrusted with absolute power over any other human beings.[62] Christianity therefore, for him, absolutely forbade anyone 'holding property in man'. Thomson drew on the 'jubilee' tradition of the Old Testament, which ransomed and released those bonded by debt or war every seven years. He embraced what had become common coin in the churches, by regarding slavery as 'sin' and he crucially took this further. 'To say we will come out of sin by degrees . . . to postpone the duty of doing justly and loving mercy', he affirmed, 'is to trample on the demands of obligation, and to disregard the voice that speaks to us from heaven.'[63]

Armed with this theological certainty that was to give a strong impetus to the abolition movement, Thomson sought to secure the moral claims of emancipation above the security of life in the colonies. He was contemptuous of the prospect of millions of pounds of compensation being paid to the slave owners, terming it as a reward for murder and pillage. He was equally sceptical over the threat of revolution in the West Indies being used to prolong slavery. 'If there must be violence', he thundered, 'let it come . . . give me the hurricane rather than the noisome pestilence.'[64] Thomson touched enough raw nerves to be quoted with disdain in Jamaica, and was credited with advancing the abolition movement in Britain to a crucial final stage.[65]

Among those who gave public criticism to this uncompromising stance were the phrenologist George Combe, and the minister of Ruthwell and founder of the Commercial Savings Bank, Dr Henry Duncan. Both men claimed strong opposition to slavery, but they were alarmed by the prospect of any change in a policy of gradual emancipation. Combe expressed his reservations in a letter to the *Edinburgh Evening Courant* of 14 October 1830. Duncan published his in pamphlet form, as letters addressed to the Colonial Secretary, but serialised in the newspaper which he edited, *The Dumfries and Galloway Courier*.[66] While protesting that he loathed slavery, he nevertheless affirmed that scripture sanctioned it. Taking Alexander Barclay as his source, Duncan claimed that the situation of those in bondage in the West Indies had considerably improved.[67] Thomson was editor of the widely read *Christian Instructor*, which maintained regular support for the anti-slavery movement, and his long review of Duncan's pamphlet, published in the *Observer* after his sudden death in February 1831, was scathing, not least because by now, in Thomson's view, Duncan was in the pocket of the West Indians who eulogised his *Letters* and used them to claim respectability.[68]

It was the churches which had seceded from the Church of Scotland that led the movement for emancipation in its final years. Dr John Ritchie, of Potterrow United Secessionist Church in Edinburgh, had a long history of anti-slavery. He had been persuaded by Andrew Thomson to take an 'immediatist' position, and was one of the Scottish representatives to meet Government ministers in London in 1833.[69] Dr Ralph Wardlaw, the prominent Glasgow Congregationalist and founder in 1823 of the Glasgow Anti-Slavery Society, made his church in Glasgow's city centre available for the newly formed Glasgow Emancipation Society, of which he was a vice-president.[70] His anti-slavery lectures attracted the attendance of the young David Livingstone, who walked from Blantyre to hear them.[71] These men commanded the moral high ground, and they used it to effect both in pulpits and at public meetings.

By the early nineteenth century Scotland's attention was focused on many contentious issues of the day: the threat of invasion from France and the threat to imperial trade, until the naval victory at Trafalgar in 1805; the issue of Catholic Emancipation; the demand for recognition of workers' organisations; and the popular movement calling for the extension of the franchise. That the issue of slavery occupied so much public attention and such keen debate was remarkable. That the debate expressed the tangled web in which the nation found itself on this subject was not surprising.

As we have seen, Scottish self-image as a more egalitarian society than England, and pride in Scottish distinctiveness in education, religion and the law, were strong influences on attitudes towards slavery. This was reflected in different ways at times, and sometimes seen in lurid and ridiculous guises. It is questionable whether Archibald Dalzel seriously believed that the slave trade delivered Africans from cruel paganism and slaughter, and gave them the benefits of 'Christian civilisation' on the plantations. Janet Schaw's account may have been more tailored to comforting those who gave her lavish hospitality, when she contended that slaves did not feel suffering in the same way as Europeans. Both in their different ways felt it necessary to appeal to humanity and Christian 'civilisation', rather than to rely on hard commercial arguments in their acceptance of slavery. John Stewart and Alexander Barclay likewise highlighted supposed improvements in the care of slaves, and barely mentioned the economic advantages of slavery in their appeal to the public.

Against them were ranged Scots such as James Ramsay and William Dickson in the late eighteenth century, and Zachary Macaulay and James Steven in the early nineteenth, who spoke with the authority of those who had lived in the colonies, and brought zeal and commitment to a cause to which they gave a substantial part of their lives. The Scots word 'thrawn' could apply to them all, expressing a stubborn, at times almost obsessive, adherence to the task of exposing the trade and slavery to the public, and providing the factual ammunition for the abolitionists in parliament.

There is no doubt that despite the more public presence of the Glasgow West India Association in the 1820s, practical defence of slavery in Scotland was infinitely weaker than its opposition. It was only attempted in bursts, often accompanied by righteous indignation over criticism of the plantation system. It is true that there were a number of anti-slavery petitions from outside the major cities from the far North to the Solway. They often came from rural areas, where Caribbean wealth had purchased estates or built large houses. Geographically they represented a wider spread than the English ones, which emanated mainly from the ports. Nonetheless the majority of the petitions were no more than late protests, arriving as they did in mid-1833 when the abolition bill was already passing through parliament, and when the only real issue was the terms of emancipation.[72]

The *Glasgow Courier*'s credibility was compromised by its satirical venom that sometimes paralleled the broadsheets on the streets. At times it reached an element of farce, as when the anonymous correspondent 'D.C.' warned Glasgow ministers that their support for abolition might lead them to lose them their commercially supported stipends. Rev. Patrick Macfarlane of St Enoch's Parish Church in Glasgow publicly exposed 'D.C.' as the former editor James McQueen,'the well known "Defender of the Colonies," pampered and well paid supporter of the West Indian interest'.[73]

Despite some Scottish newspapers carrying warnings from the West Indies that agitation on the matter would lead to rebellions such as that of 1831 in Jamaica, many of those with commercial interests were more concerned with wringing the best deal out of emancipation than producing propaganda in its favour. Scotland was weary of the tension between commercial wealth from the sugar colonies and the inhuman system on which it depended, although some of its people were soon to make a significant contribution to the new colonial exploitation, especially in Africa, that was to be a central feature of the later nineteenth century. Scottish abolitionists had played a significant part in the victory in 1833, or more correctly in 1838, when the Apprenticeship scheme in the West Indies – slavery under a different guise – was abandoned. There would, however, be much more engagement in the most significant of Britain's former colonies in the decades to come, when Scotland's ambivalent relationship with slavery was brought into sharp focus once again across the Atlantic, as the United States was forced to confront its own 'peculiar institution', and to tear the nation apart in the process.

NOTES

1. M. P. Brown (ed.), *Decisions of the Lords of Council and Session from 1776 to 1791*, collected by Lord Hailes (Edinburgh, 1826), p. 777.
2. Ibid., p. 779.
3. Eric Graham, *Burns and the Sugar Plantocracy of Ayrshire* (Edinburgh: MDPD, 2014), pp. 1, 2.
4. T. M. Devine, *To the Ends of the Earth; Scotland's Global Diaspora 1750–2010* (London: Penguin, 2011), pp. 50–1; D. Hancock, *Citizens of the World* (Cambridge: Cambridge University Press, 1995), p. 195.
5. Iain Whyte, *Scotland and the Abolition of Black Slavery 1756–1838* (Edinburgh: Edinburgh University Press, 2006), pp. 26, 27.
6. Lacy K. Ford, *Deliver Us from Evil: The Slavery Question in the Old South* (Oxford: Oxford University Press, 2009).
7. John Cairns, 'The Scottish Law of Slavery', unpublished lecture, University of Edinburgh, 6 December 2000.
8. Bill of Advocation on behalf of James Montgomery, 22 May 1756. NRS CS 234/S3/12.1.
9. Memorial for Robert Sheddan of Morricehill, 9 July 1756. Session Papers, Campbell's Collection Vol. 5, p. 9.
10. *American National Biography*, Vol. 23 pp. 704–6; W. McGinty, *An Animated Son of Liberty: A Life of John Witherspoon* (Bury St Edmunds: Arena, 2012), pp. 148, 244.
11. National Records of Scotland (NRS), 3 March 1770, CS 236/D/4/3; NRS Wemyss Parish Church, Register of Discipline (Kirk Session), 22 December 1771, NAS OPR 459/3; A. S. Cunningham, *Rambles in the Parishes of Scoonie and Wemyss* (Leven, 1905), pp. 155–6.
12. Sir John Wedderburn's Memorial (Defender against Joseph Knight, a Negro, Pursuer), February 1775, NAS CS 235/K/2/2, p. 9.
13. Memorial for Joseph Knight, NAS CS 235/K/2/2, pp. 26–30; William Robertson, *The Situation of the World at the Time of Christ's Appearance and its Connection with the Success of his Religion Considered* (Edinburgh, 1744), pp. 41, 44.
14. Brown, *Decisions of the Lords of Council and Session*, p. 778.

15. C. D. Rice, *The Scots Abolitionists 1833–1861* (Baton Rouge: University of Louisiana, 1981), p. 19.

16. T. H. Green and T. H. Grose (eds), David Hume, *Essays Moral, Political and Literary* (London: [1742] 1889), vol. 2. pp. 244–52.

17. Frances Hutcheson, *A System of Moral Philosophy* (Glasgow, 1755), Book 3, p. 201; John Millar, *The Origin of the Distinction of Ranks* (Edinburgh, 1806), p. 293.

18. William Wilberforce to William Robertson, 20 February 1788. National Library of Scotland, MSS 3943, ff. 230–4.

19. D. B. Davis, *The Problem of Slavery in Western Culture* (Ithaca: Cornell University Press, 1966), pp. 377, 391–421, 424.

20. James Beattie, *Elements of Moral Science* (Edinburgh, 1845), Book 3; On the Lawfulness and Expediency of Slavery particularly that of Negroes. 1788. Aberdeen University Library, Safe 3. Box B49.

21. Rice, *The Scots Abolitionists*, p. 120; The Edinburgh Speculative Society debated the subject annually from the 1780s, generally agreeing that slavery was 'contrary to nature' (*History of the Speculative Society* (Edinburgh, 1845).

22. E. W. Andrews (ed.), Janet Schaw, *Journal of a Lady of Quality, being the Narrative of a Journey from Scotland to the West Indies, North Carolina, and Portugal in the years 1774–1776* (New Haven: Yale University Press [1776] (1939), pp. 127, 128).

23. Viscountess Knutsford, *Life and Letters of Zachary Macaulay* (London, 1900), p. 8.

24. Zachary Macaulay to Selina Mills, Journal January–May 1797, Box 20. Macaulay Papers, Huntingdon Library, San Marino, CA; Iain Whyte, *Zachary Macaulay 1768–1838: The Steadfast Scot in the British Anti-Slavery Movement* (Liverpool: Liverpool University Press, 2011), pp. 12–16.

25. James Ramsay, *An Essay on the Treatment and Conversion of West Indian Slaves in the British Sugar Colonies* (London, 1784).

26. Folarin Shylon, *James Ramsay, The Unknown Abolitionist* (Edinburgh: Canongate, 1977), pp.14–17, 84, 97–113.

27. Whyte, *Scotland and the Abolition of Black Slavery*, p. 85.

28. *Glasgow Courier*, 23 February 1792.

29. Ibid., 28 February 1792.

30. Ibid., 8 March, 15 March 1792.

31. Ibid., 10 March 1792.

32. Edinburgh Chamber of Commerce, Minutes, 1788. Edinburgh City Council Archives, ED005/1/3, p. 245.

33. *Caledonian Mercury*, 9 February 1792.

34. Ibid., 1 March 1792.

35. Those from Glasgow, Edinburgh, Paisley, Hamilton, Perth, Dundee and Cupar.

36. Presbytery of Edinburgh Minutes, 29 February 1792, NAS, CH2/12/19.

204   RECOVERING SCOTLAND'S SLAVERY PAST

37. William Dickson, 'Diary of a Visit to Scotland 5th January–19th March 1792 on behalf of the Committee for the Abolition of the Slave Trade', Friends Library, London Temp. Box 10/14.
38. M. Armstrong, *The Liberty Tree* (Edinburgh: Wordpower, 2014), pp. 25–30.
39. Presbytery of Glasgow Minutes, 7 March 1792, Mitchell Library, Glasgow, CH2/171/14.
40. Presbytery of St Andrews, 7 March 1792, NAS, CH2/1082/4.
41. Dickson, 'Diary', 4 February, 14 February, 6 March 1792.
42. James Adair, *Unanswerable Arguments against the Abolition of the Slave Trade with Defence of the Proprietors of the British Sugar Colonies* (London, 1790).
43. Ibid., pp. 148, 195–9, 220.
44. J. D. Fage (ed.), A. Dalzel, *The History of Dahomey – An Inland Kingdom of Africa, Compiled from Authentic Memories* (London [1789], 1967).
45. Dalzel, *The History of Dahomey,* pp. 22, 25, 121, 130, 158.
46. Catherine Hall, *Macaulay and Son, Architects of Imperial Britain* (New Haven: Yale University Press, 2012), pp. 84–5; Whyte, *Zachary Macaulay,* pp. 28–48, 185–7.
47. James Stewart, *A View of the Past and Present State of the Island of Jamaica; with remarks on the Moral and Physical Condition of Slaves and on the Abolition of Slavery in the Colonies* (Edinburgh, 1823), pp. x, 220.
48. Alexander Barclay, *A Practical View of the Present State of Slavery in the West Indies or an Examination of Mr Stephen's 'Slavery in the West Indian Colonies', containing more particularly an Account of the Actual Conditions of the Negroes in Jamaica* (London, 1826); James Stephen, *The Slavery of the British West India Colonies Delineated as it exists, both in Law and Practice and compared with the Slavery of other Countries, Ancient and Modern* (London, 1824, 1830), 2 vols.
49. Barclay, *A Practical View,* pp. 40, 321, 417.
50. Minutes of the Glasgow West India Association (GWIA), Mic P. 3290–3294, vol. 3, Mitchell Library, Glasgow, February 1825, January 1826.
51. *Glasgow Courier,* 3 July 1824, 7, 9, 12, 16, 21 October 1824.
52. *Glasgow Courier,* 18 April, 15, 17, 22 June 1826.
53. Minutes of GWIA, 7 March 1823.
54. *Edinburgh Evening Courant,* 17 March 1792; *Edinburgh Advertiser,* 24 February 1792; *Glasgow Courier,* 17 January 1792.
55. Minutes of GWIA, April 1823, September 1823.
56. Ibid., April 1826.
57. *Journals of the House of Commons,* 26 May 1824, 10 June 1824, 19 May 1826, 9 June 1827, 20 June 1827.
58. *The Anti-Slavery Monthly Reporter,* October 1825, April 1826, December 1827.
59. Iain Whyte, 'Can we Come out of Sin by degrees? The Contribution of Andrew Thomson and John Ritchie to the Anti-Slavery Movement in

Scotland 1820–1840', *Scottish Church History Society Records*, vol 35, 2005, pp. 119–20.

60. Andrew Thomson, *Substance of the Speech delivered at a Meeting of the Edinburgh Society for the Abolition of Slavery* (Edinburgh, 1830), pp. 27–8.

61. Ibid., p. 39; William Robertson, *The Situation of the World at the Time of Christ's Appearance and its Connection with the Success of his Religion* (Edinburgh, 1755), p. 41.

62. Andrew Thomson, *Slavery not Sanctioned but Condemned by Christianity – A Sermon* (Edinburgh, 1830), p. 6; Thomson, *Substance of the Speech*, p. 6.

63. Thomson, *Substance of the Speech*, p. 4.

64. Ibid., pp. 33, 39.

65. Rice, *The Scots Abolitionists*, p. 23; David Brion Davis, 'The Emergence of Immediatism in British and American Anti-Slavery Thought', *The Mississippi Valley Historical Review,* vol. 42, no. 2 (September 1962), p. 221.

66. Henry Duncan, *Presbyter's Letters on the West Indian Question addressed to the Rt Hon George Murray* (London, 1830).

67. Ibid., pp. 13, 17, 20, 38–50.

68. *Christian Instructor*, January 1831, pp. 49–75.

69. Charles Buxton, *Memoirs of Sir Thomas Fowell Buxton* (Philadelphia, 1849), p. 271.

70. Glasgow Emancipation Society Minutes, December 1833, Smeal Collection, Mitchell Library, Glasgow.

71. Andrew Ross, *David Livingstone, Mission and Empire* (London: Hambledon & London, 2002), p. 12.

72. For different perspectives on the incidence and effectiveness of anti-abolitionist and anti-slavery activity in Scotland, see Douglas. J. Hamilton, 'Defending the Colonies against the malicious attack of Philanthropy: Scottish campaigns against the abolition of the Slave Trade and Slavery', in A. J. Macinnes and D. J. Hamilton (eds), *Jacobitism, Enlightenment, and Empire 1680–1820* (London: Pickering & Chatto, 2014), pp. 196–208; Whyte, *Scotland and the Abolition of Black Slavery*, pp. 163–75, 248–55.

73. *Glasgow Chronicle*, 12 November 1830.

10

'The most unbending Conservative in Britain': Archibald Alison and Pro-slavery Discourse

Catherine Hall

IN FEBRUARY 1832, while abolitionists rallied their troops for a final attack on the institution of slavery, Archibald Alison, a 40-year-old Scot, issued a dire warning to the nation on the appalling consequences that would follow emancipation. Reeling from the 'destruction of the constitution' as a consequence of the Reform Bill, he argued that Britain was now facing 'the dismemberment and dissolution of the empire'. 'The vast and splendid colonial possessions of Great Britain, encircling the globe with their stations, and nourishing its commerce by their productions', were, he warned, 'menaced with destruction'. 'The rash innovations of the mother country' were enraging the West Indian colonists and driving them into the arms of the Americans. If slavery was abolished, he was convinced, the white colonists would abandon Great Britain.[1] But sugar islands were not separate colonies of settlement, they should be thought of as a part of the mother country. The majority of West India proprietors lived in Britain and brought their riches home. A separation between the sugar islands and the mother country would be a disaster, not just for them, but also for Britain. In a flourish of his rhetorical imagination, Alison declared that the old country would be mortally wounded if the islands were lost.

His dramatic rendition of the dangers facing Britain in the event of emancipation was only part of the nightmare scenario that Alison evoked. The idea of abolition, he reported, was breeding terror among the West Indians. It came from 'the same spirit of rash, ignorant, and impetuous innovation' that had inspired the madness of parliamentary reform. Such a spirit was particularly dangerous in the Caribbean, 'as the passions are more violent, and reason less powerful, under a tropical sun and among an enslaved population, than under the cloudy atmosphere and among the free inhabitants of northern regions'. 'We' have the interests of the negroes at heart, he insisted, and do not love slavery. But slavery was 'a necessary step in the progress of improvement in the early ages of mankind.' This was a truth demonstrated by history; slavery was coexistent with the human race. It was hopeless to imagine that slavery could be abolished in a society that was not civilised. It had taken a thousand years to establish law and regular government in Britain, to subjugate the passions and establish not only a highly civilised upper class but an opulent and industrious middle class. Without 'developed habits of industry' and 'long established artificial wants' the overthrow of authority would lead to the annihilation of industry, the unfettering of passions and the extermination of improvement. It was only necessary to look at the examples of history – the horrors of the Jacquerie, or of St Domingo – to know that this was the case. The abolitionist appeal to religion, he insisted, was deranged. Any notion that Christianity proclaimed equality was totally mistaken. Negroes must by slowly encouraged to progress from the state of savage infancy to that of civilised man. West Indian negroes were 'in a situation so extremely low' that they were clearly

> incapable of understanding what freedom is, the duties with which it is attended, the restraint which it imposes, and the labour which it induces. They have none of the artificial wants which reconcile men to the severe and uninterrupted toil which constitutes the basis of civilised prosperity ... To them, freedom conveys the idea of the immediate cessation of all restraint, the termination of every species of labour, the undisguised indulgence of every passion ... Nature never intended that men in this stage of society should be free ...[2]

The inflammatory speeches of the Government on this subject were, to his mind, grossly irresponsible. Combined with the 'reckless and ambitious popular leaders in this country' and the 'ignorant and fanatical missionaries in the West Indies', there was a danger of lighting a powder keg and provoking not only a repetition of the American War of Independence but also a servile uprising.[3] It was essential to step back from the brink and learn the lessons of history.

Archibald Alison's defence of slavery was in no sense original. He was reiterating the arguments that had been made by pro-slavery forces since the 1770s and 1780s, ever since abolition first of the slave trade and then of slavery had become serious political issues. It was the questions from abolitionists that first provoked the colonists to articulate a defence of their practices. Though there were voices from the earliest days of the development of the slave trade challenging the enslavement of Africans, these were initially lone voices. It took Granville Sharp's testing of the legitimacy of slavery on English soil in the Somerset case to provoke two substantial pamphlets in 1772 exploring the legal, historical and political foundations of slavery in both the colonial and metropolitan worlds, in an attempt 'to reconcile colonial settler claims to an identity as free-born Britons with their enslavement of the vast majority of their colony's inhabitants'.[4] Edward Long, who had spent twelve years as a slave owner and colonial official in Jamaica, and Samuel Estwick, assistant agent for Barbados who owned extensive plantations, challenged Lord Mansfield's judgement and the growing anti-slavery literature.[5] They argued that English common law, numerous parliamentary statutes, and the slave codes all legitimated slavery as a necessary part of the colonial system. Furthermore, British prosperity depended on it. Slavery would over time civilise Africans who were fortunate, they maintained, to have been rescued from the barbarism of Africa and taken to a better world. Two years later, Edward Long published his *History of Jamaica*, a text that was to become a standard point of reference for all those engaged in debates over slavery. Long took an extreme view of racial difference, arguing that Africans were fundamentally different from and inferior to Europeans: white and black were 'two tinctures which nature has dissociated, like oil and vinegar'. Indeed, he was convinced 'the White and the Negroe are two distinct species'.[6] At the very same time that Long was attempting to codify racial difference, Joseph Knight, an enslaved man brought by John Wedderburn from Jamaica to Scotland, having heard of the Somerset judgement, was claiming in the courts of Perthshire that he was not a slave. The initial judgement was in his favour: 'the state of slavery is not recognized by the laws of this kingdom'.[7] Wedderburn appealed against this and the case was heard in Scotland's highest courts between 1775 and 1778. A sustained justification of slavery was presented by Wedderburn's lawyers, including the notion that Africans represented a threat to the white race, but a majority of the judges decided in Knight's favour. Slavery, they declared, was not recognised in Scotland.[8] This did not mean, however, that Scots would not recognise it elsewhere: slavery could be tolerated at a distance (see Introduction).

By the 1830s, when Alison was writing, few pro-slavery advocates argued publicly on explicitly racist grounds. Rather, they adopted a long-term stadial view: Africans were not a different species, they could become civilised but only over an extremely long period and with European authority to discipline and improve them. But the key arguments of the pro-slavers were remarkably consistent and Long's text remained iconic: slavery was essential to British prosperity, it had been legitimated by the crown, parliament and the common law. Africans were incapable of freedom, subject to passion and superstition. Thanks to the plantation system which was encouraging industry, artificial wants and domesticity, 'negroes' – the word 'slaves' was rarely used – were very slowly advancing from a state of barbarism. After the events of the French Revolution, the horrors of Haiti and St Domingo provided all the evidence that was necessary to convince sceptics of the hell that would be let loose if 'negroes' were emancipated before they were prepared for freedom.

In recent years, as this volume makes clear, historians have begun to explore Scotland's relation to slavery and have established the scale of Scottish involvement with the Caribbean – as indentured servants, as slave owners, as bookkeepers and attorneys, as merchants and bankers, as widows and daughters living off the proceeds of King Sugar. Considerable work has also been done on the Enlightenment figures who critiqued slavery and the Scottish abolitionists who challenged it.[9] So far, however, there has been little investigation of the contribution of Scots to the defence of the slave trade and slavery. Yet Scots were active both in defence of the trade and of the institution itself. Connections with slavery ran deep in Scottish economy and society: its legitimacy might have been in question by the late eighteenth century, yet it was clearly also regarded as a perfectly normal practice, especially if it took place somewhere else. What were the attitudes to race that made it possible to pursue these forms of exploitation, justified by an understanding of the differences between white men and black, between Britain, Africa and the West Indies? Who were the Scots who contributed to pro-slavery discourse? Archibald Alison was extremely well known in his lifetime, as a lawyer and state official, as an historian and as a prolific writer. He still figures in contemporary discussions of historiography and conservatism. His pro-slavery views, however, have for the most part been ignored, seen as irrelevant either to his history writing or to his politics.[10] In this chapter I argue that ideas about race, slavery and empire were integral to his thought and that more attention needs to be paid not only to the circulation of such ideas in early nineteenth-century Scotland but also to the centrality of race to British social and political thought. It was men such as Alison who not only defended slavery but crafted visions of racial hierarchy after emancipation that influenced generations.[11]

Alison's passionate intervention against emancipation in 1832 was part of his much wider campaign against reform. He was born in England in 1792, the second son of a well-known Scottish Episcopalian cleric, Rev. Archibald Alison, whose *Essays on the Nature and Principles of*

Taste (1790) had enjoyed a considerable success. His mother, Dorothea Gregory, was the daughter of another well-known cleric whose improving text on femininity, a *Father's Legacies to his Daughters*, was a favoured evangelical offering. Dorothea had become the young companion of the celebrated blue stocking, Elizabeth Montagu, after the death of first her mother, then her father. Before her marriage she had moved in an elevated intellectual circle.[12] She had, however, absorbed nothing of the blue stocking, and according to her son had 'an abhorrence for learned ladies', often quoting a favourite saying of Jeffrey's (the famed editor of the *Edinburgh Review*), who 'had no objection to blue stockings, provided the petticoats were long enough to conceal them'.[13] One of Dorothea's trustees was Sir William Johnstone Pulteney, a slave owner, politician and property developer, who became her husband's patron. The Alisons' first son, William, was named Pulteney after him, while one of their daughters was named Eliza Montagu, again a recognition of connection and influence. Thanks to the patronage of Sir William, Rev. Archibald Alison enjoyed his first appointments in England, in Leicestershire, then Shropshire. Pulteney's daughter, Laura, was said to be the richest heiress in England thanks to an inheritance through her mother. Laura, who was later to become the Countess of Bath, acted as William Pulteney's godmother and spent considerable time in the Alison household.[14] Alongside these landowning and slave-owning family connections were the Enlightenment figures who also frequented the Alison home, including Duguld Stewart, Rev. Archibald Alison's closest friend. In 1800 Rev. Archibald Alison was appointed to the ministry of the Episcopal church in Cowgate, Edinburgh and the family returned to Scotland, where Alison senior had been born and educated. His father, also Archibald Alison, had been Lord Provost of Edinburgh.

The young Archibald the third was initially educated by his father along with his brother William. They read *The Wealth of Nations* together and enjoyed long country walks discussing books, history and politics. Rev. Archibald Alison was horrified by the French Revolution and by Malthus with his mechanistic assumptions – both were issues which Archibald junior was to write about extensively. After a stint at Edinburgh University he began legal studies and was called to the bar in 1814. As a promising young lawyer he was welcomed into the Whig circle in Edinburgh but soon recognised that this was not the group for him. He was travelling on the continent, was fascinated by the war and the revolutions of 1820, was reading history systematically, and rapidly becoming a staunch Tory. Thanks to his burgeoning support for the Tory administration he was appointed Advocate-Depute in 1823, a crown appointment associated with the preparation of indictments and decisions about prosecutions. Two years later he married Elizabeth Tytler, cousin of one of his closest friends, Patrick Fraser Tytler, who was to become a well-known historian of Scotland. This was 'the most important and most fortunate event of my life', he later wrote. 'Never was evinced in a clearer manner the beneficial effect of marriage, in detaching the mind from dangerous excitements, and bracing it up to the real duties of life, than in my case.'[15] It was now time to settle down and to enjoy domesticity in the new house he had built in Edinburgh. His brother's serious illness, however, provoked a crisis for him. It was a warning from Providence not to waste his time on earth and he decided 'to devote myself to the elucidation of the unbounded wickedness, the disastrous results of the French Revolution'. He had become convinced 'that affairs were hurrying on to some great social and political convulsion in this country, of which it was easy to see the danger, but impossible to foresee the termination'. The passion for innovation, the Government's pursuit of popularity, 'the loosening of the constitution in its most essential parts, and progressive vesting of political power in new and inexperienced hands', all made him extremely pessimistic. 'I saw that a revolution was approaching in Great Britain, and that the means of resisting it did not exist in the nation.'[16] He had just finished a volume critiquing Malthus, and now he decided he would write a history of Europe from the French Revolution that would act as a rallying call for those who wished to conserve rather than reform.

The fall of the Tory Government in 1830 meant that he lost his official position and was faced with immediate financial problems. He decided to give up any political ambitions and devote himself to writing: the 'cramped political partisan' would be able to become 'the independent thinker'.[17] Always an extremely hard worker, he speedily authored a successful criminal law textbook after which William Blackwood proposed to him that he should write regularly for his magazine. *Blackwood's* was targeted at Tory readers who were critical of the liberalism of the *Edinburgh Review*. It had established itself after 1827 as the most articulate voice of the ultra Tories, with a monthly sale in the 1820s of between 6,000 and 7,000 but a much wider readership.[18] The thirteen-part series of essays on parliamentary reform and the French Revolution that Alison wrote between 1831 and 1833 established him as the magazine's principal political contributor, admired by luminaries such as Coleridge. The radical press was seen as a significant danger by the Tories, one which must be countered. Alison was fearful of 'the democratic tendency of the daily press'. The great majority of the public, he was convinced, were incapable of making political judgements, yet 'printing has extended to the whole people the passions of a mob'.[19] It was the duty of responsible men to intervene. The only way to effectively challenge the immense circulation of the popular press was by engaging with that press which had established itself as critical to the formation of public opinion, shaping debates 'out of doors' and informing those within. Alison might not be able to speak in the House of Commons, but he could be sure that his essays would appear in the drawing rooms and reading rooms of the Tories, for the political journals were an essential part of the political world. He was always looking for a wide readership for his work, hoping that his writings would find a place 'in the cottage or by the fireside'.[20] His first article appeared in January 1831, marking 'the commencement of a new career – it was my first speech in the great Parliament of the nations'.[21]

The analysis of reform that he developed was built on his conviction that the French Revolution had been a disaster and that Britons must learn from that experience: 'history', 'experience' and 'the dangers of innovation' were his watchwords. The desire for reform was to his mind delusional, a frenzy that had seized the nation. The real love of freedom, he argued, was quite distinct from the passion for democratic power. To the end of his life he remained convinced that the only practicable basis of government was by the propertied and that 'the consequences of vesting political power, suddenly and irrevocably, in a million of electors – a great part of whom, especially in that distracted isle [Ireland], and the manufacturing districts of Great Britain, were wholly unprepared to exercise it', could not but be ruinous.[22] Years later, his account of parliamentary reform in his volumes on the contemporary history of Europe reiterated his horror at the dangers associated with popular power but recognised that the Whigs had stepped back from excessive democratic change – their alliance with 'savages', as he termed them, had strict limits. The Anglo-Saxon race (with whom he clearly aligned the Scots), he declared, 'eminently practical and domestic in its disposition', sought what he described as '*home* benefits'. 'The vague idea of liberty and equality, powerful on the other side of the Atlantic, had little influence beside the English fireside.'[23]

In the years of crisis between 1830 and 1833, when parliamentary reform, the abolition of slavery and the reform of the East India Company were all on the political agenda, threatening stability at home and abroad, Ireland erupted once again. Catholic emancipation in 1829 had been intended to solve 'the Irish problem' but left multiple grievances untouched at the same time as having split the Tory party and left the Ultras enraged. Alison's essays in these years were littered with references to the 'savage Irish' whose racial characteristics he saw as central to the island's distemper. As a young man he had travelled in Ireland and become convinced that the miseries of over-population were a result of 'the innate character of the unmixed Celtic race, averse to labour and little inclined to improvement'. He recognised problems associated with English rule of the island – the confiscation of land, the problems of absenteeism, and the injustices of English law. But the 'impassioned, volatile Irish race' were not ready for the responsibilities of a representative political system.[24] His assumptions as to the degraded character of 'the Irish race' and the 'distracted and unhappy' country of Ireland were integral to his political analysis. 'Incessant' Irish immigration was a disaster, 'an evil peculiar to Britain, and perhaps greater than any which now afflicts any civilised state'. Between 1801 and 1821 over a million 'redundant' and 'miserable' Irish had arrived in Britain. 'There is no instance of the influx of barbarous settlers on record to such an extent,' he argued, 'even when the Goths overwhelmed the Roman empire.'[25] Catholic emancipation, in his view, had been a disaster, bringing 'midnight conflagration, dastardly assassination ... universal insurrection against the payment of tithes'. By 1833, with Ireland in a state of turmoil and O'Connell leading the call for repeal of the union, he pointed to the 'enormous evils' which arose from the principles of 'anarchy and insubordination' rampant in that island. The Irish were 'a semi-barbarous and impassioned people', three-quarters of the population were 'little better than savages'.[26] Immigration was blighting Britain, a major source of distress, but the sister kingdom could not be abandoned; there was no choice but to rule Ireland properly. The truth was, he believed, that Ireland had never been properly conquered. He pointed to the contrast with Scotland, ruled by an aristocratic and unrepresentative Government, yet prosperous. The Irish had been given privileges for which they were not ready, what was needed was

> a regular and severe administration of justice; a coercion of the lawless spirit and extravagant passions of the lower classes; a steady and unflinching repression of popular excitation; and a gradual preparation of the nation, by the habits of industry, and the acquisition of property, for the moderation and self-control indispensable for the safe discharge of the duties of a popular government.

It had been a terrible mistake to forget the lessons of experience, to be so blind to the 'difference between such different races and situations of mankind'. Foolishly, the Whigs had done this: 'They have given the same sovereign powers to the impassioned Catholic cottar, guided by his priest, and execrating the Protestants, as to the sober English yeoman, inheriting from a long line of ancestors attachment to his King and country.'[27]

Alison's conception of a racial hierarchy headed by the English and Scots and with the Irish linked to savagery was hardly unusual. The bright young man of the Whigs, Thomas Babington Macaulay, who had been in the forefront of arguments for a limited reform of the franchise and whose parliamentary speeches had been the toast of the town, shared many of these sentiments.[28] But while Macaulay had no love for Africans, despite his father Zachary's lifelong commitment to abolitionism, he was opposed to slavery, seeing it as the antithesis of British freedom. While Macaulay had grown up in an evangelical and anti-slavery household, an experience that left him averse to those he saw as sentimental 'negrophiles', Alison's familial world was different. His father's patron, Sir William Pulteney, who also provided significant support to his brother William, was part of the Johnstone family who had extensive interests in the West Indies. On the death of his older brother John Johnstone in 1794, Pulteney inherited the Westerhall plantation in Grenada. He was a staunch supporter of the slave trade and in 1805 argued against Wilberforce in the House of Commons that the West Indies could not be cultivated by Europeans. It was therefore necessary, he insisted, utilising the language of Long, that the labour was performed 'by some other class of the human species'.[29] Pulteney had appointed as manager of Westerhall James MacQueen, who was to become one of the most significant Scots defending slavery. At the time of abolition in 1834, when £20 million compensation was granted to the slave owners, Pulteney's heir received nearly £5,000 for 176 enslaved men and women in Grenada.[30] Even closer to home, Alison's sister Montagu had married Lieutenant Colonel John Gerard in 1810. He had made a fortune in India and invested both in Scotland and St Vincent. By the time of emancipation, Gerard was dead but Alison, along with his brother, was acting as a trustee for him and a successful claim was entered for 152 enslaved men and women on the Bellevue Estate. Alison received the compensation money of over £4,000.[31] West Indian slave owners and merchants constituted a significant population in early nineteenth-century Edinburgh, Glasgow and Leith. While the Whiggish circle around *Edinburgh Review* were supportive of the abolition of the slave trade and of slavery, Tory circles were much closer to the West India interest. As a young man pursuing legal studies, one of Alison's close associates had been Nathaniel Hibbert, 'son of Mr Hibbert, a

gentleman of large fortune, the able advocate of the West India interest in the House of Commons'.[32] They both belonged to a reading and
discussion society in Edinburgh and this was the period which Alison
himself described as being formative for all the key principles which his
writings were later to expound.

His alignment with pro-slavery forces in 1831 was, therefore, not
surprising. In preparation for his first volume on the French Revolution
he had been reading on St Domingo. The first account he gave of the
horrors and mayhem there was published in 1832 in *Blackwood's* and
was to be repeated in the volume he published later that year, *History of
the French Revolution from 1789–96*. It echoed the history produced by
Bryan Edwards, another staunch defender of the slave trade and slavery,
whose horrific account of the events in St Domingo claimed its authenticity on the basis of eye-witnesses.[33] St Domingo, Alison maintained,
had been a wonderfully happy colony but the slaves had been 'agitated'
by the news they got from Paris and 'early manifested symptoms of
insubordination'. Their passions were excited by the Society of Friends
of the Blacks and the mulattoes, injudiciously advised, organised an
insurrection. They had expected to be able to control 'the ferocity of
the slaves ... they little knew the dissimulation and the cruelty of the
savage character'. The rebellion broke out, coffee and sugar plantations
were burnt down, 'the unfortunate proprietors hunted down, murdered,
or thrown into the flames by the infuriated negroes'.

> The unchained African signalized his ingenuity by the discovery of new
> and unheard-of modes of torture. An unhappy planter was sawed asunder
> between two boards; the horrors inflicted on the women exceeded anything
> known even in the annals of Christian ferocity. The indulgent master was sac-
> rificed equally with the inhumane; on all alike, young and old, rich and poor,
> the wrongs of an oppressed race were indiscriminately wreaked. Crowds of
> slaves traversed the country with the heads of the white children affixed on
> their pikes; they served as the standards of these furious assemblages.[34]

Faced with these events, the French Assembly granted political rights
to men of colour. After the outbreak of war with Britain, French army
commanders felt compelled to liberate the enslaved, in an attempt to
avoid disaster.[35] The intention behind emancipation, argued Alison, had
been philanthropic, but it was 'carried into execution without regard
to the capacity of those for whom it was intended'.[36] 'A child does not
acquire the strength of manhood in an hour.'[37] An 'ignorant slave population' had been granted freedom and a calamitous history had ensued:
'The independence of its population has been established; but with it

they have relapsed into a state of degradation, combining the indolence and recklessness of savages, with the vices and corruptions of civilised life.' There was the most frightful dissoluteness of manners alongside a rapid decline of population, a total cessation of industry, and 'general suffering among the unhappy victims of premature freedom'.[38] Negroes, 'naked and voluptuous', were 'fast receding into the state of nature from which their ancestors were torn, two centuries ago, by the rapacity of Christian avarice.'[39] Cultivation was down, sugar was being imported, profligacy was everywhere. It was this dreadful example which had 'penetrated the West India proprietors with a sense of the danger which threatens them'.[40]

The first volume of Alison's *History* was greeted with very modest success, though later he was to become a seriously popular historian, providing the Tories with an antidote to Macaulay's story of progress. He had, however, established himself as a leading Scottish Tory, and in 1834 his fortunes changed with the fall of the Whigs. A Unionist, he was also an ardent Scot, enthusiastic about Scottish history, strongly in favour of national monuments, and seeing the rivalry of the two nations as a source of strength. As Michael Michie argues, he can be understood as a transitional figure, wanting to preserve an agrarian commercial Scotland, paternalist in some respects, yet committed to professionalism and public service.[41] With no family money, official appointments were important to his income, though in later years he made very considerable amounts from his writing. He was offered the significant position of Sheriff of Lanarkshire and moved with his family to Possil House, a large establishment with grounds on the outskirts of Glasgow, previously occupied by a leading West India merchant. Glasgow offered Alison a very different context and new opportunities. The town had expanded massively in the preceding fifty years, particularly because of the development of cotton textiles. In a country that was still predominantly agricultural, its manufacturing base was unusual. Commercial men provided the elite, rather than the professionals who were so significant in Edinburgh life. Observers constantly commented on the spirit of industry, though the town council was run by a corrupt oligarchy of tradesmen and merchants, and many of the new industrialists were the sons of farmers or small lairds from the surrounding districts in the West of Scotland. Alison soon recognised the clear hierarchy within the city's commercial sectors. At the apex were the 'sugar aristocracy', he noted, five or six families who 'lived almost exclusively with each other'. Then there were the cotton magnates, next the calico masters and then the iron and coal masters.[42] Unlike the 'tobacco lords' of a previous era, the West Indians had never achieved political hegemony but their investments spanned both Caribbean plantations and Scottish landed estates, many of them in the immediate environs of the town.[43] The sugar merchants had fought hard against abolition and for compensation. The threat of emancipation had unified planters and merchants and they had used the Glasgow West India Association, formed in 1807, to make their case. In the early 1820s they had asked James MacQueen to spearhead their campaign. MacQueen had left Grenada and settled in Glasgow around 1810. He worked as a West Indian wholesaler and began to write for the *Glasgow Courier*, launched in 1791 to profit from the Atlantic trade. *The Courier* championed the ultra Tories, protection and High Church interests. The Glasgow West India Association was to become 'the strongest pro-slavery group outside London'.[44] They complained bitterly about how the British public had been 'excited and deluded on the subject of slavery', and about 'the inveterate and persevering enemies of the colonies'.[45] MacQueen's two pro-slavery books, *The West India Colonies* and *The Colonial Controversy*, established him as a leading figure in the debates over slavery, with its reiteration of the racist stereotypes of 'the ignorant population of Africa' who could 'only be raised to the blessings and advantages of freedom through personal slavery'.[46] In the late 1820s several of the West Indians had been Tory MPs, but 1832 had changed the political landscape of Glasgow and the West of Scotland and brought in Whigs and Liberals, an unwelcome shift for Alison.

The new sheriff arrived in the immediate wake of reform and was soon dismayed by the failure of the elite groups to work together when faced with challenges. This was a time when he was writing in *Blackwood's* on the need for the middle classes, thinking men, to cohere behind the forces of conservatism and to adjust to the new political landscape. Alison saw himself as a self-made man, one who worked hard to achieve a competence and independence, those central attributes of early nineteenth-century manliness. 'An extensive and opulent middle class', he was convinced, was a necessary 'connecting link' between the refined and civilised rich and the 'lower classes'.[47] They must unite to 'uphold the remaining institutions of the country'.[48] To his chagrin he found the Glasgow and Lanarkshire elite quite unwilling to back him in what he conceived as the imminent threats to social and political stability. 'Commercial cities are merely workshops of wealth', he noted ruefully; great wealth could be accumulated very fast but did not bring with it a proper sense of responsibility.[49] He was convinced that 'history' and 'experience' had demonstrated that the weakness of the ruling class was a fundamental cause of the French Revolution: that must not be allowed to happen in Britain.

Glasgow proved to be his first encounter with the new world of industry and a major test of his authority. As sheriff he was an official of the British state with responsibility for aspects of public order. A factory-based cotton textile industry had begun in Glasgow in the early 1780s and by 1830 the town had 98 cotton mills, about 40 firms and 10,000 workers in a population of over 200,000.[50] About a thousand of these men were spinners, often with their children working under them. They had been unionised since the early 1800s. The great concern of these skilled workers in the 1830s was to keep a firm hold on entry into the trade and ensure that they did not suffer the fate of de-skilling which had befallen the weavers. The employers, however, were keen to lower their costs by taking on 'outsiders', including the Irish who had flocked into Glasgow. The unions, as Alison later explained it to the parliamentary inquiry of 1838, were simply committed to maintaining their hold on access to their trades, determined to exclude 'a hundred thousand of unskilled workmen . . . it is just a system of the aristocracy of skilled labour against the general mass of unskilled labour'.[51] In his view they depended on secretive organisation and despotic power. But the employers, far from facing up to this challenge, were feeble and lacking in courage. 'The capitalist', he was convinced, 'is the most timid animal in existence.'

An economic boom in 1836 was followed by a downturn and the union decided to strike against one of the largest firms. The strike was broken and the union weakened. Taking advantage of this situation, the employers met and decided to reduce wages. A strike was threatened but in April the employers decided on further reductions, seriously threatening the position of the spinners. They struck and Alison watched with dismay the 'vast accession of force to the numbers of the idle and discontented'. The unions were determined, he believed, 'to set the law at defiance' and large bands of men with drums and banners were 'denouncing their masters as the most oppressive of tyrants'. Serious disorder threatened, and 'anarchy was rapidly approaching'.[52] There were no police in Lanarkshire at this time and only 280 in Glasgow. 'The higher classes' would not act. He knew that he could only call in the military in a situation of severe danger. According to his own account, Alison watched the situation closely, waiting until 'some serious invasion on life or property was committed, which would rouse the indignation of all classes' and he could move with force.[53] After three months, with the strike funds virtually exhausted, a crisis erupted when one of the new hands who had been brought in, John Smith, was killed. Alison used the opportunity to employ the military to break the strike, which had now spread to the iron and coal workers. He led troops to break up the pickets and arrest the spinners' leaders, insisting that they were engaged in a conspiracy against property, the bulwark of freedom. For Alison this was a form of class war with unionists cooperating with dangerous radicals. A high-visibility trial of the leaders had an unsatisfactory result from Alison's point of view, but the strike and the trial had proved very useful to the authorities and the employers. The barrier to technological change in the mills was broken and new machines came in, worked by youths and women. The Scottish unions had been tarred with a reputation for violence and had to struggle over decades for respectability.[54] In Alison's own judgement, his actions had been entirely beneficial. The cotton spinners returned to work and 'about 30,000 persons in and around Glasgow were at once raised from a state of idleness, destitution, and despair, to industry and comfort'.[55]

Alison was convinced his curtailment of the power of the unions was once again called for in the context of the Chartist agitation and miners' strike of 1842. These were 'formidable attacks on property' and he was certain his own speedy action against 'insurrection and intimidation', backed by the yeomanry, had been essential to the maintenance of good order.[56] But his efforts to crush radicalism were only one aspect of his conservative interventions – questions of race and slavery did not go away.

His hope that emancipation could be averted by the dire warnings he issued had been doomed to failure. The abolitionists had triumphed in 1833, albeit with the twin successes for the slave owners of compensation and apprenticeship.[57] Like many others in the 1830s, Alison was extremely enthusiastic about emigration as a cure for the nation's ills. Speaking at a dinner in Glasgow on the occasion of the first colonists leaving the Clyde for New Zealand in 1839, he waxed lyrical on the providential future of 'the British race, peopling alike the western and the southern hemispheres'. He could 'already anticipate the time when two hundred millions of men on the shores of the Atlantic, and in the isles of the Pacific, will be speaking our language, reading our authors, and glorying in our descent. Who ... can avoid the conclusion that the British race is indeed the chosen instrument for mighty things, and that to it is given to spread the blessings of civilisation and the light of religion, as far as the waters of the ocean extend?' What was more, the bad old days of conquest were over and now the British would 'humanise', not enslave, others.[58] 'To the Anglo-Saxon race', he declared, 'is destined the sceptre of the globe.'[59] But if this was to be achieved, the colonies needed to be attended to and the 'parent state' needed to redress the terrible damage it had done to the West Indies.

By the late 1830s the abolitionist assumption that free labour would be successfully established and the West Indian economies flourish was coming under sustained attack from the West Indians. Faith in the 'great experiment' was waning and the case for the introduction of Asian indentured labour being made. Alison pitched into these arguments in *Blackwood's*. Of course he recognised the evils of slavery, he averred, but it had resulted in something good. The horrors of the Middle Passage were over and negroes had 'become permanently located on fixed estates; they had acquired homes, and all the endearments and enjoyments of domestic existence'. The Government had done well in abolishing the slave trade, but slavery was 'the necessary state between savage manners and civilised industry' . . . a 'transition state necessarily enduring several centuries'. Emancipation had been a disaster, leading to the 'almost total ruin' of the colonies. Government compensation had been totally inadequate, in the majority of cases covering a third of the real value of 'their property'. In Jamaica, Africans would not work for wages and had no discipline. It was essential to introduce 'some other race' and leave the negroes to 'lead a life of savage indolence'. It was a delusion to think it was possible to impose freedom – the transition might take five hundred years. 'To men in the stage of advance which the African Negroes exhibit, liberty is the same thing as it would be to a herd of cattle or a troop of camels – the signal for the immediate abandonment of the restraints and the enjoyments of domestic life, and resumption of the want, the penury, and independence of the prairie or the desert.'[60]

Alison, it was clear, had in no sense abandoned his belief in slavery.[61] This remained central to his creed and he was unapologetic about it, though well aware that he was at odds in some respects with the 'increasing *Liberal* spirit of the age'.[62] At the time of the American Civil War he remained convinced that slavery, 'in certain climates and with certain races of mankind, . . . is part of the system of nature'. It was right to attempt to mitigate its severities, but foolish to abolish it. Negroes would not work without compulsion and

> compulsory labour in the tropics is . . . the condition of national existence and of social progress. The experiment of emancipation in the British West India Islands, which has terminated after the experience of a quarter of a century in their ruin, has dispelled the pleasing illusion, so dear to republicans of every age, that all men are equal by nature. So far from being so, they are enormously unequal.[63]

Negroes were born to be the servants of Europeans. This was the order intended by nature, just as

> the richer and more educated classes, guided by the instincts of property and enlightened by the lessons of history, should direct and rule the greater numbers of the working classes, who are impelled only by the wants of poverty ... The people may occasionally establish for a brief season the dogma of democratic government, but it will only be to furnish an additional proof of its dangers, and terminate more speedily its destructive sway.

In Alison's 'order of things', Anglo-Saxons should rule the world, Celts be disciplined, negroes act as servants, property must govern, the working classes be governed.

Thinking about slavery was never separate from other aspects of social and political thought. Alison indeed deserved the title of 'the most unbending Conservative in Great Britain', bestowed upon him in his *Blackwood's* obituary, but his conservatism was centrally concerned not only with questions of class and nation but also those of empire, race and slavery.[64] Being pro-slavery was always part of a wider set of attitudes to race and the social order, and while abolitionists successfully challenged the institution of slavery, they only partially unpicked understandings of racial difference. The conviction of white superiority ran very deep, and continues to trouble us today.

NOTES

1. Archibald Alison, 'The West India Question', *Blackwood's Edinburgh Magazine*, 31:191 (February 1832), reprinted as 'Negro Emancipation' in Alison, *Essays, political, historical and miscellaneous*, 2 vols (Edinburgh: Wm Blackwood & Sons, 1850), i, pp. 208–38, 208–10.
2. Ibid., pp. 214, 219, 221.
3. Ibid., p. 230.
4. Jack P. Greene, 'Empire and Liberty', in Greene (ed.), *Exclusionary Empire. English Liberty Overseas, 1600–1900* (Cambridge: Cambridge University Press, 2010), p. 65.
5. Edward Long, *Candid reflections upon the judgement lately awarded by the Court of King's Bench in Westminster Hall on what is commonly called The Negroe Cause by a Planter* (London, 1772); T. Lowndes and Samuel Estwick, *Considerations on the Negroe Cause commonly so called* (London: J. Dodsley, 1772).
6. Edward Long, *The History of Jamaica. Or, General Survey of the Ancient and Modern State of That Island: with Reflections on its Situation, Settlements, Inhabitants, Climate, Products, Commerce,*

Laws, and Government, 3 vols (London: T. Lowndes, 1774), ii, pp. 332, 336.

7. Cited in Emma Rothschild (2011), *The Inner Life of Empires. An Eighteenth-Century History* (Princeton, NJ: Princeton University Press, 2011), p. 93.

8. Ibid. for an account of the Joseph Knight case, pp. 91–6.

9. See the recent historiography considered in the text and references of the Introduction and Chapter 1.

10. Michael Fry's biography in the *ODNB* is an honourable exception. Michael Fry, 'Alison, Sir Archibald, first baronet (1792–1867)', *Oxford Dictionary of National Biography*, Oxford University Press, 2004, http://www.oxforddnb.com/view/article/349 (accessed 31 December 2014). The one contemporary biography, Michael Michie, *An Enlightenment Tory in Victorian Scotland. The career of Sir Archibald Alison* (East Lothian: Tuckwell Press, 1997), has one reference in his discussion of his attitudes to poor relief, p. 116. He noted the poor had always been protected, 'in the rude stage of society it was by means of slavery, which, incidentally, he thought was still appropriate for such societies (including Ireland) in his own day'.

11. For the writing of Alison and other pro-slavers after emancipation, see Catherine Hall, 'Reconfiguring Race: The Stories the Slave-owners Told', in Catherine Hall, Nicholas Draper, Keith McClelland, Katie Donnington and Rachel Lang, *Legacies of British Slave-ownership. Colonial Slavery and the Formation of Victorian Britain* (Cambridge: Cambridge University Press, 2014) pp. 163–202.

12. Norma Clarke, 'Gregory, Dorothea (bap. 1754, d. 1830)', *Oxford Dictionary of National Biography*, Oxford University Press, 2004, http://www.oxforddnb.com/view/article/65052 (accessed 31 December 2014).

13. Archibald Alison, *Some Account of my Life and Writings. An Autobiography*, edited by his daughter-in-law, Lady Alison, 2 vols (Edinburgh: Blackwood, 1883), i, p. 292.

14. Sir William Pulteney was born William Johnstone. He married Frances, daughter and heir of Daniel Pulteney, and she inherited the fortune of General Harry Pulteney in 1767. The Johnstones immediately adopted the Pulteney name. M. J. Rowe and W. H. McBryde, 'Pulteney, Sir William, fifth baronet (1729–1805)', *Oxford Dictionary of National Biography*, Oxford University Press, 2004; online edn, January 2008, http://www.oxforddnb.com/view/article/56208 (accessed 31 December 2014); M. J. Rowe and W. H. McBryde, 'Pulteney, (Henrietta) Laura, suo jure countess of Bath (1766–1808)', *Oxford Dictionary of National Biography*, Oxford University Press, 2004; online edn, January 2008, http://www.oxforddnb.com/view/article/59519 (accessed 31 December 2014); Norma Clarke, 'Gregory, Dorothea (bap. 1754, d. 1830)', *Oxford Dictionary of National Biography*, Oxford University Press, online edn, January 2008, http://www.oxforddnb.com/view/article/65052 (accessed 27 August 2014).

15. Alison, *Some Account*, i, p. 233.
16. Ibid., pp. 245, 253–4.
17. Ibid., p. 298.
18. Maurice Milne, 'Archibald Alison: Conservative Controversialist', *Albion: A quarterly journal concerned with British Studies*, 27/3, Autumn 1995, pp. 419–43.
19. Archibald Alison, 'The Reform Bill', May–September 1831, reprinted in *Essays*, i, pp. 41, 46.
20. Ibid., p. 120.
21. Ibid., p. 304.
22. Ibid., p. 306.
23. Archibald Alison, *History of Europe from the Fall of Napoleon in 1815 to the Accession of Louis Napoleon in 1852*, 5 vols (Edinburgh: Blackwood, 1856), v, p. 335.
24. Ibid., p. 137.
25. Alison, 'The Reform Bill', p. 12; 'Ireland', *Blackwood's*, January 1833, reprinted *Essays*, i, p. 240.
26. Alison, 'Ireland', pp. 248, 256–7.
27. Ibid, p. 270.
28. Catherine Hall, *Macaulay and Son. Architects of Imperial Britain* (London: Yale University Press, 2012). See particularly Chapter 4.
29. Quoted in Rothschild, *The Inner Life*, p. 163.
30. National Archives, T71/880. Grenada 865 (Westerhall Estate), http://www.ucl.ac.uk/lbs/claim/view/10589 (accessed 30 December 2014). On the question of compensation, see Nicholas Draper's chapter in this volume.
31. National Archives, T71/892. St Vincent. Bellevue Estate, http://www.ucl.ac.uk/lbs/claim/view/27151 (accessed 30 December 2014).
32. Alison, *Some Account*, i, p. 56.
33. Bryan Edwards, *An Historical Survey of the French Colony in the island of St Domingo, comprehending an account of the revolt of the Negroes in the year 1791 and a detail of the military transaction of the British army in that island in the years 1793 & 1794* (London: W. B. Whittaker, 1819).
34. Archibald Alison, *History of the French Revolution from 1789–96* [1832], 10 vols (Paris: no publisher, 1852), i, pp. 192–3.
35. Alison's account of these events was severely truncated.
36. Alison, 'Negro Emancipation', pp. 222–6.
37. Alison, *History of the French Revolution*, p. 192.
38. Alison, 'Negro Emancipation', p. 226.
39. Alison, *History of the French Revolution*, p. 193.
40. Alison, 'Negro Emancipation', p. 222.
41. Michie, *An Enlightenment Tory*, explores his critique of political economy, his desire to reform the Scottish poor laws and his enthusiasm for landownership for the poor.

42. Alison, *Some Account*, i, p. 344.
43. T. M. Devine, 'An Eighteenth-Century Business Elite: Glasgow West India Merchants, c.1750–1815', *The Scottish Historical Review*, vol. 57, 163, Part I (April 1978), pp. 40–67. See also Stephen Mullen, 'A Glasgow-West India Merchant House and the Imperial Dividend, 1779–1867', *Journal of Scottish Historical Studies*, 33:2 (2013), pp. 196–233.
44. Stephen Mullen, *It Wisnae Us: The Truth about Glasgow and Slavery* (Edinburgh: Royal Incorporation of Architects of Scotland, 2009), p. 66.
45. Quoted in Anthony Cooke, 'An Elite Revisited: Glasgow West India Merchants, 1783–1877', *Journal of Scottish Historical Studies*, 32:2 (2012), pp. 127–65, 141.
46. James MacQueen, *The Colonial Controversy, containing a Refutation of the Calumnies of the Anticolonists* (Glasgow: no publisher, 1825), p .86; for details on MacQueen, see David Lambert, *Mastering the Niger. James MacQueen's African Geography and the Struggle over Slavery* (Chicago: Chicago University Press, 2013).
47. Alison, 'Negro Emancipation', p. 220.
48. Quoted in Milne, 'Archibald Alison', p. 434.
49. Alison, *Some Account*, i, p. 349.
50. W. Hamish Fraser, 'The Glasgow Cotton Spinners, 1837', in John Butt and J. T. Ward (eds), *Scottish Themes. Essays in honour of Professor S. G. E. Lythe* (Edinburgh: Scottish Academic Press, 1976), pp. 80–97. My account relies heavily on Fraser's work.
51. *P. P. 1837–8*, vol. 8, p. 130, quoted in T. C. Smout, *A History of the Scottish People 1560–1830* [1987] (London, 1969), p. 386.
52. Alison, *Some Account*, i, pp. 350, 372–3.
53. Ibid., p. 375.
54. Ibid., pp. 96–7.
55. Ibid., i, p. 386.
56. Ibid., i, pp. 487–9
57. Hall et al., *Legacies*, Introduction.
58. Archibald Alison, 'Ships, Colonies, and Commerce', Speech at dinner in Glasgow on occasion of first colonists leaving Clyde for New Zealand, in the vessel 'Tory', 20 October 1839. In *Essays*, ii, pp. 658–74.
59. Archibald Alison, 'Colonial government and the West India Question' [1839], *Essays*, i, pp. 302–30, 304.
60. Ibid., pp. 319, 322, 327.
61. Hall, 'Reconfiguring race: The stories the slave-owners told', in Hall et al., *Legacies*.
62. Alison, *Some Account*, ii, p. 237.
63. Ibid., ii, p. 291.
64. *Blackwood's*, obituary 102 (1867), pp. 125–8.

11

Did Slavery make Scotia Great?
A Question Revisited[1]

T. M. Devine

I

IN HIS MAGNUM OPUS, *The Wealth of Nations*, Adam Smith famously declared: 'Under the present system of management, therefore, Great Britain derives nothing but loss from the dominion which she assumes over her colonies.' Yet even Smith's authority could not lay to rest the question whether empire in the later eighteenth century was a drain on the metropole or a priceless resource of great material advantage to the mother country as it progressed towards economic transformation and industrialisation.

More recently, in 1944, Eric Williams published his seminal *Capitalism and Slavery*.[2] In it he not only made a stimulating contribution to the intellectual debate which Smith's assessment had encouraged, but raised the issues to a more polemical and controversial level. His focus in part centred on the role of African slavery in the origins of the world's first Industrial Revolution in Britain. Williams himself described his book as 'an economic study of the role of negro slavery and the slave trade in providing the capital which financed the Industrial Revolution in England'.[3] Ironically enough, however, despite its later fame, if not notoriety, this thesis formed a relatively small section of a much broader study which also included the argument that mature industrial capitalism was ultimately responsible for the destruction of the slave system itself. At first the book provoked little published reaction in scholarly circles and only in the 1960s were significant responses forthcoming. They were unambiguously hostile. A series of thoroughly researched and carefully argued articles stretching from the 1960s to the 1980s sought to demonstrate that the 'Williams thesis' did not stand up to serious scholarly scrutiny.[4] Thus, one estimate published in volume two of the *Oxford History of the*

British Empire series concluded that the slave trade, though immense in scale, might only have added a mere 1 per cent to total domestic investment in Britain by the later eighteenth century.[5] Scholarship seemed to have delivered a final verdict on the Williams ideas.

But that judgement was premature. From the 1980s new perspectives began to emerge. Most importantly, some scholars argued that the approach of the sceptics was much too narrow. Not only should the slave trade itself be considered but also (as Williams himself had implied) the total impact of the slave-based plantation economies of America and the Caribbean on Britain. These could not have existed and, even more importantly, have grown enormously in scale over time, but for the labour input of untold numbers of black slaves. If the American colonies and the islands of the British Caribbean contributed markets, profits, capital and raw materials to industrialism in the Mother Country, then those gains ultimately depended on their enslaved workers.[6] It was an important shift of conceptual direction which gave a new and invigorating lease of life to the entire debate.

A stream of books and articles by Blackburn, Inikori, Solow and others proceeded to place 'the Williams thesis' firmly back on the historical agenda. Even long-term sceptics, such as David Eltis and Stanley Engerman, were forced to partially recant.[7] They did not exactly swallow the revisionist view hook, line and sinker, but root-and-branch opposition was now replaced by a cautious realignment of argument: 'African slavery thus had a vital role in the evolution of the modern West, but while slavery had important long-run economic implications, it did not by itself cause the British Industrial Revolution. It certainly "helped" that Revolution along, but its role was no greater than that of many other economic activities'.[8] Others were less restrained. In 2002 Joseph E. Inikori published a lifetime's research on the subject under the title *Africans and the Industrial Revolution in England*.[9] Inikori's conclusion, after presentation of an impressive array of statistical and empirical evidence, was unequivocal: 'the contribution of Africans was central to the origin of the Industrial Revolution in England'.[10] The critical responses to his work nonetheless demonstrated that the debate was far from over.[11]

The Scottish dimension never featured in these discussions, although significantly, it was mentioned in Williams' own book. Perhaps this was hardly surprising given the persistent anglocentricity of modern English history, the *cordon sanitaire* between much of the modern historiography of England and Scotland, and the continued commitment of many Scottish historians to stick to their own patch and for the most part avoid engagement in major British and international debates. This is a pity because, as will be argued in this chapter, the Scottish experience has much to contribute to an assessment of the broader issues of slavery and industrial capitalism which currently interest a wide audience of historians across the world. Several of the participants in the ongoing debate refer to 'British' or 'Britain' in their contributions. Yet what they really mean by that term is England. There is precious little sign in the discourse of evidence being deployed for and against opposing views derived from studies north of the Border.

II

The results of recent research, reported in the earlier chapters of this book, confirm the extent of Scottish engagement at every level of the slave trade and slave system as a whole. Yet, while the business may have made some profits for a few Scots merchants, the relatively small *direct* scale of slave trafficking from Scottish ports was hardly likely to have had much effect on the overall economy of Scotland itself. To evaluate the connection between slavery and Scottish development, it is therefore necessary to extend the range of the enquiry from the trade in slaves to the plantations of the West Indies and the Chesapeake colonies whose very existence depended on enslaved labour. The sugar, tobacco, indigo, rice, rum and cotton produced by these slave-based economies were central components in Scottish overseas commerce for most of the eighteenth century and the dominant factors in the country's international trade to a much greater extent than the equivalent sectors in England.

The importation and re-export of tobacco became the most remarkable example of Scottish commercial enterprise in the imperial economy during much of the eighteenth century. In one year, 1758, Scottish tobacco imports from the American colonies exceeded those of London and the English outports of Bristol, Liverpool and Whitehaven combined. Three years later, the highest-ever volume of tobacco leaf was landed in Scotland, a staggering 47 million lbs, amounting to a third of all the nation's imports and when sold on to European and Irish markets no less than two-thirds of national exports. On the eve of the American Revolution in 1773–4 the Scots were reckoned to control over half the trade in the key areas of new colonial tobacco production in the Chesapeake. Little wonder then that one influential planter, William Lee, could proclaim: 'I think it self-evident that Glasgow has now almost monopolised Virginia and its inhabitants.'[12]

Lee's reference to Glasgow was telling. Although in earlier years other Scottish towns, such as Ayr, Dumfries, Bo'ness, Leith, Dundee and

Aberdeen, were actively importing tobacco, the Glasgow merchants, through their two outports of Greenock and Port Glasgow, increasingly established a virtual stranglehold on the trade. As early as the 1710s the Clyde's share of Scottish imports was already around 90 per cent, and by the 1760s had climbed further to 98 per cent. Glasgow was Scotland as far as the tobacco trade was concerned. It was not simply that the city's merchant houses were adept at crushing competition within the country, they were also formidable rivals within the broader transatlantic economy. Over the middle decades of the century they carved out an ever-larger share of the British trade. As late as 1738 the Scots controlled only 10 per cent of official UK tobacco imports. But that figure then rose to 20 per cent in 1744, stood at 30 per cent by 1758 and topped 40 per cent in 1765. Alarmed voices were raised in London, Bristol and elsewhere that if the trend continued for much longer, Glaswegians would surely dominate one of Britain's most lucrative Atlantic trades in its entirety.[13]

In this period the population of Scotland was around 9 per cent of that of Great Britain but the country's share of British tobacco imports was more than four times that figure. This confirmed the crucial point that the external trade economy of Scotland from the 1740s to the 1770s was much more reliant than the rest of Britain on a commodity which was dependent for its cultivation on slave labour. Colonial imports and re-exports were also disproportionately represented in Scottish overseas commerce. In 1771, for instance, 60 per cent of Scottish imports by value were shipped from America and the West Indies. Tobacco alone also made up 51 per cent of all Scottish exports in that year, dwarfing the second-ranked commodity, home-produced linen, which stood at 27 per cent. These figures can be contrasted with the pattern of external trade in the UK as a whole. There the import of tropical and semi-tropical produce, sugar, tea and tobacco, despite rapid recent growth, was at 30 per cent of the total in the early 1770s, around half the Scottish figure for the share of these commodities. This was a trend continued when West India sugar and raw cotton imports superseded the previous dominance of the tobacco trade after 1783 and the Caribbean became Scotland's largest overseas market into the early nineteenth century.

In an important sense, however, the tobacco business was much more than the simple acquisition of tobacco leaf from colonial planters followed by sale to burgeoning consumer markets in France, Scandinavia, Holland and the German states. In essence, the tobacco trade had developed to become Scotland's first global enterprise. To establish and refine their competitive position in the international marketplace, Clyde merchants serviced the needs of the colonial planter class for domestic articles, plantation equipment, household plenishings, clothing, luxuries and a host of other items. American consumers became increasingly sophisticated purchasers as their material standards rose in the wake of expanding markets in Europe for American produce. Some sense of the new consumerism comes from the New York press. In the 1720s merchants in that city described only fifteen different manufactured goods for sale in newspaper articles. By the 1770s they were marketing over 9,000 different imported items. Expanding custom in the tobacco colonies, therefore, increasingly meant that Scottish factors and storekeepers had to offer the widest possible range of goods to satisfy the new demands. That in turn meant that their Glasgow principals had to create secure lines of supply for the vast array of consumer goods selling across the Atlantic.

A global enterprise blossomed as a result. Wines came from Madeira and the Canary Islands; sugar and rum from the Caribbean; linen from Ireland; luxuries from Holland; and so on. The sources of supply ran from the Mediterranean to Russia and across the Atlantic to the West Indies and British North America: 'the great shipping routes stretched out from Glasgow like the ribs of a fan'.[14] And, at home, tobacco houses set up many of their own centres of production by investing heavily in tanneries, bottleworks, linen manufactures, sugar-refining, breweries, ironworks, collieries, printworks and many other economic activities in Glasgow and the hinterland of the city.[15]

The impact was deeply felt too on the other side of the Atlantic. If the needs of the colonial planter class for consumer goods and agricultural tools were great, their requirements for short-term credit were even more pressing. Especially in the newer areas of tobacco cultivation, where the poorer planters concentrated, credit was the lifeblood of the local economy. With capital provided by British merchants, planters could purchase some slave labour and the tools necessary to expand cultivation and clear virgin land. Credit also ensured that the colonists could work through the months between harvests without denying themselves clothing, food and other items. It enabled them to cope with the inevitable differences in timing inherent in the tobacco economy – before the return for one year's crop had been harvested, the planter had to maintain himself, his family and his holding and also plant the next. In a sense, then, by extending liberal credit the Scottish houses helped to provide the development capital for the back country of the Chesapeake. The resulting level of debt owed to the Scots rose steeply from an estimated £500,000 in the early 1760s to around £1.3 million when the American Revolution broke out in 1775.[16]

Credit on this scale provided evidence of yet another close Scottish link with the slave economies. It was not simply the merchant houses who gained but those at home on whom they relied for sources of capital for transatlantic investment. While the three new Glasgow banks provided short-term support, longer-term funding originated elsewhere. As a late eighteenth-century historian of Glasgow put it, 'the strength of the monied interest of the west of Scotland was embarked in it [tobacco]'.[17] The account books of the big companies reveal their capacity to attract interest-bearing loans on personal and heritable bonds from a very wide social circle outside the active managers and partners of the firms. The funds which helped to lubricate the Chesapeake trade were drawn from Scottish landowners, trustees, tradesmen, physicians, military officers, spinsters, widows and university professors, among many others. That also meant the profits of the slave-based tobacco business were widely distributed through these financial networks well beyond the ranks of the active merchant community itself.[18]

III

The connection with the West Indies functioned in parallel with the American relationship in terms of trade, slaving, and the Glaswegian mercantile syndicates which straddled both colonial economies.

As well as trading with the Caribbean islands, Scots were heavily involved there in the ownership of plantations (less common in the American colonies) and, as already noted earlier in this volume, were also much engaged in their management as attorneys, surgeons, physicians, shopkeepers and overseers. It was also striking that although the commercial relationship went back to the seventeenth century, it strengthened markedly from the 1760s. This was especially so after the end of the Seven Years War in 1763, precisely at the time when the transformation of the Scottish domestic economy itself gathered pace. In total there were an estimated 4,500 Scots in the Caribbean at the Union of 1707. These numbers remained relatively stable until mid-century and then rose steeply to c. 17,000 new emigrants between c. 1750 and 1800.[19]

Especially after the collapse of the tobacco trade in 1775–6, followed only by a muted recovery after 1783, the Scottish commercial relationship with the Caribbean also achieved a huge new significance. The export share of all goods from Scottish ports to the islands expanded dramatically, rising from 21 per cent at official values in 1781, to 42 per cent by 1801 and then to 65 per cent in 1813. By that date the official value of sugar and cotton imports was even higher than tobacco had been during the zenith of that trade in the early 1770s. Sugar imports increased by around 400 per cent between 1783 and 1800, while the official value of cotton imports from both America and the West Indies rose more than thirty-two times between 1783 and 1801. In addition, the tonnage of Scottish shipping bound for the Caribbean by that last date was 50 per cent greater than that to all European countries combined and this during the key decades of transformational economic change in Scotland itself.[20] Again, as with the tobacco era, the extreme dependency of Scottish overseas commerce on commodities which were the product of transatlantic slave labour is very striking.

Scottish links with the West Indies had important parallels with those to the American colonies.[21] If the American trade had its rich 'tobacco lords', West Indian commerce could eventually boast its 'sugar princes'. Both produced merchants and firms of immense wealth with the financial surpluses which allowed large-scale investment in the Scottish domestic economy. Glasgow's sugar merchants were a small élite numbering around eighty individuals in the partnerships which dominated the trade. Among them was an inner group of only a couple of dozen families who ran much of the business. The giant firm for a time was Alexander Houston & Co., with assets in trade, land and industry in both Scotland and the West Indies valued at £630,000 in 1809. When this colossus showed potential signs of collapse in the 1790s, the Government itself was forced to step in, so disastrous would a bankruptcy have been for the imperial trading system as a whole. Immediately below the vast Houston organisation were houses such as John Campbell, senior, & Co. (with assets of £179,000 in 1814: see Chapter 6 for a detailed account); Robert Dunmore & Co.; Dennistoun, Buchanan & Co.; Leitch and Smith; Robert Mackay & Co.; and Stirling, Gordon & Co.

Several of the merchant dynasties who made up these partnerships also owned Caribbean plantations, but their primary role was to act as the selling agents in the UK and Europe for sugar, rum, cotton, indigo and coffee, provide credit and advances for slave purchases and organise the Scottish export trade to the West Indies. From their ranks were also drawn Glasgow's political élite after c. 1783, the provosts, councillors and officers of the Merchants' House and the Chamber of Commerce who governed the city down to the early nineteenth century. They established the Glasgow West India Association in 1807, which as already seen had become the most vocal and energetic opponent of the crusade for slave emancipation.[22] While anti-slavery petitions were being generated from all over Scotland, the Association and its loyal press ally, the

Glasgow Courier, vigorously defended the interest of the slave owners against 'the spread of evil, so much to be dreaded' which, if emancipation came, would be catastrophic for the fortunes of the city.[23]

The evidence surveyed thus far, therefore, suggests that Scotland had a deep association with the two principal slave-based economic systems in the eighteenth-century Atlantic empire: Virginia, Maryland and North Carolina on the American mainland, and the sugar islands of the Caribbean. This pattern differentiated the Scottish involvement in slavery from that of Bristol and Liverpool. In these English slaving ports the primary orientation was to Africa and the West Indies. Crucially, however, the Scottish connection was not simply to the Caribbean but also with North America, especially before the American War of Independence.

What impact did these relationships have on Scotland's domestic history in this period?

IV

In England, the debate on slavery and industrial capitalism, despite the innovative work of Inikori, Solow and others, remains unresolved. Indeed, one recent contribution to the discussion has still insisted that 'sugar cultivation and the slave trade did not form an especially large part of the British economy'.[24] Such a conclusion is hardly surprising because the revisionists who search for a key link between slavery and capitalism in England face considerable evidential and conceptual difficulties.

On the eve of the Industrial Revolution, England was already a comparatively developed and sophisticated economy with substantial urban growth and a commercialised agriculture system which made it one of the most advanced societies in eighteenth-century Europe.[25] English industrialism probably had less need of finance from external sectors to move forward by that period. The domestic system was capable of replenishing itself from re-ploughing of profits to provide for further growth while also drawing on any surplus wealth of the contemporary domestic economy. In addition, econometric studies suggest that the idea of a radical change in economic direction in England, implied by the term 'revolution', may be overdrawn. The country's route to modernity was long and evolutionary rather than an experience of short-term dramatic transformation. In this perspective, once again, the resulting modest increments in capital supply could easily be achieved from within the existing domestic system. As the economic historian Michael Postan once asserted, 'there were enough rich people in the country [England] to finance an economic effort far in excess of the modest activities of the leaders of the Industrial Revolution'.[26]

It might be that Scotland could provide more fertile ground for the revisionists. As a poorer country it was in much greater need of external supplies of capital during the industrialisation process than its neighbour to the south. North of the Border, and until the 1840s, when convergence between the two countries became more evident, the structures of the Scottish economy remained distinctive and different. First, as indicated by contrasting wage rates and the persistence of subsistence relationships in much of agriculture, Scotland c. 1750 was a less-developed society in economic terms.[27] Indeed, a few decades earlier in the 1690s, a series of harvest failures and trade crises had unambiguously demonstrated the fragility of the nation's economy. Some argue that it took nearly a generation for Scotland to achieve sustained recovery from those disasters.[28] Second, the current consensus among most Scottish historians is that from around the 1750s and the 1760s a clear and decisive break with the past occurred. The comparative evidence suggests that not until forced Soviet state industrialisation in the 1920s and 1930s could any country in Europe equal the speed and scale of the Scottish transformation.[29] In brief, the concept of an 'Industrial Revolution' may still be considered to have legitimate resonance in a Scottish context even if it has lost some of that resonance in English history.

Third, the fundamental extent of these rapid changes needs to be stressed. Growth was not simply confined to a 'leading sector' of cotton and linen manufacturing. The whole of Scottish society was being recast between the mid-eighteenth and early nineteenth centuries. A key indicator of the dash towards modernity was the pace of urbanisation. In 1750 only one in eight Scots lived in towns (defined as urban communities of 4,000 or more inhabitants), a very much lower proportion than that of England. By the 1820s it was more like one in three.[30] Further, the transformation was not confined to manufacturing industry and the urban areas. In the two decades after c. 1760 the Scottish countryside rapidly took on a recognisably modern form with enclosed fields, trim farms and separated holdings, a set of changes which had taken generations to achieve south of the Border. North of the Highland line, too, Gaeldom moved from tribalism to capitalism over less than two generations.[31]

Fourth, again unlike England, the Scottish domestic market was relatively small and grew only slowly in the eighteenth century. In the 1750s the population was around 1.25 million and had only risen to 1.6 million in 1801. The annual growth rate of 0.6 per cent was just over half that of England, primarily because of high net levels of emigration, and significantly behind the Irish increase of 2.1 per cent over the longer period 1791 to 1821. Not surprisingly, therefore, historians of Scotland place much more emphasis on external markets, partly in England but also across the Atlantic, as the strategic sources of demand for the vastly increasing flow of goods now turned out by the nation's mills, weaving shops and iron works. Throughout the early nineteenth century this overseas orientation became even more evident.

Against this background it can be argued that the slave-based econo-mies of the Atlantic had a powerful impact on Scottish economic growth as a source of raw materials for industrialism, market expansion and capital transfers to manufacturing, mining and agriculture.

Before the 1830s the industrial transformation concentrated on tex-tiles. Metal manufacture was laggard and only came into its own from the later 1830s and 1840s onwards. The establishment of the famous Carron Company in 1759 and a flurry of iron works opened before 1801 proved to be a false dawn. No new companies were floated between that date and 1824. While output did rise for a time, the rate of expansion was markedly slower than that in England.[33] On the other hand, textiles were dominant, accounting for the employment of 257,900 workers, or 89 per cent of all recorded manufacturing jobs. Much the fastest rise was in mechanised cotton spinning, which in turn depended on expansion of raw material supplies from the plantation economies of the West Indies and the American South.[34]

In fact, the connection was potentially catalytic. During the American War, several Glasgow tobacco houses switched their interests to the sugar islands of the Caribbean. Merchant correspondence reveals that while the most lucrative opportunities lay in the importation of sugar, planters drove hard bargains and forced firms to take raw cotton as well. In consequence, cotton coming into the Clyde virtually halved in price between 1776 and 1780: it is suggested that 'this was one of the factors which appears to have persuaded numerous former linen and silk merchants and manufacturers to concentrate activities on cotton spinning and weaving'.[35] Until well into the 1790s, 'sea island' cotton from the Caribbean provided the leading sector of the Scottish Industrial Revolution with the vital raw material for its mills and workshops until being replaced after that period by the southern states of the USA, another slave-based economic system.[36]

These economies were also key markets for Scottish textile producers and other manufacturers. Eltis and Engerman stress that 'All scholars recognise the [English] domestic market to have been much larger than the Caribbean.'[37] Perhaps so, but it was a different story for Scotland, especially when the populations of the American tobacco colonies are added to those of the West Indian islands. Between 1651 and 1851 the population of England rose from 5.2 million to 16.7 million.[38] The Scottish population was 1.2 million in 1755 and by 1801 had only grown to 1.6 million. In 1851 the total stood at 2.8 million.[39] For such a relatively small country, the Atlantic markets came as a much bigger and more decisive bonus than for England. In 1770 the population of the British American colonies was 2.7 million, and that of the British Caribbean 760,000 in 1801; most of the latter were slaves, who represented a potentially enormous market for provisions and cheap clothing. By 1810 the number of Africans in the sugar islands and the plantations of North America had risen to just over two million, significantly more than the population of Scotland as a whole.[40]

Scottish exports to the American mainland colonies at official values averaged £97,962 in 1740–4, then tripled to £298,922 from 1770 to 1814.[41] This was significant, but much more crucial to the domestic economy, however, was the market for 'slave cloth' in the Caribbean. Demand there helps to explain why, as already seen, the West Indies took such an increasing share of exports from Scotland of home-produced goods in the later eighteenth century, rising to 65 per cent in 1813.[42] Here, the strategic factor was linen manufacture. Linen was by a long way Scotland's largest manufacturing industry and biggest industrial employer in the eighteenth century. Between 1746 and the 1790s the output of cloth more than doubled in volume and trebled in value. Even after the 1780s, when the dramatic expansion of cotton captured attention, linen production continued apace. Official output again rose threefold to reach nearly 27 million yards annually in 1813–17. Work in linen spinning, weaving and finishing was critical to the way of life of countless Scottish families. Contemporary estimates suggest that about 40,000 weavers worked for the market in the 1780s and just under 170,000 women found their 'chief employment' in the spinning of linen yarn. When some of the finishing trades are included, full-time and part-time linen employment in that decade may have occupied more than 230,000 men, women and children.[43] Little wonder that John Naismith could remark in 1790: 'The linen manufacture has been the most universal source of wealth and happiness introduced into Scotland. To how many thousands has it afforded bread for these forty years past?'[44]

In broad terms, manufacturing was divided into two types of specialisation. Most Scottish production concentrated on the cheaper and coarser lines, which in turn were heavily geared to satisfying the needs of the export market. Fife, Angus and Perthshire were the dominant centres for these trades. Fine manufacture for lawns and cambrics tended to focus more on Glasgow and the western counties of Renfrewshire and Lanarkshire. The finer production was more oriented to the home market than in the regions of east-central Scotland. It was in that area that the imperial factor was crucial in three ways.

First, the industry enjoyed the protection of a high tariff wall against European competition. Second, the system of bounty payments set up by the state in 1743 to boost cloth exports to the colonies was vital. From 1745 bounties were also extended to low-priced cloth, which generated a dramatic increase in linen exports to the plantations across the Atlantic in the years that followed. Throughout the eighteenth century 80 to 90 per cent of these exports were supported by the bounty, and when it was temporarily withdrawn in 1754 the output of some of the coarser lines halved, only to recover vigorously when the subsidy was restored two years later.[45] Third, the colonial markets were critical to growth. European consumption was marginal and Ireland's of minor consequence. Nine-tenths of all Scottish linen exported from Scotland went to North America and the West Indies. After the American War the Caribbean became even more important. In the last quarter of the eighteenth century the standards of living of countless working-class families in the eastern Lowlands of Scotland came to depend on the huge markets for cheap linen clothing among the slave populations of Jamaica and the Leeward Islands.[46] Moreover, out of this specialisation eventually came the global industry of jute, for sacking and packaging production, centred on Dundee. Jute was to that city in the Victorian era what shipbuilding was to Clydeside. Eventually Dundee would rejoice in the title 'Juteopolis'.

A final issue to be considered is that of capital transfers from the slave-based economies to Scotland. Previous work by this author has revealed very significant investment by tobacco and West Indian traders in Scottish industry, commercial infrastructure and land in the key decades of economic transformation between c. 1750 and c. 1800.[47] Manufacturing industry in Glasgow and the West of Scotland gained significantly from colonial merchant capitalisation after c. 1730. Around eighty industrial ventures in iron working, sugar houses, glassworks, soapworks, printworks, collieries and the like were funded in whole or in part, so providing a bridge between the old trading world and the new age of both commerce and industrialism.

West India merchant capital was often vital for the big cotton-spinning firms which dominated the industry in the region before 1815. Two

houses, Leitch and Smith, and Stirling, Gordon & Co., were key shareholders in James Finlay & Co., which by the early nineteenth century
owned three major mill complexes and had probably become the single
largest producer of cottons in Scotland.[48] Similarly, two of the partners
in John Campbell, senior, & Co. and one of the members of Dennistoun,
Buchanan & Co. contributed £70,000 of total capital of £150,000 to
the famed New Lanark Company between 1810 and 1812.[49] The two
last-mentioned West India firms were also connected through Alexander
Campbell and Robert Dennistoun with Robert Humphrey & Co., cotton
spinners of Hutcheson town, Glasgow, in which West India interests held
£20,000 of the £32,000 capital in 1816.[50] The Dennistoun family were
involved in a variety of other firms, including John Monteith & Co. and
Reynolds, Monteith & Co., cotton spinners of Renfrewshire (c. 1795),
and, more importantly, in the formation of the company which developed the major Stanley Cotton Mills in Perthshire.[51] Monteith, Bogle &
Co., the owners of the cotton complex at Blantyre in Lanarkshire, also
drew on the resources of two West India houses – Alexander Garden,
of the Caribbean firm of Francis Garden & Co., became a partner of
Monteith, Bogle & Co. through his marriage with the daughter of
its leading partner, Henry Monteith.[52] Adam Bogle, the other major
partner, was not only a scion of one of the most renowned merchant
families in Glasgow from the tobacco era, but was also a member of
Robert Bogle, junior, & Co., a leading West India house in the city.[53]
Furthermore, it was reckoned that Alexander Houston & Co., the pre-
eminent Caribbean firm, had about £20,000 invested in the cotton industry at the time of the firm's bankruptcy, while Robert Dunmore was
the leading figure behind the establishment of the Ballindalloch Cotton
Company in Stirlingshire.[54] Other spin-offs from the tobacco and sugar
trades were infrastructural developments of Glasgow's first three private
banks and sustained investment in shipping and port facilities on the
Clyde and the Forth & Clyde and Monklands canals. The Glaswegian
financial scene was revolutionised by the foundation of the Ship, Thistle
and Arms banks, all capitalised by Atlantic merchants, the development
of insurance, and invigorated markets in personal and heritable bonds by
which the moneyed classes through interest-bearing were able to share in
the new commercial bonanza. All of this came together as integrated critical mass with very potent consequences for regional economic growth.
A huge outflow of funds from colonial commerce was also channelled
into the purchase of landed properties. Some repatriated their wealth
to London and the Home Counties, but the transfer of fortunes to the
homeland was also very extensive. Well over half of the Glasgow colonial

merchant élite bought up land between 1770 and 1815, with a grand total of more than 140 estates acquired around the town itself and the four surrounding counties of its hinterland in Ayrshire, Dumbartonshire, Lanarkshire and Renfrewshire.[55] Even this impressive figure, however, does not do full justice to the capital repatriated from the Caribbean, because being confined to merchant portfolios it does not take account of the investment by plantation and slave owners in Scottish landed estates. Some West India fortunes were certainly spent on the purchase of major properties in England but, as earlier chapters have shown, the majority who acquired land bought throughout the length and breadth of Scotland and did not confine their purchases to any one region or locality. They, like the wealthy nabobs returning from India at the same time, had the resources to spend on agrarian improvement and so can be seen as prime sources of finance helping to fuel the Scottish agricultural transformation of the eighteenth century.[56]

V

This chapter has attempted to describe a strategic connection between the Atlantic slave-based economies and Scotland's Great Leap Forward before 1830. The relationship was arguably a potent one, especially in relation to raw material supply for cotton manufacturing, vigorous expansion of new and larger markets, and large-scale capital transfers to industry and agriculture. It has been argued that these external influences were especially important to Scottish development because of the country's relative poverty before c. 1750 and the small size of its own internal market. Moreover, current understanding of the Industrial Revolution throughout Britain suggests that it was essentially regional in impact. Some areas, such as South Lancashire, West Yorkshire and the West Midlands, were in the vanguard, at the same time as others, such as the South of England and the Scottish Highlands, experienced industrial and economic decline. One of the key regional economic engines of Britain was Glasgow and the hinterland of the city, precisely that part of Scotland where the effects of the Atlantic slave-based economies were most decisive and strategic in their impact.

It would be naïve, of course, to argue that transformation derived only from these crucial drivers.

First, the origins of industrialism were far from being monocausal. The commitment of the landed élites to economic improvement, indigenous levels of literacy, the practical impact of improving Enlightenment thought, English markets within the Union, new technologies and the indigenous natural endowment of coal and ironstone resources, *inter alia*, were all part of the mix.

Second, recent research has identified the Indian Empire as an important generator of external funds in the eighteenth century; the Atlantic trades most certainly did not have a monopoly. Yet, in the present state of knowledge, it would seem that Asian resources, repatriated by Scots in the East India Company's service and by private merchants, tended on the whole to be invested in landownership throughout Scotland (or in the English shires) rather than directly into manufacturing in the western Lowlands for much of the period.[57] On the other hand, resident Glaswegian merchant families, located in the heartland of the new industrialism, had the best personal connections and more knowledge of opportunities for profit than others.

Third, the slave-based economies were of much more importance to the first textile-dominated phase of Scottish industrialisation than to the second after c. 1830, which was primarily, though by no means exclusively, founded on iron, steel, shipbuilding and engineering. One reason for this was that the capital resources of the nation had by the later decades been radically enhanced through internal economic growth. Indeed, surplus indigenous capital was now available to borrowers beyond Scotland on a quite extraordinary scale. This was confirmed by the massive growth in external investment from Scottish sources from c. 1850 to territories across the globe. Remarkably, between 1885 and 1910 nearly half – 44 per cent – of the increase in Scottish capital took the form of such overseas investment.[58]

One author has recently argued the case for the continued relevance of West India finance into the later nineteenth century, particularly in railway investment, but the sums adduced in evidence were of minor value compared to the overwhelming dominance of capitalisation from mainly domestic sources during the later Victorian era. Nicholas Draper's chapter also shows how slave compensation monies to Scots comprised but a fraction of the overall resources later invested in railway development in the 1840s.[59]

So the story is a complex one, but even when all the qualifications are taken on board, the central argument remains that the Atlantic slave-based economies can be considered key factors in Scotland's eighteenth-century transformation.[60] A brief comparison with their impact on Ireland and Wales places the Scottish experience of burgeoning markets and returning profits in clearer perspective. Irish merchants were banned for most of the eighteenth century from direct importation of sugar and tobacco under the British Navigation Laws, which only allowed these 'enumerated commodities' to be landed at mainland British ports. Nevertheless, for much of the period, Irish salt beef, exported on a huge scale from the port of Cork, became a staple diet of the slave populations. Also, there were numerous Irish indentured servants in the Caribbean in the eighteenth century and Ireland's age-old commercial connections with the west coast ports of France ensured that many Irish merchant families became involved in the slave trade to the French Caribbean, particularly to St Domingue. One of the most famous was Antoine Walsh, who was reckoned to have shipped more than twelve thousand Africans to the West Indies during his career. Walsh gained historical immortality in 1745 when he equipped a slaver, the *Du Teillay*, and sailed for Scotland with Prince Charles Edward Stuart. Thus began the last Jacobite rising.

Like the Scots, the Irish were active as sea captains and traders in the slaving centres of Bristol and Liverpool, and several merchants with Irish names who were deeply involved in the Africa trade have been identified in the two ports.[61] However, as one historian of Ireland and slavery has argued, these Irish emigres in both England and France contributed little to the economic development of their homeland. For the most part they and their successors remained permanently overseas and so, to quote the most recent authority, 'not much in the way of slave trade profits trickled back to Ireland'.[62]

It was a broadly similar pattern in Wales. The Welsh copper and woollen industries produced goods for sale by slave traders along the African coast and many cargoes were also sent directly to the Caribbean to provide slave clothing. But the relative importance of these markets in relation to domestic and other outlets remains problematic in Welsh historiography. Moreover, unlike the ubiquitous Scots, Welsh planters, managers and merchants were notable by their virtual absence from the plantations. Hence, the impact of slavery on Welsh economic development, though relevant in certain sectors and localities, never assumed the strategic importance which it did in Scotland.[63]

These comparisons are not yet final or definitive. However, already they bring into sharp focus the distinctive relationship between Scotland and the Atlantic slave economies when considered in the context of the other nations of the British Isles.

NOTES

1. This chapter is an amended version with additional material of my 'Did Slavery make Scotia Great?', published in *Britain and the World*, 4.1 (2011), pp. 40–64.

2. Eric Williams, *Capitalism and Slavery* (London: André Deutsch, 1944; 1964 edn).
3. Ibid., p. v.
4. See, *inter alia*, R. P. Thomas, 'The Sugar Colonies of the Old Empire. Profit or Loss for Great Britain', *Economic History Review*, 21 (1968), pp. 30–45; S. L. Engerman, 'The Slave Trade and British Capital Formation in the Eighteenth Century: A comment on the William Thesis', *Business History Review*, 46 (1972), pp. 430–43; Roger I. Anstey, *The Atlantic Slave Trade and British Abolition, 1760–1810* (London: Macmillan, 1975), pp. 38–57; R. P. Thomas and N. Bean, 'The Fishers of Men: The Profits of the Slave Trade', *Journal of Economic History*, 34 (December 1974), pp. 885–914; C. H. Feinstein, 'Capital Accumulation and the Industrial Revolution', in R. Floud and C. McLuskey (eds), *The Economic History of Britain since 1700. Volume 1* (Cambridge: Cambridge University Press, 1981), p. 131.
5. David Richardson, 'The British Empire and the Atlantic Slave Trade, 1660–1807', in Peter J. Marshall (ed.), *The Oxford History of the British Empire. Volume 2: The Eighteenth Century* (Oxford: Oxford University Press, 1998), p. 461.
6. See, *inter alia*, L. Solow, 'Caribbean Slavery and British Growth. The Eric Williams Hypothesis', *Journal of Development Economics*, 17 (1985), pp. 99–115; Joseph E. Inikori and Stanley L. Engerman (eds), *The Atlantic Slave Trade* (Durham, NC: Duke University Press, 1992); R. Blackburn, *The Making of New World Slavery* (London: Verso, 1997); Barbara L. Solow and Stanley L. Engerman (eds), *British Capitalism and Caribbean Slavery: The Legacy of Eric Williams* (Cambridge: Cambridge University Press, 1987).
7. David Eltis and Stanley L. Engerman, 'The Importance of Slavery and the Slave Trade to Industrialising Britain', *Journal of Economic History*, vol. 60 (March 2000), pp. 123–44. See also Pat Hudson, 'Slavery, the slave-trade and economic growth: a contribution to the debate', in C. Hall, N. Draper and K. McLelland (eds), *Emancipation, Slave-ownership and the Remaking of the British Imperial World* (Manchester: Manchester University Press, 2014), pp. 36–59; Ronald Findlay and Kevin H. O'Rourke, *Power and Plenty: War, Trade and the World in the Second Millennium* (Princeton, NJ: Princeton University Press, 2009); C. K. Harley, 'Slavery, the British Atlantic Economy and the Industrial Revolution', Paper presented at the conference 'New Perspectives on the Life and Work of Eric Williams', Oxford University, 24–25 2011.
8. Eltis and Engerman, 'Importance of Slavery', p. 141.
9. Joseph E. Inikori, *Africans and the Industrial Revolution in England* (Cambridge: Cambridge University Press, 2002).
10. Ibid., p. 482.
11. 'Roundtable' on Inikori's work, *International Journal of Maritime History*, 15 (2003), pp. 279–361.

12. Quoted in A. Herman, *The Scottish Enlightenment: The Scots' Invention of the Modern World* (London: Fourth Estate, 2002), p. 138.

13. T. M. Devine, 'The Golden Age of Tobacco', in T. M. Devine and G. Jackson (eds), *Glasgow. Vol .I. Beginnings to 1830* (Manchester: Manchester University Press, 1995), pp. 140 ff. The UK trade data, discussed here and the next paragraph, come from C. Knick Harley, 'Trade: discovery, mercantilism and technology', in Roderick Floud and Paul Johnson (eds), *The Cambridge Economic History of Modern Britain. Volume I: Industrialisation, 1700–1860* (Cambridge: Cambridge University Press, 2004), pp. 175–203.

14. I. C. C. Graham, *Colonists from Scotland: Emigration to North America 1707–1783* (Ithaca: Cornell University Press, 1956), p. 127.

15. Devine, 'The Golden Age of Tobacco', in Devine and Jackson (eds), *Glasgow*, pp. 139–83.

16. Glasgow City Archives, Speirs Papers, TD 131/10-12, Diary of Alexander Speirs, 2 March 1778.

17. Andrew Brown, *History of Glasgow* (Glasgow, 1795), vol. II, p. 143.

18. T. M. Devine, 'Sources of Capital for the Glasgow Tobacco Trade, c. 1740–80', *Business History*, 16 (1974).

19. Trevor Burnard, 'European Migration to Jamaica, 1655–1780', *William and Mary Quarterly*, vol. 53, no. 4 (1996), pp. 769–96; A. L. Karras, *Sojourners in the Sun: Scottish Migrants in Jamaica and the Chesapeake 1740–1800* (Ithaca: Cornell University Press, 1992), pp. 43–5; Douglas Hamilton, *Scotland, the Caribbean and the Atlantic World, 1750–1820* (Manchester: Manchester University Press, 2005), pp. 23–4.

20. National Archives, Customs 14 and 17/12. Copies in National Archives of Scotland, RH 2/4/22 and 40.

21. This paragraph summarises T. M. Devine, 'An Eighteenth Century Business Elite: Glasgow West India Merchants, c. 1750–1815', *Scottish Historical Review*, lvii, no. 163 (April 1978).

22. Glasgow City Archives (GCA), West India Association Minutes, Miscellaneous Papers, 3290–3294.

23. Quoted in Iain Whyte, *Scotland and the Abolition of Black Slavery, 1756–1838* (Edinburgh: Edinburgh University Press, 2006), p. 86.

24. T. G. Burnard, '"Prodigious Riches": The Wealth of Jamaica before the American Revolution', *Economic History Review*, IIV, 3 (2001), p. 506.

25. Joel Mokyr, 'Accounting for the Industrial Revolution', in R. Floud and P. Johnson (eds), *The Cambridge Economic History of Modern Britain, Volume I: Industrialisation, 1700–1860* (Cambridge: Cambridge University Press, 2004), pp. 1–27.

26. N. F. R. Crafts and C. K. Hanley, 'Output, Growth and the British Industrial Revolution', *Economic History Review*, vol. 43, pp. 103–30; M. M. Postan, 'Recent Trends in the Accumulation of Capital', *Economic*

History Review, vol. VI, no. 1 (October 1935). For an opposing perspective, see Inikori, *Africans and the Industrial Revolution*, pp. 405–72.

27. Compare the content of my chapter, 'Scotland', in Floud and Johnson (eds), *Cambridge Economic History of Modern Britain*, pp. 388–416, with the rest of that volume.

28. Christopher A. Whatley, 'The Issues facing Scotland in 1707', in S. J. Brown and C. A. Whatley (eds), *The Union of 1707. New Dimensions* (Edinburgh: Edinburgh University Press, 2008), p. 13.

29. T. M. Devine, *The Scottish Nation: A Modern History* (London: Penguin, 2012), pp. 105–23.

30. T. M. Devine, 'Urbanisation', in T. M. Devine and Rosalind Mitchison (eds), *People and Society in Scotland. Volume 1 1760–1830* (Edinburgh: John Donald, 1988), pp. 27–52.

31. T. M. Devine, *The Transformation of Rural Scotland. Social Change and the Agrarian Economy, 1660–1815* (Edinburgh: Edinburgh University Press, 1994, 1999); T. M. Devine, *Clanship to Crofters' War. The Social Transformation of the Scottish Highlands* (Manchester: Manchester University Press, 1994).

32. R. H. Campbell, 'The Making of the Industrial City', in Devine and Jackson (eds), *Glasgow*, pp. 184–213.

33. J. Butt, 'The Scottish Iron and Steel Industry before the Hot-Blast', *Journal of the West of Scotland Iron and Steel Industry*, 73 (1966); Christopher A. Whatley, *The Industrial Revolution in Scotland* (Cambridge: Cambridge University Press, 1997), p. 31.

34. Norman Murray, *The Scottish Handloom Weavers, 1790–1850* (Edinburgh: John Donald, 1978), p. 23.

35. National Library of Scotland, MS8793, Letter Book 'E' of Alexander Houston & Co., *passim*; T. M. Devine, 'A Glasgow Tobacco House during the American War of Independence', *William and Mary Quarterly*, 3rd ser., xxxiii (July 1975), no. 3; Whatley, *Industrial Revolution in Scotland*, p. 42.

36. Inikori, *Africans and the Industrial Revolution*, pp. 377–8.

37. Eltis and Engerman, 'The Importance of Slavery', p. 125.

38. E. A. Wrigley and R. S. Schofield, *The Population History of England, 1541–1871* (Cambridge: Cambridge University Press, 1986), pp. 208–9.

39. *Census 1971 Scotland: Preliminary Report*.

40. Inikori, *Africans and the Industrial Revolution*, pp. 192–5.

41. Jacob M. Price, 'New Time Series for Scotland's and Britain's Trade with the Thirteen Colonies and States, 1740–1791', *William and Mary Quarterly*, XXXII, 2 (April 1975), pp. 301–25.

42. See above, p. 15.

43. Alastair J. Durie, *The Scottish Linen Industry in the Eighteenth Century* (Edinburgh: John Donald, 1979), pp. 158–60.

44. John Naismith, *Thoughts on Various Objects of Industry pursued in Scotland* (Edinburgh, 1790), p. 93.

45. Durie, *Scottish Linen Industry*, pp. 151–2.
46. T. M. Devine, *Scotland's Empire, 1600–1815* (London: Allen Lane, 2003), pp. 336–7.
47. T. M. Devine, 'The Colonial Trades and Industrial Investment in Scotland, c. 1700–1815', in P. Emmer and F. Gaastra (eds), *The Organisation of Interoceanic Trade in European Expansion, 1450–1800* (Aldershot: Ashgate, 1996), pp. 299–312.
48. James Finlay & Co., Glasgow, Balance Book of J. Finlay & Co. 1789–1800: the firm's capital rose from £30,000 in 1795 to £75,000 in 1810.
49. National Archives of Scotland (NAS), GD64/1/274, (Copy) Contract of Copartnery of New Lanark Company, 5 October 1810.
50. GCA, Campbell of Hallyards Papers, Minute of the Meeting of the Trustees of Alexander Campbell, 16 April 1819; Trustees of R. Dennistoun to Campbell's trustees, 15 December 1823.
51. NAS, Particular Register of Sasines (Renfrew), 42/217.
52. *Glasgow Courier*, 31 December 1812.
53. GCA, Bogle MSS, Genealogy of the Bogle family; Minute Books of West India Association of Glasgow, Individual and Firm Subscriptions.
54. NAS, GD237/134, Minute of a Meeting of the Creditors of the House of A. Houston & Co., 23 September 1806; Signet Library, Court of Session Process 368/21, Petition of Robert Dunmore, 1–4.
55. T. M. Devine, *Clearance and Improvement. Land, Power and People in Scotland, 1700–1900* (Edinburgh: John Donald, 2006), pp. 54–92.
56. Based on a preliminary survey by my research assistant, Alex Hendrickson, in 2008 of records of landed families with eighteenth-century Scottish West India interests held in both public and private archives.
57. George McGilvary, *East India Patronage and the British State* (London: I. B. Tauris, 2008), pp. 180–202.
58. Christopher Schmitz, 'The Nature and Dimensions of Scottish Foreign Investment 1860–1914', *Business History,* vol. 39, no. 2 (1997), pp. 42–68; T. M. Devine, *To the Ends of the Earth: Scotland's Global Diaspora 1750–2010* (London: Allen Lane the Penguin Press, 2011), p. 232.
59. Anthony Cooke, 'An Elite Revisited: Glasgow West India Merchants, 1783–1877', *Journal of Scottish Historical Studies*, vol. 32, no. 2 (2012), pp. 127–66, esp. p. 146. See also Stephen Mullen, 'A Glasgow-West India Merchant House and the Imperial Dividend, 1799–1867', *idem*, vol. 33, no. 2 (2013), p. 228.
60. An important start in advancing knowledge was made in March 2010 at the Royal Society of Edinburgh Workshop on Scottish connections to the slave trade and slavery, sponsored by both Edinburgh and Glasgow universities. It involved Scottish historians, archivists and key researchers from outside the country with expertise on the subject from non-Scottish perspectives.
61. Nini Rodgers, *Ireland, Slavery and Anti-Slavery* (London: Palgrave Macmillan, 2007), pp. 95–106.

62. Ibid., p. 113. See also Nicholas Draper, '"Dependent on Precarious Subsistences": Ireland's Slave Owners at the Time of Emancipation', *Britain and the World*, 6 (2), pp. 220–42.
63. Chris Evans, *Slave Wales. The Welsh and Atlantic Slavery 1660–1850* (Cardiff: University of Wales Press, 2010), pp. 130–3.

Conclusion

History, Scotland and Slavery

T. M. Devine

T HOSE WHO HAVE WRITTEN this book are aware that they have not engaged in any ordinary academic exercise. Its findings may provoke not only interest but also argument and controversy well beyond the world of scholarship. This would not be surprising. The study deals with big issues: a suggested reinterpretation of part of a nation's past, its beliefs and sense of itself. Readers of the book therefore should be assured that all contributors are bound by the classic credo of historical scholarship – to aspire towards convincing conclusions based on professional scrutiny of relevant and representative evidence without either fear or favour.

The immense scale and duration over two centuries of the Atlantic slave trade in the British Empire was bound to leave its mark on the history of the four nations of the United Kingdom. Equally, the depth and range of the impact was likely to vary significantly between them. This study suggests that the effect was relatively minor in the case of Ireland and Wales but much more significant for England and Scotland.

The relationship between England and slavery has long been recognised and understood, the linkages with Scotland much less so. Indeed, for more than a century and a half, any such connections were mainly lost to history as a comforting myth took root and then flourished that the Scots had little to do with the history of the enslaved. It was believed that the 'nefarious trade' in human beings within the Empire was always an English monopoly and never a Scottish preserve. After all, Scots had long taken pride in the Calvinist tradition of the equality of souls before God and the sentiments of shared humanity articulated most eloquently in the immortal words of the national bard, Robert Burns, 'a Man's a Man for a' that . . . That Man to Man, the world o'er Shall brothers be for a' that'.

Moreover, the Christian values of the nation coupled with the progressive thought and humane sympathies of the Scottish Enlightenment eventually inspired many Scots to play a leading and well-documented role in the successful campaigns for abolition of the slave trade in 1807, slavery itself within the British Empire in 1833 and then to become passionately involved in the global crusade to confront that moral evil throughout Africa and the Americas in the second half of the nineteenth century. It was this edifying story which was celebrated in commemoration events and became lodged in the memory of the nation.

After abolition, all European countries which had extracted handsome profits from transatlantic slavery, whether England, France, Holland, Portugal or Spain, soon managed to distance themselves from their unsavoury past. But Scotland was different. Not only did it succumb to amnesia like the rest but also to an explicit denial of ever having had any part in the business of transatlantic slavery: 'It wisnae us', as the Scots vernacular had it. The evidence presented throughout this book directly challenges these old assumptions.

First, the time-honoured denial of a Scottish role in slavery is comprehensively refuted. Scotland's connection was deep, long-lasting and not simply confined to the Atlantic trades of Glasgow. The analysis here supports, amplifies and extends the findings of other contributions over recent years by showing that few aspects of Scottish society at the time were insulated from the impact of the slave-based economies.

Second, some evidence in the study points to an even greater per capita Scottish stake than any of the four nations of the UK in British imperial slavery. This is clearly the case in relation to Ireland and Wales but perhaps also to England when the different population size of the two countries is taken into account. More work is needed to confirm this important point conclusively but, if the argument prevails, slavery can no longer be regarded as a side issue in Scottish history but rather has to be seen as integral to the weft and woof of the national past from the seventeenth to the early nineteenth centuries.

The involvement was not based on slave trafficking by ships from Scottish ports. Rather it was founded on the central presence of Scots and Scottish trade in the transatlantic slave economies and the custom of Scottish-born slavers to conduct their business from English centres or from the Caribbean islands directly to west Africa rather than from the homeland itself. The thesis of a close and enduring engagement between Scotland and transatlantic slavery is supported by the following six summative arguments which have already been rehearsed in more detail throughout the book.

First, systematic evidence from the *Legacies of British Slave-Ownership* (LBS) project at University College London demonstrates that Scottish absentee slave owners were more likely to be rewarded on a per capita basis than their counterparts elsewhere in Britain and Ireland for property in slaves at the end of slavery in the Empire in 1833. Scotland's population was 10 per cent of that of the UK at the census of 1831 but accounted for 15 per cent of identified absentee slave owners – or a thousand awards from seven thousand absentees throughout the British Isles. In contrast, Ireland, with a population of nearly 8 million, or almost a third of the UK total, accounted for just over 2 per cent of absentee slave owners in 1833. Chapter 8, where these issues from the LBS database were considered in forensic detail, concluded: 'Scotland played a disproportionately larger part [than elsewhere in the United Kingdom] in the story of British and Irish slave ownership', and that 'slavery and slave ownership ... permeated Scottish commerce and finance' in a similar way to patterns in the City of London (see pp. 174, 181).

But the compensation evidence, though invaluable, cannot capture the total scale of the Scottish connection over time, as Nicholas Draper stresses in his chapter. Some Scottish absentees did not return to Scottish addresses but to residence in England and so would not necessarily be picked up as Scots returnees in the overall analysis. Also, the compensation data are inevitably partial, based as they are on a limited snapshot at the end of slavery and at that point confined only to the ownership of slaves. Self-evidently other key aspects, such as the Caribbean markets for Scottish commodities, the supply of raw cotton to domestic manufacturing from the West Indies and the southern United States, and the remitted profits of merchanting and plantation ownership, cannot feature. In addition, it may be that slave ownership in some islands over the decades of slavery is itself underestimated by evidence from the 1830s. Disinvestment from property in slaves might have occurred as the abolitionist campaigns reached a political climax in the years immediately before emancipation. For instance, the compensation claims suggest a comparatively lower level of Scottish slave ownership in Jamaica in the 1830s relative to the rest of Britain. Yet, earlier, in the later eighteenth century, as shown in Chapter 4, the island was the pre-eminent source of sugar production and the very epicentre of Scottish business in the West Indies.

Second, it was argued the famous Williams thesis on the connection between profits from slavery and the origins of British industrialisation considered in Chapter 11 may have more intellectual purchase when applied to eighteenth-century Scotland than to England in the same period. The poorer Scottish economy before c. 1760 had much more need of imperial markets and inward capital flows from the transatlantic plantations than its richer and more developed southern neighbour to enable progress towards modernity. That conclusion, which covers the decades down to c. 1830, may, however, only be the end of the beginning of the story. Researchers of the future will have to turn for a comprehensive perspective to those slave-based societies across the Atlantic which continued after 1833. Slavery was not abolished in the American South until 1865, Cuba in 1886 and Brazil in 1888. We already know that Scotland depended on these countries for supplies of raw cotton, sugar, tobacco, coffee and much else in the later nineteenth century; but how far were they also key markets for Scottish industry and overseas investment? Knowledge of the full links between Scotland and slavery will remain incomplete until this and related questions are tackled.

Third, Scotland was deeply involved in not one but two of the transatlantic colonial systems where slavery was fundamental to the functioning of economic activity: the West Indies, considered at length in this book, but also, particularly before 1776, the plantations of mainland America in Virginia, Maryland and North Carolina. Both relationships were well established before the American War of Independence, with the Chesapeake tobacco business more dominant in the first half of the century and the Caribbean sugar and cotton trades assuming more strategic significance after 1783. Chapter 11 showed that the plantation economies of those regions provided profits, capital, markets, raw materials and overseas careers to the homeland from before the Union of 1707 until the end of slavery within the Empire. In the decades before 1776 the tobacco trade was by far Scotland's largest source of imports and re-exports. After 1783 it was mainly replaced by sugar and cotton from the West Indies as the centrepiece of the nation's maritime commerce. Both these sectors, however, could not have flourished without human bondage on a massive scale. The comparison with England also indicated that Scotland's external commerce was in relative terms much more reliant than its neighbour on colonial commodities produced by slave labour, both for imports and exports over the period from the 1740s to the early decades of the nineteenth century. This dependency reached a peak of overwhelming dominance in the overseas trade sector precisely at the same time as the 'take off' of the new Scottish industrial and agrarian economy during the last quarter of the eighteenth century. The linkages between the two developments were overt and unambiguous.

Fourth, in some Caribbean colonies Scots were significantly over-represented after c. 1750 as governors, civil functionaries, plantation

owners, merchants, overseers, attorneys and physicians. This was especially so in Jamaica, the richest and most productive island of all, which
eventually accounted for more than half the slave population of the
entire British West Indies, but also the Ceded Islands of Grenada, St
Vincent and Tobago and, later, the territories of British Guyana, where
the slave system reached its apogee within the Empire from the 1790s.
Some, probably a small minority, became rich but in terms of the impact
of their fortunes on the homeland, however, it should be remembered
that several who had done well for themselves in the plantations returned
to spend the rest of their days with their wealth, not to Scotland, but
rather to London and the spa towns of England. Equally, it would be
wrong to conclude that only those directly involved in the slavery business gained from it. The compensation claims of 1833–5 confirm the
very large number of creditors from the moneyed classes and beyond
who owned slaves as security for interest-bearing loans. They included
minors, widows, annuitants, clergy, lawyers, university professors, merchants, industrialists, tenant farmers and others. The social mix of those
profiting from slavery in Scotland was wide and deep.

Fifth, some of the biggest and most profitable slave-trading syndicates
in English ports by the early nineteenth century, according to the evidence presented in Chapter 8, were managed and financed by Scots or
founded initially by Scottish mercantile families. No similar transfer of
slaving capital or enterprise from England to Scotland has been identified to date.

Sixth, Scottish resistance to abolition in the years before 1833 seems to
have been more widespread geographically than that in England. There,
the campaign against emancipation for the most part concentrated on
the slaving ports of Bristol, Liverpool and London. In Scotland, on the
other hand, petitions to delay or abandon abolition were generated
across several regions, from the rural parishes of the far North to the
towns and cities of the South, particularly where landed estates had
been bought and great houses built on the profits of West India slavery.
Predictably, Glasgow was well represented but so too were locations
as far apart as the western Highlands, the Black Isle (north-east of
Inverness), Aberdeenshire, Angus, Edinburgh and Dumfries. Scots from
the Highlands and the North were still investing extensively in slavery
throughout the 'frontier lands' of British Guiana only a few years before
emancipation was enacted in law. There can be no doubt, of course,
that the cause of abolitionism was certainly much stronger and more
popular in Scotland by the 1830s than anti-abolitionism. Indeed, it was
the enthusiastic Scottish movement in support of emancipation which

helped to deliver the famous victory in Britain in 1833. The nation also produced in Zachary Macaulay, James Ramsay and James Stephen some of the most famous, charismatic and effective abolitionists of the entire campaign. Nevertheless, the now-forgotten activities of the anti-abolition lobby confirmed the continued presence of significant vested interests in support of Caribbean slavery throughout Scotland even on the very eve of emancipation. They had become embedded over several generations from the time that the first Scottish connections with the West Indies were forged in the seventeenth century.

Index

Page numbers in **bold** refer to figures and those in *italics* refer to tables. Page numbers including 'n' refer to notes.